"I found it fascinating. A long-overdue idea presented with skill, charm, and common sense. The self-tests are particularly exciting. Every Christian should own a copy, certainly every Christian leader. In short, invaluable!"

Marjorie Holmes

In the New Testament, the apostle Paul teaches about three groupings of spiritual gifts. These include the motivational—or personality — gifts: perceiving, exhorting, serving, teaching, giving, administrating, and having compassion. How fulfilled or frustrated you are depends on your use or neglect of your motivational gifts. Therefore, it's imperative (and enjoyable, too) to know with which gifts you have been blessed. Through charts, tests, and information, Don and Katie Fortune help you recognize your gifts. In addition, *Discover Your God-Given Gifts* reveals:

- why you relate to people the way you do
- what your primary and secondary gifts are
- the character traits associated with each gift
- typical problem areas for each gift
- biblical characters who demonstrate each gift

You'll experience great joy as you *Discover Your God-Given Gifts* and learn to use them as He intended.

DISCOVER YOUR GOD GIVEN GIFTS

Biblical handbook to help you discover . . .

Why you think and act the way you do
How gifts affect your relationships
What career or ministry suits you best
How using your gifts will bring you joy

Don & Katie Fortune

Chosen Books
A Division of Baker Book House Co
Grand Rapids, Michigan 49516

The accounts in this book are factual; however, to protect confidentiality, some names and identifying details have been changed.
Scripture quotations are taken from:

TAB: The Amplified New Testament, © The Lockman Foundation 1954, 1958. The Amplified Old Testament © Zondervan Publishing House, 1965.
NAS: The New American Standard Bible, © The Lockman Foundation 1960, 1962, 1963, 1968, 1971, 1972, 1973, 1975, 1977.
NIV: The Holy Bible, New International Version, © 1978 by the International Bible Society, used by permission of Zondervan Bible Publishers.

Material taken from the "Dear Abby" Column by Abigail Van Buren is Copyright © 1977, Universal Press Syndicate. Reprinted with permission. All rights reserved.

Library of Congress Cataloging-in-Publication Data

Fortune, Don.
    Discover your God-given gifts.

    1. Gifts, Spiritual.   2. Spiritual life—1960–
I. Fortune, Katie.   II. Title.
BT767.3.F67   1987   234'.13   87-20543
ISBN 0-8007-9108-8

Copyright © 1987 by Don & Katie Fortune
Published by Chosen Books
a division of Baker Book House Company
P.O. Box 6287, Grand Rapids, Michigan 49516-6287

ISBN: 0-8007-9108-8

Twenty-sixth printing, October 2003

Printed in the United States of America

For current information about all releases from
Baker Book House, visit our web site:
http://www.bakerbooks.com

CONTENTS

Contents

Part III: Practical Applications

INTRODUCTION

It was in 1974 that friends of ours, Lynn and Glenn Koontz, invited us over to their home to share with us what they had learned about the motivational gifts during the advanced Basic Youth Conflicts seminar taught by Bill Gothard. We were excited as Glenn went through his notes. We could suddenly see why we were so different from one another. It helped us to understand things about ourselves that had eluded us before.

"Ah!" Don said to me. "Now I understand why you are always eager to organize things, including me and the kids!"

"Uh huh," I replied, "and I see why you are always telling everyone to look for good in every situation."

I soon recognized that administration was my primary gift. For the first time in my life I understood why I always felt such zeal for whatever I was involved in. I could see that it was "all right" for me to prefer to delegate tasks instead of doing them myself. I could at last release myself from self-imposed guilt for not measuring up to the "ideal homemaker" image. I felt relieved that my interest in pioneering projects outside the home was within the range of expected and acceptable behavior for my particular gift. I also recognized some of the problem areas of my life as being characteristic of the administrator. Now I would be able to work on them with greater understanding.

Don identified his primary gift as that of exhortation. He could see why he was so eager to give advice to people . . . sometimes whether they asked for it or not. He realized that the Lord had equipped him to be an encourager, to build people up in the Body of Christ, and that he needed to persevere in doing so even when no immediate results were visible.

"I could begin to accept some of Katie's puzzling-to-me ideas and behavior," he admitted later. "Knowing that she was operating within the motivational gifts that God had given her, I could stop trying to convert her to my way of thinking and doing."

For my part, I realized I needed to release Don to be what God has made him to be. Our differences no longer needed to be a threat to either one of us. Rather, we could delight in them, knowing that God has brought us together in marriage with different gifts that will enrich both of our lives if we allow it.

We began also to recognize the unique giftedness in each of our three children. Linda is a classic compassion person. David is an interesting mixture of his parents' gifts, an administrator-teacher-exhorter. Dan is a perceiver modified by compassion. How much fun it was to see their personalities grow and blossom as we allowed them to be what God created them to be. It helped us to know better both how to discipline and how to encourage.

We became sensitive to the gifts of friends and colleagues too. We could better understand why some of our actions caused a reaction rather than a response in others, and why we sometimes felt threatened by certain people. Former personality conflicts diminished—in many cases even disappeared.

Soon we were applying our new understanding to all our interpersonal relationships. We saw why our pastor's sermons typically gravitated to certain themes. Why a particular person who had been placed in a leadership position couldn't handle it. Why our older son cultivated a large group of friends while our younger son was happier with one or two close ones. Why our daughter consistently befriended the unlovable.

It all began to make sense!

ADDITIONAL RESEARCH

Our perspective was further enriched when we received a set of tapes on the biblical gifts by the Rev. Don Pickerill, president of Life Bible College in California. The more we searched the Scriptures the more excited we became. The biblical characters came alive. Their ministries, motives, and methods began to fall into the broader framework of the purpose and plan of God for their lives.

At the same time, the Holy Spirit began to confirm that this was a subject He wanted me to teach. (I'd identified a secondary gift of teaching.) So, taking what others had discovered and adding what we were learning from the Scriptures and from experience, I began to teach about these gifts in women's groups, Bible studies, wherever the Lord opened up doors of opportunity.

And of course, the more I taught, the more I learned. The feedback from the groups was fantastic. More insights! More indication that the teaching was indeed essential and life-changing. I collected data from each group I taught, and developed a scoring method (my administration gift in action) that enabled people to identify their gifts.

Several other women from our area began to teach on the subject and we decided to get together each month to share findings and to brainstorm. I told Margaret Ann Hardwick, Judy Walker, Bobbie Elmore, and Barbara Walsh that I was preparing a book on the subject and asked for their input. We had some wonderful times together, researching, revising, enlarging.

Special thanks go to those who later helped with the research compilations, Colleen McGowan, Lydia Mathre, and Carol Miller. Gigantic thanks to Helen Bishop who gave endless hours of help on the computer. I also want to thank Elizabeth Sherrill for her sensitive and thorough editing.

BROAD EXPOSURE OF THE TEACHING

During the past twelve years Don and I have taught our motivational gift seminar across the country, from Washington to Florida, and from California to New York. We have also taught it in Canada, New Zealand, Australia, England, Scotland, Germany, Panama, India, Singapore, Hong Kong, Korea, Japan, and the Philippines.

The testing materials have been translated into German, Spanish, French, Korean, Polish, Finnish, and Japanese.

We have been privileged to work with some wonderful interpreters. In Panama, one would have thought Karen Hines (wife of evangelist Mike Hines) had been teaching the subject for years. In Germany, Waltraud Keil (a teacher with the Berlitz School of Languages) picked up our very gestures and inflections. In Japan young pastor Kai interacted with us in a way that could only have been the work of the Spirit.

In Korea, Archer Torrey, grandson of the theologian-writer R. A. Torrey and himself a theologian, was our interpreter at the Jesus Abbey. When we asked why his interpretations were often longer than the original, he explained that he was getting such clear insights from the Holy Spirit that he added those too.

We've also had some funny things happen, like the time Don was saying, "A perceiver will often fast and pray." Our missionary friend, Ron Sisco, jumped in with a quick correction when the interpreter said, "A perceiver will often pray fast."

We have found that the teaching appeals to and applies to not only people in every nation and culture, but also to people from every type of church, denomination, and parachurch organization. We get enthusiastic responses from teenagers, college groups, adults, senior citizens. All tell us basically: "This seminar has changed my life!"

GOOD TIDINGS OF GREAT JOY

There is a simple acrostic often used in Christian circles: **J ESUS**
O THERS
Y OU

It is because *Jesus*, our Lord, has tugged on our hearts to do so that we have written this book.

It is because *others*, in fact hundreds of you, have asked us to commit this teaching to writing that we have written this book.

It is because we have seen so many lives changed and enriched by this understanding that we know it will enrich *you*.

We know without a doubt that the end product of the adventure you are starting today will release *joy* in your life in a new and exciting dimension!

Joy is the byproduct of operating in the sphere of *your* God-given gifts!

Preface

In the '70s and '80s people in the Body of Christ have become concerned with getting to know themselves better so they can be fulfilled, happy, and be their best for the Lord. They want to know how other people function, so they can relate to them better. As we understand our own giftedness we can enjoy our work, and do it well.

Some working in the field of human behavior have looked at the list of gifts in Romans twelve and been surprised to find there the seven basic personality types they had already categorized in secular studies. God must enjoy tucking truths away in His Word to be revealed and understood at a later date, because it happens regularly. It's gratifying, too, when the secular world and the religious world can have a basis for communication.

This book is about "motivational gifts." Don and Katie are offering us a biblical way of looking at the inborn gifts God has given to us and to others. The tests that go with the teaching are most detailed, accurate, and effective. There are tests for adults, teens, and children, and they are even available in many different languages. Katie's teaching and administration gifts shine here! No one seems to have been forgotten.

The teaching in this book and the tests that go with it will help you better understand yourself and others. You will find it easier to forgive and be less critical of others, and such helps with interpersonal relationships will enable the Body of Christ to function better. If we're going to be good witnesses to the world, we *must* learn to understand, love, and affirm one another.

The Fortunes treat their subject as "gifts that shape our personalities." It will be evident to the reader that the Holy Spirit has breathed a fresh touch on the Scriptures they share. There will always be those who will criticize new ways of looking at Scripture, saying, "Jesus, Paul, and the other apostles didn't see it that way!" My answer is, no, and Jesus didn't use electric lighting to read the Scripture, but that doesn't mean it's a sin for me to use electricity in this Twentieth Century. God created light in the first place, and then He allowed Edison to discover and harness a way to make that light available in a new way. It seems logical that our Lord would give us fresh insights for our own day.

I've known Don and Katie for many years. I was involved in the beginning, in 1967, of what has become the Women's Aglow Fellowship International, and Katie was the first editor of the *Aglow* Magazine. I've always been impressed with her loving good-nature, and her numerous talents in writing, speaking, art, and photography. (She took the picture for the cover of the first edition of my book, *I'm Glad You Asked That*.)

About a year ago I went to Don and Katie's Motivational Gifts Seminar at their church. I enjoyed the way they took turns teaching—team teaching. Katie's research, attention to details, and enthusiasm about her discoveries was very obvious, as was her enjoyment of her subject. Don, retired from the Postal Service, and now in charge of mission outreach for his church, is a "down home," relaxed person. He would give appropriate examples, usually from real life experience, and joke a little so everyone would relax. So Don prepared them to hear further interesting facts and illustrations from Katie.

When I took their test, I found that, as with Katie, administration was my number-one motivational gift. Second was teaching, and my third, compassion. Katie says that if you score highly on what she calls the "speaking gifts"—such as my first two—it's good when a "serving gift"—such as compassion—balances it out. I had always thought of administration as a field primarily for men, but as I thought further I could see how the Lord had used this gift in my life. I realized, for instance, how God had given me ability to organize the travel invitations that had been blanketing our dining room table! To see to it the letters didn't take a long time to process, and people would get a quick reply. I came to realize my way of studying and working was different from Dennis's. He writes and learns inductively, dipping in here and there and then drawing things together; I enjoy learning and writing deductively, step by step.

Since I'm active in prayer-counseling ministry I could see the importance of administration there, since I usually see the overall picture easily, and keep copious notes on prayer experiences. But compassion must be added to administration. I'm aware that the person I pray with must feel loved, or he or she will not be as open for healing. Yet a person who rates number one in compassion may be effective in praying with people, but may not be best in the role of one who coordinates a prayer ministry—who hears the numerous needs and determines how to bring the counselee and counselor together. He may take all the needs to his or her own heart, and in a year or so may be worn out by it.

Judy Blankenship, a friend of mine, was at the seminar I attended. She had taken the test three years earlier and had now taken it the second time. She showed me the graphs of the two tests, and they were exactly the same in contour, which was impressive; but on the later test I was interested to see how each gift extended further, showing Judy's growth in the respective areas.

As a clergy wife for twenty-two years, I see that this teaching on Motivation Gifts is important for churches to function properly. Many clergy are not gifted with administrative ability, but find they are expected to do it as part of their job. They don't know where to ask for help, and everyone wonders why the church can't get off the ground. That same minister may have great gifts as an exhorter, and part of the congregation enjoys his sermons but another part expects him to excel as a teacher (or vice versa). When he tries to be what he isn't, frustration can result, both for him and for his hearers: "Well, the pastor just couldn't get with it today!" A wise minister will not only discover his own gifts, but the gifts of members of his congregation, so they can assist him to the fullest, and so he can get on with the work he is called to do. Then, too, if he chooses an assistant, he can pick one who has the gifts he himself may lack, and so, as a good shepherd, see to it that his sheep have a balanced diet.

I have two cautions. One, be careful not to put people in boxes, but rather use this study of the gifts as a measuring tool to understand and help one another. The other, remember that the motivational (inspired, natural) gifts do not take the place of the manifestation (supernatural) gifts, and the two should not be confused.

God bless you as you set out with Don and Katie Fortune to *Discover Your God-Given Gifts*.

Rita Bennett

PART
1

PERSPECTIVE

THREE CATEGORIES OF GIFTS

1

If you have a basket of apples, oranges, and bananas—what do you have? A basket of apples? No. You have a basket of fruit. So it is with the three categories of gifts enumerated in the New Testament. All three groups are composed of gifts but, like the fruit in the basket, each group is unique and distinct from the others.

One of these groups of God-given gifts holds the key to understanding many things about yourself—why you think and act the way you do, how you relate to other people and circumstances around you, and what makes you the special individual you are. This group of gifts will be the focus of this book, the gifts we feel are primarily spoken of in this verse from 1 Peter:

> As each of you has received a gift (a particular spiritual talent, a gracious divine endowment), employ it for one another as [befits] good trustees of God's many-sided grace—faithful stewards of the extremely divers [powers and gifts granted to Christians by] unmerited favor.
>
> *1 Peter 4:10, TAB*

Here, unmistakably, is a statement that every believer has been given a gift. Here, also, is a command to employ it for the benefit of others. We can be confident that God would not command us to use something we do not possess—but how do we get it?

The Greek word for "gift" in this verse is *charisma*, defined in my Greek dictionary as "a divine gratuity . . . a spiritual endowment . . . a free gift." So this is not something we can earn; in fact, the command is not to try to deserve it, but to *use* it. This kind of gift is a possession, something already given to each one of us by God at our creation.

And as I mentioned, this is true of only one of the groups of gifts found in the New Testament. Let's look briefly at each listing to see which one falls into this category of special gifts that reveal so much about the way God made us.

THE MANIFESTATION GIFTS

The first group of gifts is found in 1 Corinthians 12:

> But to each one is given the manifestation of the (Holy) Spirit—that is, the evidence, the spiritual illumination of the Spirit—for good and profit. To one is given in and through the (Holy) Spirit [the power to speak] a message of wisdom, and to another [the power to express] a word of knowledge and understanding according to the same (Holy) Spirit; To another (wonder-working) faith by the same (Holy) Spirit, to another the extraordinary powers of healing by the one Spirit; To another the working of miracles, to another prophetic insight—that is, the gift of interpreting the divine will and purpose; to another the ability to discern and distinguish between [the utterance of true] spirits [and false ones], to another various kinds of [unknown] tongues, to another the ability to interpret [such] tongues.
>
> *Verses 7–10, TAB*

There are nine gifts listed here:

1. *The word of wisdom*, a revelation of wisdom beyond natural human wisdom that enables a person to know what to do or say.

2. *The word of knowledge*, a revelation of information for a person, group, or situation that could not have been known by any natural means.

3. *Faith*, the kind of wonder-working faith that moves mountains and waits expectantly for results.

4. *Gifts of healings*, the many different ways and varieties of degrees in which God manifests healing.

5. *Working of miracles*, the demonstration of the power and action of God that goes beyond natural laws.

6. *Prophecy*, an anointed proclamation of God through an individual to encourage, exhort, or comfort.

7. *Discerning of spirits*, a person's ability to perceive what type of spirit is in operation in a given situation.

8. *Various kinds of tongues*, the languages given to the believer by the Holy Spirit but not learned or understood by the speaker.

9. *Interpretation of tongues*, the supernatural ability to express the content of what has been spoken in tongues.

Some call these the manifestation gifts because Paul used the Greek word *phanerosis*, meaning "an exhibition, expression, or manifestation." In other words, Paul defined these as supernatural manifestations of the Holy Spirit at work through a believer.

This listing of gifts is not the object of our study. The first reason is the Bible shows that it is the person being ministered to who actually receives the gift (such as when Jesus heals the blind or lame). The second reason is no one can dictate when the gift is to be used; the Holy Spirit is the One in charge of the gift working through an available and expectant vessel. These, then, are not the primary possessions indicated in 1 Peter.

THE MINISTRY GIFTS

The second listing of gifts is found in Ephesians 4. In this instance, the word for gift in verse 8—". . . He ascended up on high . . . and gave gifts [*doma*] unto men" (KJV)—means literally "a present." Looking at this verse in context we see that after Jesus ascended to the Father He presented gifts of *people* who were called and gifted to lead and train the rest of the Body of Christ.

While many versions do not repeat the implied word "gift" in verse 11, the Amplified Bible does:

> And His gifts were [varied; He Himself appointed
> and gave men to us,] some to be apostles (special
> messengers), some prophets (inspired preachers
> and expounders), some evangelists (preachers of
> the Gospel, traveling missionaries), some pastors
> (shepherds of His flock) and teachers.
>
> *Ephesians 4:11*

It is important to note that in this verse the words "men" and "some" are used in the sense of "mankind"—men and women. Therefore, both can be *domas* to minister to the Body of Christ.

There are five ministry gifts listed in this passage:

1. The *apostle*, one who establishes and strengthens churches.
2. The *prophet*, one who speaks forth the message of God.
3. The *evangelist*, one who is called to preach the Gospel.
4. The *pastor*, one who feeds and shepherds the believers.
5. The *teacher*, one who instructs believers in the Word of God.

We purposely list these gifts in lower-case type to emphasize the fact that these are not titles, but functions. A person does not become a prophet by being given the name. Rather, he becomes a prophet as he develops his God-given ability to function in prophet-like ways, responding to God's specific call with a willing heart.

The purpose of these ministry gifts is clear. The New American Standard Bible states it this way:

> And He gave some as apostles, and some as
> prophets, and some as evangelists, and some as
> pastors and teachers, for the equipping of the
> saints for the work of service, to the building up
> of the body of Christ; until we all attain to the

unity of the faith, and of the knowledge of the
Son of God. . . .

Ephesians 4:11–13

These five ministry gifts might equally well be called "equipping" gifts, enabling the saints (believers) to do the work of the ministry so that Christ's Body on earth (the Church) can function as His true representative.

Therefore, neither are these gifts the possessions—the things that belong to us—spoken of in 1 Peter 4:10. Rather they are *people* who are gifted to be equippers of the rest of the Body of Christ.

THE MOTIVATIONAL GIFTS

Now turn to the third listing of gifts in the New Testament found in the book of Romans.

> Having gifts (faculties, talents, qualities) that differ according to the grace given us, let us use them: [He whose gift is] prophecy, [let him prophesy] according to the proportion of his faith; [He whose gift is] practical service, let him give himself to serving; he who teaches, to his teaching; (He who exhorts, encourages), to his exhortation; he who contributes, let him do it in simplicity and liberality; he who gives aid and superintends, with zeal and singleness of mind; he who does acts of mercy, with genuine cheerfulness and joyful eagerness.

Romans 12:6–8, TAB

Charisma is the Greek word here, the same word used in 1 Peter 4:10. We believe this is the category of gifts that Peter was referring to when he said we were to employ them to benefit one another. Notice the Romans passage urges us to use them. This verse is like a repetition, an echo of Peter's statement.

This is the list of gifts that is the focus of this book. These are the gifts we *possess*. These are the gifts that God has built into us, made part of us, to be used for the benefit of others and for His glory. Like all the others, they are grace gifts. We do not deserve them. But because God loves us He gives them to us. Since they provide the motivating force for our lives, they have been called motivational gifts. They are the gifts that *shape our personalities*.

Because God has created us with free will we can choose to use our motivational gifts appropriately, or we can choose to neglect them, or even to abuse them. To be able to choose to use these gifts according to the will of God, it is important to have some understanding of what they are and how they function. That will be our goal in the following pages. Here we will just touch on the seven gifts briefly by presenting the seven key words we have chosen to identify the various recipients.

1. *Perceiver*, one who clearly perceives the will of God. We have purposely chosen this word rather than the word "prophet" to avoid confusion, since the same root word is also used in the two other categories of gifts.

2. *Server*, one who loves to serve others. Another appropriate word is "doer."

17

3. *Teacher*, one who loves to research and communicate truth. We almost selected the word "researcher" since that motivation is so strong.

4. *Exhorter*, one who loves to encourage others to live a victorious life. These are extremely positive people who can equally well be called "encouragers."

5. *Giver*, one who loves to give time, talent, energy, and means to benefit others and advance the Gospel. Another word could be "contributor."

6. *Administrator*, one who loves to organize, lead, or direct. Other words could be "facilitator" and "leader."

7. *Compassion person*, one who shows compassion, love, and care to those in need. We say "compassion" instead of "mercy" since this word is more comprehensive in today's usage.

THE GIFTS IN CONTEXT

It is always important to look at any verses you plan to study in the context of the entire passage. In this case, we should focus briefly on the first five verses of the twelfth chapter of Romans, the verses preceding the list of motivational gifts.

> I appeal to you therefore, brethren, and beg of you in view of [all] the mercies of God, to make a decisive dedication of your bodies—presenting all your members and faculties—as a living sacrifice, holy (devoted, consecrated) and well pleasing to God, which is your reasonable (rational, intelligent) service and spiritual worship.
>
> Do not be conformed to this world—this age, fashioned after and adapted to its external, superficial customs. But be transformed (changed) by the [entire] renewal of your mind—by its new ideals and its new attitude—so that you may prove [for yourselves] what is the good and acceptable and perfect will of God, even the thing which is good and acceptable and perfect [in His sight for you].
>
> For by the grace (unmerited favor of God) given to me I warn every one among you not to estimate and think of himself more highly than he ought—not to have an exaggerated opinion of his own importance; but to rate his ability with sober judgment, each according to the degree of faith apportioned by God to him.
>
> For as in one physical body we have many parts (organs, members) and all of these parts do not have the same function or use,
>
> So we, numerous as we are, are one body in Christ, the Messiah, and individually we are parts one of another—mutually dependent on one another.
>
> *Romans 12:1–5, TAB*

In the first verse Paul, writing the Christians in Rome, states that all believers are to present themselves to God as living sacrifices. It is only by this wholehearted dedication that our motivational gifts can be used as they were intended.

In the second verse we learn that we need to have our minds renewed. How do we do this? By the Word of God. As we prayerfully read and study the Bible, it becomes a living, personalized revelation of God to each believer, and our minds are cleansed and renewed.

In the third verse we learn, first, that we are to have a right attitude about ourselves—gratefulness and humility rather than conceit, and an objective sense of value rather than self-abasement. And we learn, second, that each of us has been given a degree of faith that will allow us to operate effectively in our motivational gifts: The *perceiver* has faith that God will answer petitions; the *server* has faith that enables him to complete whatever task is started; the *teacher* has faith that he can ferret out the facts of any matter; the *exhorter* has faith that there is a solution to every problem; the *giver* has faith that God will supply all needs; the *administrator* has faith that any project can be accomplished if the right people are brought together to do it; and the *compassion person* has faith that he can help people work together in love.

In the fourth and fifth verses we learn that we need to discern the various gifts in the Body of Christ and work together in mutual interdependence.

In this context we can see the importance of using our motivational gifts for the glory of God for this is the only way we will find fulfillment. These gifts—of which we have mostly been unaware—are the motivating forces of our lives, and unless they are channeled properly we cannot help but feel frustrated. But once we discover them, we discover a tremendous potential for happiness.

This book will show you not only how to identify your gifts but also how to release these gifts more effectively. You will see how your particular gifts have been evident in your actions even from early childhood. You will understand that the gifts give you your basic motivation for what you like to do and they affect the way you do it. You will also find that when you use your special gifts only for your own selfish ends, they will tend to become polluted. But, when you use your gifts for the benefit of others, cooperating with God's plan for your life, they will produce the greatest joy you can experience.

There is one more list of gifts in the Bible. It is not a new list, but rather a composite of the three lists already mentioned. It is found in 1 Corinthians 12:28–30, (NAS):

> And God has appointed in the church, first apostles, second prophets, third teachers, then miracles, then gifts of healings, helps, administrations, various kinds of tongues. All are not apostles, are they? All are not prophets, are they? All are not teachers, are they? All are not workers of miracles, are they? All do not have gifts of healings, do they? All do not speak with tongues, do they? All do not interpret, do they?"

Perspective

Here Paul is using as examples gifts from each of the three categories:

MOTIVATIONAL GIFTS	MINISTRY GIFTS	MANIFESTATION GIFTS
Helps (serving)	Apostles	Miracles
Administrations	Prophets	Healings
	Teachers	Tongues
		Interpretation

The passage is immediately followed by the famous "love chapter," 1 Corinthians 13. Paul is making an important point, that whether or not you are operating in the motivational gifts, the ministry gifts, or the manifestation gifts, if you don't do it in *love*—God's agape love—you are doing *nothing*! An apt admonition to remember at all times.

EVERYONE HAS A GIFT!

2

Good news: *Everyone has a motivational gift!* No one has been left out. We have tested tens of thousands of people and each one has discovered his specific giftedness, falling under one of the seven categories, or sometimes under more than one. (We have never found anyone who fits into an eighth category. In fact, there is no eighth category.)

But don't take our word for it. Look at God's Word:

> As *each one* has received a special gift, employ it in serving one another, as good stewards of the manifold grace of God.
>
> *1 Peter 4:10, NAS.*

> And since we have gifts that differ according to the grace given to us, let *each* exercise them accordingly: if prophecy, according to the proportion of his faith; if service, in his serving; or he who teaches, in his teaching; or he who exhorts, in his exhortation; he who gives, with liberality, he who leads, with diligence; he who shows mercy, with cheerfulness.
>
> *Romans 12:6–8, NAS*

There you are. Seven motivational (that is, motivating) gifts. And *each one of us* receives one (or more). So, what do we do with them?

21

WE ARE COMMANDED TO USE OUR GIFTS TO BENEFIT OTHERS.

Scripture stresses that our motivational gifts are given to us *to benefit others.* They are not to be used for selfish purposes. It is only by the grace of God that we are gifted in the first place; therefore we are to use our giftedness to help and bless others.

The contrast of the two seas in Israel shows that an outflow is essential for life. The Sea of Galilee has water flowing not only into it but *out* of it. Therefore the lake is fresh and useful; it supports life. But the Dead Sea has no outlet. It holds in all of the water it receives. Through evaporation this lake has become the saltiest in the world: there is no life in it at all.

So it is with the motivational gifts. They were designed by the Creator to overflow from us to those around us.

OUR GIFT WAS BUILT INTO US WHEN GOD FORMED US.

Our giftedness was not an afterthought. It was a part of God's plan to shape us for our role in the building of His Kingdom.

One of the most beautiful creation passages in the Old Testament is found in Psalm 139:13–16:

> For You did form my inward parts, You did knit me together in my mother's womb.
> I will confess and praise You, for You are fearfully wonderful, and for the awful wonder of my birth! Wonderful are Your works, and that my inner self knows right well.
> My frame was not hidden from You, when I was being formed in secret and intricately and curiously wrought [as if embroidered with various colors] in the depths of the earth [a region of darkness and mystery].
> Your eyes saw my unformed substance, and in Your book all the days of my life were written, before ever they took shape, when as yet there was none of them.
>
> *TAB*

What a magnificent expression of the design and development of the child in the womb!

God uses what scientists now call DNA in the process. When a child is conceived half of his DNA inheritance comes from the father and half from the mother. And in that microscopic fertilized egg the joined DNA forms a helix-shaped genetic ladder that is literally six feet long. Yet it is marvelously compacted within that tiny egg. How incredible!

Every detail of our physical being is programmed by DNA. Its intricacies far outweigh the most sophisticated computer system on the market today. The color of your hair was pre-programmed by your DNA. The shape of your nose, your height, your body frame, all your physical characteristics were determined at that moment of conception.

If God has so precisely planned for the development of your physical body—which is eventually subject to degeneration and death—how much more has He planned for your giftedness. We believe that our motivational gifts are given to us at conception and that just as DNA eventually brings forth our physical characteristics, so our motivational gifts bring forth the interests, abilities, enthusiasms, and actions that make us effective members of the Body of Christ.

One of the things that has convinced us that motivational gifts are a part of our initial creation is our study of twins.

The first time I tested a twin was nine years ago in Montana. Judy, a young mother in her thirties, commented at the time that she was sorry her identical twin sister, Jane, lived too far away to come to the seminar. Judy scored highest as "exhorter." Other women present who knew both twins insisted that Jane would probably score the same.

A year later I was invited to teach the motivational gift seminar in another Montana town that happened to be where Jane lived. While she had heard Judy speak of the seminar she had not seen Judy's scores or profile sheet. "I thought it would be best if I didn't see Judy's results until after I had a chance to do the test myself," Jane explained.

After the seminar Jane brought her profile sheet to me. Her primary gift was exhorter! What surprised me more, her second and third gifts matched Judy's too.

Since then, each time twins have taken the test their primary gifts have been identical.

For instance, one pastor's wife was strongest in the serving gift. Her favorite part of her ministry was hospitality. She loved entertaining people in her home and having house guests.

Her twin sister had married a wealthy businessman. She could afford domestic help but preferred to take care of her home herself. She loved entertaining her husband's business associates. She too was a server.

In another instance, Deanne was tested in Washington state and her identical twin sister, Dianne, by mail on the East Coast. Both proved to be perceivers.

The Reader's Digest carried an article on twins that presented even stronger evidence that motivational gifts are born in us, not added later. One revealing paragraph:

> Identical twin boys, born in Ohio some 40 years ago, were adopted by different families shortly after birth. A year ago, after 39 years apart, they were reunited. It was discovered that each had been named James; that each had had law-enforcement training; that each liked mechanical drawing and carpentry. Each married a woman named Linda, had a son—one named James Alan and the other James Allan—had divorced, and then married a second wife named Betty. Both had dogs named Toy. Also, both favored the same St. Petersburg, Florida, vacation beach.[1]

It is significant for our study that these twins were raised apart in different homes, leaving no opportunity for family or school to influence their identical choices of jobs, hobbies, and recreation. Clearly something more fundamental than external influence was involved—something, we believe, built in at conception.

OUR GIFT CAN BE OBSERVED IN CHILDHOOD.

> Train up a child in the way he should go: and
> when he is old, he will not depart from it.

Proverbs 22:6, KJV

As we began raising children we took this Scripture seriously, endeavoring to raise our youngsters morally and scripturally.

Then when the boys were eight and ten years old we discovered the motivational gifts and began to realize there was more to Proverbs 22:6 than a teaching about discipline and training. The Amplified Bible version of this Scripture gave us new insight: "Train up a child in the way he should go [and in keeping with his individual gift or bent], and when he is old he will not depart from it."

The original Hebrew included the insight that each child has a *gift*—a motivational gift—and a *bent*— direction to be fulfilled by using his motivational gift(s). We as parents then, have a responsibility to discover our child's giftedness and to "train him up" in it, to encourage the development of that gift, so that when he comes of age he will be using that giftedness to the glory of God and for his own true fulfillment.

We are grateful that we found this out before our boys were fully grown. We could easily see that Dave was an administrator (with a secondary gift of exhortation). We could encourage his leadership at school. Dan was completely different from his older brother: a perceiver, with a modifying effect from the gift of compassion. We could encourage him to take strong stands on issues and ideals.

Not only have they expressed gratitude that we encouraged them in their giftedness, but over the years they have brought friends and schoolmates home to take the motivational gift test as well.

Linda was already grown and married when we learned about the motivational gifts. But, in retrospect, we could see that she had a strong gift of compassion. As a child she was always drawn to others who were hurting or friendless. And her love for animals was exceptional. She wanted to be a veterinarian so she could work with animals, but when she learned they also did surgery she couldn't bear the thought of performing operations.

WE ARE NOT TO NEGLECT OUR GIFT.

> Neglect not the gift [*charisma*] that is in thee,
> which was given thee by prophecy, with the lay-
> ing on of the hands of the presbytery.

1 Timothy 4:14, KJV

Of the fifteen times the word *charisma* is used in the New Testament, we find that it is not uncommon for more than one gift category to be referred to at the same time. (The term, as with any term, must be understood within the context in which it is used.) In this reference, for instance, see the three categories of gifts expressed: The supernatural gifts may have been more fully released or manifested by the laying on of hands on Timothy, the manifestation gift of prophecy flowed through an elder who had the ministry gift of a prophet, and the motivational gift Timothy had been endowed with was identified and released in greater measure at this special time of his ordination. A careful examination of this verse as given in *The Interlinear Greek-English New Testament*[2] brings out an interesting rendering: "Be not negligent of the in thee gift which was given thee through prophecy with the laying on of the hands of the elderhood."

First of all, notice that the original Greek refers to the "in thee gift," indicating that the gift was already "in" Timothy when the elders prayed for him. The word "given" in the

Greek is *didomi* which has a wide range of meanings according to *Strong's Exhaustive Concordance of the Bible*[3] including "to be brought forth, shown, and uttered." It is likely that Timothy, being a young man, had not yet identified his primary motivational gift. So, when the elders were ordaining him (utilizing the various manifestation gifts of prophecy and word of knowledge), the gift that was already "in him" was identified verbally. (His primary motivational gift seems to have been that of teacher as evidenced by many later references to Timothy's ministry of teaching. See 1 Timothy 4:6, 11, 13–16; 2 Timothy 2:2, 15; 4:2.)

That Paul was probably one of those who prophesied over Timothy is indicated by his reference in 1 Timothy 1:18 to "prophetic intimations which I formerly received concerning you, that inspired and aided by them you may wage the good warfare" (TAB).

But more important than the timing of the gift is the fact that to neglect it is to neglect God's purpose and plan for our lives. Each of us has an "in thee" gift and, like Timothy, we need to use it for the glory of God and the benefit of others.

OUR GIFT COLORS ALL WE SEE.

If you put on a pair of sunglasses, all you see will be colored accordingly.

So it is with a person's motivational gift. A perceiver will look at life through a perceiver's eyes. Everything will look either good or bad, right or wrong, in God's will or out of God's will. It is impossible for the perceiver to see life in any other way.

A server on the other hand will approach reality with the question, "What can I do to help in this situation?" He constantly notices opportunities to do things for others.

A teacher will search for truth in everything he encounters. Like the persistent Diogenes of Greek literature searching with a lantern for an honest man, the teacher will investigate, seek, and research.

An exhorter will see opportunities to encourage people at whatever they do.

The giver will look for ways in which he can invest his time, talent, and money providing for the needs of others.

The administrator with his broad vision will grasp the overall dimensions of a situation.

The compassion person will recognize hurts and wounds that need to be healed and see endless opportunities to express love.

And each one may think, "Why don't others see things the way I see them? It's clear to me!"

OUR GIFT GIVES ONLY ONE PERSPECTIVE OF THE WHOLE.

God has purposely limited and focused our giftedness so that we must work together and remain dependent on each other in order to grasp the whole truth.

Remember the six blind men who went to "see" an elephant? One felt the side and said an elephant is like a wall. The next felt the tusk and claimed an elephant is like a spear. The third felt the trunk and likened it to a snake. The fourth felt a leg and said an elephant is like a tree. The fifth, touching an ear, declared an elephant is like a fan. The sixth felt the tail and insisted an elephant is like a rope. No one was altogether right, yet neither was he entirely wrong. It was only when they got all their observations together that they "saw" the whole elephant.

Thus it is with our motivational gifts. Each of us is somewhat blind to the other perspectives. We are wrong to say our way of seeing is the only true one. We are each partly right. But we are not totally right all by ourselves. We need each other's viewpoints in order to see the complete picture.

In our presentation of the motivational gifts we not only want to help you to discover *your* gifts but also to become familiar with the *other* gifts, how people with differing gifts think, how they operate, and how they benefit the whole Body of Christ. We believe you will be enriched both personally and in your relationships by gaining these insights.

EACH GIFT IS OF EQUAL VALUE.

Draw a circle in the space
provided at the right.

Let's suppose the circle represents a pie. Obviously it's easier to cut a pie into six or eight segments, but we want you to cut the pie above into seven *equal* slices. A challenge? See how well you can do.

Now, just in case your slices did not turn out symmetrically, write, "These are equal slices" beside the pie. Then label each slice with the name of a motivational gift: perceiver, server, teacher, exhorter, giver, administrator, or compassion person.

We want you to grasp the concept of this diagram: that all the gifts are equal. They are equal in the sight of God. They are equal in value in the Body of Christ. No gift is higher than or better than another gift. They each contribute invaluably to the collective functioning of the Body of Christ. If any one gift is not in operation there is a lack, a void.

Whatever motivational gift you have been given is the best gift God could have given you for the working out of His purposes in your life and for the benefit of the other people whose lives you will touch. Rejoice in your giftedness! Use your giftedness! Develop your giftedness! We like that oft-quoted slogan:

What we are is God's gift to us;
What we make of our lives is our gift to God.

It is true that God bestows some of the gifts more frequently than others. That's because more people are needed in certain functions. There need to be more followers, for instance, than leaders. From the data we have compiled* here is the percentage of people who have each gift:

Perceiver	12%	Giver	6%
Server	17%	Administrator	13%
Teacher	6%	Compassion person	30%
Exhorter	16%		

* This tabulation is based on detailed response sheets from 1000 people over a ten-year period, representing more than 100 groups in a variety of states, provinces, and countries.

The most prevalent gift is that of compassion—perhaps because there is so much need for love and compassion in the world.

The gifts of server and exhorter are almost tied for second place. Lots of servers are needed to get God's work done, and we all need encouragement every day.

But just because there are more with a certain gift does not mean that gift is more important. Neither does a lesser percentage mean a gift is somehow more special. All the gifts are equally important. All the gifts are necessary. All the gifts, when used properly, are a blessing.

Here's a brief review of the motivational (motivating) gifts and the needs they tend to meet:

GIFT	DEFINITION	NEEDS MET	WHAT IT DOES
PERCEIVER	Declares the will of God	Spiritual	Keeps us centered on spiritual principles
SERVER	Renders practical service	Practical	Keeps the work of ministry moving
TEACHER	Researches and teaches the Bible	Mental	Keeps us studying and learning
EXHORTER	Encourages personal progress	Psychological	Keeps us applying spiritual truths
GIVER	Shares material assistance	Material	Keeps specific needs provided for
ADMINISTRATOR	Gives leadership & direction	Functional	Keeps us organized and increases our vision
COMPASSION PERSON	Provides personal & emotional support	Emotional	Keeps us in right attitudes & relationships

The above chart offers only a bird's-eye view of how the motivational gifts function; there is, of course, the possibility of overlapping and interaction, and secondary gifts will color or modify the operation of a primary gift.

We will be going into detail on these points in Part II; for now let's lay an additional foundation by taking a look at how each gift is placed in the Body of Christ.

Placed in His Body

3

In the two verses of Scripture leading into his description of the motivational gifts Paul uses the graphic example of the human body:

> For as in one physical body we have many parts (organs, members) and all of these parts do not have the same function or use,
> So we, numerous as we are, are one body in Christ, the Messiah, and individually we are parts one of another—mutually dependent on one another.
>
> *Romans 12:4–5, TAB*

There are three points from this illustration that apply particularly to our study of the motivational gifts.

First, the body represents completeness, a whole, a totality—but a totality made up of disparate parts. Similarly, we who make up the Body of Christ have different functions. We are not all the same. We are gifted in different ways. Just as a physical body needs hands and feet and eyes and ears to enable it to function properly, so the Body of Christ needs those with different motivational gifts to enable it to function properly. We are to have unity through diversity.

It's good to know we don't all have to behave just alike. It's okay to be different.

Second, we can see in this analogy that we don't have to "do it ourselves." We do our part. Others do their part. *Together* we get the job done. *Together* we do the work of the ministry of our Lord.

I remember in my teens how I would hear a different sermon each week and try so hard to do what the preacher said. One Sunday he would preach on the importance of prayer, and all the following week I would pray strenuously. The next week he would preach on having a servant's heart, and I'd set out to serve anyone and everyone. Next might come tithe Sunday, when I'd determine to increase my giving. Or there'd be a sermon on love and I would wipe my brow from exhaustion, take a deep breath, and walk out the church door determined to be loving even if it killed me.

It almost did. I was trying so hard to be all of these things that I was approaching burn-out. I was aiming at some sort of "super-Christian" ideal that was impossible to achieve. I really believed I had to be outstanding in all these areas if I were going to please God. And when I failed, as I had to, I was a ripe target for guilt and self-condemnation.

I was so relieved, when I first discovered the variety of motivational gifts, to find that I did not have to be or do everything well, but that I could concentrate on those areas where I had been gifted by God. It also released me to appreciate the very different giftedness in others.

And third, Paul emphasizes our mutual dependence in the Body of Christ. We really need each other. No member of Christ's Body can go off on a desert island and be a victorious Christian all by himself. God has purposely made us so that we are incomplete without the interaction and ministry of our brothers and sisters.

David DuPlessis, who was known internationally as "Mr. Pentecost" for his years of building bridges of understanding between denominations around the world, used to have a wonderful saying: "Whenever I meet someone—anyone—I always ask myself, 'What can I impart to benefit this person, and what can he or she impart to benefit me?' "

THE GIFTS IN THE BODY

One day I said to the Lord, "Since Paul put this analogy of the Body before the list of motivational gifts in Romans 12, is it possible that each gift corresponds to a part of the physical body?"

The Lord not only showed me where each gift might fit in such a scheme, He also gave me Scriptures for each one.

1. Perceiver: This is the eye of the body.

"But blessed—happy, fortunate and to be envied—are your eyes, because they do see . . ." (Matthew 13:16, TAB).

It has become evident to us that perceivers, of all the members of the Body of Christ, are the most gifted with spiritual sight. They see things that the rest of us often miss completely.

"The eye is the lamp of the body. So, if your eye is sound, your whole body will be full of light; but if your eye is not sound, your whole body will be full of darkness. If then the light in you is darkness, how great is the darkness!" (Matthew 6:22–23, RSV).

Although these words of Jesus may apply to the individual, they also have direct application to the Body of Christ. The perceiver has the special responsibility of having a clear and sound eye with which to detect God's truth. Of all the members, this is the person who cannot afford pollution or sin in his life—for if he does, his sight becomes clouded. The rest of the Body counts on the perceivers to accurately identify and proclaim the will of God. If the perceiver is not walking in purity of life, his vision is impaired and what he states as truth may, in fact, be error, leading many astray. Then how great the darkness becomes!

2. Server: This is the hands of the body.

"She opens her hand to the poor; yes, she reaches out her filled hands to the needy [whether in body, mind or spirit]" (Proverbs 31:20, TAB).

Of all the gifted, we notice that servers are literally the most capable with their hands. They have great dexterity. They seem to be able to fix or build just about anything.

This is also referred to in 1 Corinthians 12:28 as the gift of helps. These people love to be helpful, anytime, anyplace . . . especially if it includes hands-on involvement.

3. Teacher: This is the mind of the body.

"Now these [Beroean Jews] were better disposed and more noble than those in Thessalonica, for they were entirely ready and accepted and welcomed the message (the word), with inclination of mind and eagerness, searching and examining the Scriptures daily to see if these things were so" (Acts 17:11, TAB).

Teachers are exceptionally gifted with intelligence. At first this may not seem fair to the rest of us, but remember that being the mind of the Body, they need to be so gifted. They are always asking questions. They want to know the basis for everything and they will search until the facts convince them that something is true. Note that the Beroeans were commended by Paul for checking out the Scriptures (what we now call the Old Testament) to be sure that their acceptance of the Good News was on a verifiable foundation.

4. Exhorter: This is the mouth of the body.

"After the reading of the Law and the prophets, the leaders [of the worship] of the synagogue sent to them saying, Brethren, if you have any word of exhortation or consolation or encouragement for the people, say it" (Acts 13:15, TAB).

Exhorters talk a lot. We have jokingly said that they have the best-oiled jaws of all the gifts. But, seriously, God has endowed them with great facility of speech. How else can an exhorter exhort, console, or encourage?

5. Giver: This is the arms of the body.

"He has shown strength and made might with His arm . . ." (Luke 1:51, TAB).

In this New Testament passage, Mary is quoting Old Testament Scriptures that couple strength with the arms. (As in Isaiah 51:9, TAB, "Awake, awake, put on strength and might, O arm of the Lord. . . .")

Givers have great strength spiritually, extending the reach of every Christian endeavor.

Remember the story about Moses holding aloft the rod so that Israel might prevail in battle over Amalek? (See Exodus 17:8–16.) When his arms grew weary he lowered them, and the Israelites began to lose. So, God provided two givers, two support people, Aaron and Hur, who held up Moses' arms until the battle was won. Givers are a strong support to those who are in spiritual battle or out on the "front lines" sharing the Gospel.

6. Administrator: This is the shoulders of the body.

"For to us a child is born, to us a son is given; and the government shall be upon His shoulder . . ." (Isaiah 9:6, TAB).

We often say that someone in leadership is shouldering responsibility. Administrators are shoulders in the body of Christ, carrying the load of leadership. Wise administrators know how to yoke up with Jesus so that He bears the burden with them.

7. Compassion Person: This is the heart of the body.

"May the Lord direct your hearts into [realizing and showing] the love of God . . ." (2 Thessalonians 3:5, TAB).

People gifted with compassion are ruled by the heart rather than the head. They reveal the true nature of God by showing kindness, care, and mercy to others.

TWO DISTINCTIONS WITHIN THE SEVEN GIFTS

When I began my study of the gifts it was 1 Peter 4:10 that helped me identify the gifts that we have been given as a lifelong endowment. For a long time I was puzzled, however, by the verse immediately following:

> Whoever speaks, [let him do it as one who utters] oracles of God; whoever renders service, [let him do it] as with the strength which God furnishes abundantly; so that in all things God may be glorified through Jesus Christ, the Messiah. . . .
>
> *1 Peter 4:11, TAB*

I knew this could, by its context, be referring to the motivational gifts. It seemed that Peter was saying that there are two basic categories of motivational gifts—those that focus primarily on speech and those that focus primarily on service. But which ones were which?

As I studied and prayed about it the Lord suggested, "Draw the human body and make a horizontal line below the shoulders and above the heart."

I drew a little cookie-cutter figure and a dotted line.

"Now look at the gifts that are represented by the parts of the body above and below the line."

I looked and it suddenly became clear. I could see that the teacher, the mind of the body, must speak in order to teach. The perceiver, the eye of the body, must speak in order to proclaim God's will. The exhorter, being the mouth of the body, obviously had a speaking gift. And the administrator, the shoulders of the body, must have facility of speech in order to lead.

These four, then, were the speaking gifts.

Looking at the gifts below the dotted line, I could see that the compassion person, the heart of the body, is usually not one who likes to get up in front of a group and speak. He would much rather work behind the scenes serving others through the abundance of love God has given him. The giver, the arms of the body, also has a supportive type of gift, shunning the limelight to serve in the background. And the server, the hands of the body, obviously excels in this area. These three were the serving gifts.

Perspective

teacher ⎫
perceiver ⎬ speaking: as for God
exhorter ⎭

administrator ⎫
compassion person ⎬ serving: with strength
giver ⎬
server ⎭

First Peter 4:11 urges those with speaking gifts to speak "as one who utters oracles of God." Such people bear the responsibility of making sure that what comes out of their mouths is what God wants said. What we say has power. God *spoke* the world into existence (Genesis 1:3). Our words have an impact on others. Anyone with a speaking gift must constantly seek to be led of the Holy Spirit as he speaks.

For those with one of the three serving gifts, the verse contains a tremendous promise. They are to serve "with the strength which God furnishes." God will give them an "abundance" of strength and energy for the work they are to do. We have observed in fact that those with serving gifts seem to have unusual amounts of stamina.

The verse also emphasizes that no matter which category our gift falls into, *all* must be done so that God is glorified.

WE MINISTER IN ALL AREAS

4

Many people asked us, "Is it possible to have all seven of the motivational gifts in my life to some extent?"

The answer is yes. We will see during the testing process that you will have some scoring, no matter how little, in each gift. We are all endowed with enough of each gift to be able to operate in that area to some degree, when called on.

Just because you do not have a particular gift as your primary giftedness does not mean that you should shrink from responding to needs around you.

For example, let's suppose your primary motivational gift is teaching and you scored the least number of points on the gift of compassion. In church one Sunday, however, you realize that the woman sitting next to you is crying. You don't know what's wrong, but you can tell she is hurting. Then you remember that compassion was your lowest score and so you say to her, "Don't expect *me* to help you. Go find someone with the gift of compassion!"

Right?

Wrong!

As part of the Body of Christ we can minister to anyone for any need, anywhere, anytime.

Don't ever let the knowledge of your particular motivational gift keep you from ministering in other areas.

While it is true that in the above scenario a compassion person would be aware of the hurting person sooner than others and move to meet the need, it does not mean that others are not able to reach out with compassion when it's needed.

33

Perspective

We will all minister in the spheres of all seven gifts.

You see, there is a difference between *being* (your motivational gift makes you what you are) and *doing* (your service to Jesus will include a wide variety of activities). Yet, the way you minister in any area will be affected by your primary motivational gift.

Also, remember that God's grace is sufficient for any circumstance we may find ourselves in. He enables. He anoints us for the task at hand. We can count on Him.

How do we know that all Christians are enjoined (and enabled) to minister in the areas of all the gifts? The Bible makes it clear:

1. Perceiving: *You* are to perceive God's will in various degrees and situations.

We should all perceive spiritual truth:
Speaking to His disciples (all of them) Jesus said, "To you it has been given to *know* the secrets and mysteries of the kingdom of heaven . . ." (Matthew 13:11, TAB).

We should all proclaim God's will with the help of the Holy Spirit:
"And it shall come to pass in the last days, God declares, that I will pour out My Spirit upon all mankind, and your sons and your daughters shall prophesy—telling forth the divine counsels . . ." (Acts 2:17, TAB).

We should all seek wisdom:
"That people may know skill and godly wisdom and instruction, discern (perceive) and comprehend the words of understanding and insight" (Proverbs 1:2, TAB).

2. Serving: *You* are to serve the Lord and other people in a variety of ways.

We should all serve God:
"Serve the Lord with gladness! Come before His presence with singing!" (Psalm 100:2, TAB).

We should all serve others:
". . . Through love you should serve one another" (Galatians 5:13, TAB).

We should all serve Jesus:
"If any one would serve Me, he must continue to follow Me—to cleave steadfastly to Me, conform wholly to My example, in living and if need be in dying—and wherever I am, there will My servant be also. If any one serves Me, the Father will honor him" (John 12:26, TAB).

3. Teaching: *You* are to teach others in appropriate ways.

We should all be prepared to teach:
"Study and be eager and do your utmost to present yourself to God approved . . . a workman who has no cause to be ashamed, correctly analyzing and accurately dividing— rightly handling and skillfully teaching—the Word of Truth" (2 Timothy 2:15, TAB).

We should all teach one another:
"Let the word [spoken by] the Christ . . . have its home (in your hearts and minds) and dwell in you in [all its] richness, as you teach and admonish and train one another in all insight and intelligence and wisdom [in spiritual things] . . ." (Colossians 3:16, TAB).

We should all teach others to obey the commands of Jesus:

"Go then and make disciples of all the nations, baptizing them into the name of the Father and of the Son and of the Holy Spirit: Teaching them to observe everything that I have commanded you . . ." (Matthew 28:19–20, TAB).

4. Exhorting: *You* are to exhort, admonish, and encourage others.

We should exhort one another whenever we gather together:

"Not forsaking or neglecting to assemble together [as believers], as is the habit of some people, but (exhorting) admonishing—warning, urging and encouraging—one another, and all the more faithfully as you see the day approaching" (Hebrews 10:25, TAB).

We should all devote ourselves to exhortation:

"Till I come, devote yourself to [public and private] reading, to exhortation—preaching and personal appeals—and to teaching and instilling doctrine" (1 Timothy 4:13, TAB).

We should all exhort every day:

"But instead warn (admonish, urge and encourage) one another every day, as long as it is called Today, that none of you may be hardened . . . by the deceitfulness of sin . . ." (Hebrews 3:13, TAB).

5. Giving: *You* are to give of your resources and energies to God and to others.

We should all be generous:

"Give, and [gifts] will be given you, good measure, pressed down, shaken together and running over . . ." (Luke 6:38, TAB).

We should all give freely:

". . . Freely (without pay) you have received; freely (without charge) give" (Matthew 10:8, TAB).

We should all be responsible for the support of ministry:

"Contribute to the needs of God's people—sharing in the necessities of the saints—pursuing the practice of hospitality" (Romans 12:13, TAB).

6. Administering: *You* are to lead as God calls you to do so.

We should all lead with a servant's heart:

". . . You know that those who are recognized as governing and are supposed to rule the Gentiles (the nations) lord it over them—ruling with absolute power, holding them in subjection—and their great men exercise authority and dominion over them. But this is not to be so among you; instead, whoever desires to be great among you must be your servant. (Mark 10:42–43, TAB).

We should all begin by administering right where we are:

"His master said to him, Well done, you upright and faithful servant! You have been faithful and trustworthy over a little; I will put you in charge of much . . ." (Matthew 25:21, TAB).

We should all look to God for a leadership position:
"But God is the judge! He puts down one and lifts up another" (Psalm 75:7, TAB).

7. Showing Compassion: *You* are to show love, compassion, and mercy to others.

We should all abound in mercy:
"Blessed are the merciful, for they shall obtain mercy" (Matthew 5:7, KJV).

We should all be loving:
"Finally, all [of you] should be of one and the same mind (united in spirit), sympathizing [with one another], loving [each the others] as brethren (of one household), compassionate and courteous—tenderhearted and humble-minded" (1 Peter 3:8, TAB).

We should all show compassion to others:
"Thus has the Lord of hosts spoken: Execute true judgment and show mercy and kindness and tender compassion every man to his brother" (Zechariah 7:9, TAB).

In all these ways the Bible admonishes us to minister in all areas of giftedness. This helps to bring balance into our lives. We will still function mainly in our primary motivational gift (that's what motivates us, remember?) but we are able to—and we must—minister in the other areas as well.

IF I HAVE A GIFT, WHY HAVEN'T I KNOWN IT?

5

The best way to measure whether or not you are operating in the sphere of your motivational gift is by this simple test:

Joy is the byproduct of operating in your motivational gift. *Frustration* is the byproduct of trying to operate outside it.

Joy is always a byproduct of doing what is in the will of God for you. Joy can never be sought as a goal or an end in itself. But as you function in the giftedness that God has given you, you will have joy.

REASONS WHY YOU MAY NOT KNOW YOUR MOTIVATIONAL GIFT

1. You were never taught about it.

This is probably the major reason for most people. It was certainly true for us. Until twelve years ago when our friends introduced us to the list of motivational gifts in Romans 12:6–8, we knew nothing about them. We had read that passage many times but never recognized it for what it is.

We estimate that fewer than two percent of American churchgoers know that motivational gifts even exist. Of those fewer than half have discovered their particular gifts. In other places it would be far less. In many of the countries where we have taught, we were, to the best of our knowledge, the first ones to teach about them.

This is why we feel it is so important to make this information available on a wider scale.

We hope you will share the teachings of this book with friends, relatives, study groups, your pastor (or your flock if you are the pastor), and anyone else you think would be helped.

2. You have never received Jesus Christ as your personal Savior and Lord.

While every person is gifted by God whether he is a Christian or not, the receiving of Christ releases the motivational gifts in far greater measure and opens up the way for the gifts to be used as God intended them to be used.

Before a person becomes a Christian his motivational gift will be functioning, at least to some extent, but often in ways that are self-centered and self-serving. Before Christ becomes central in our lives, we are central.

3. You are not being fed spiritually.

Just as a newborn baby needs nourishment, so the person who is "born again" needs spiritual sustenance in order to grow. Many people have been led to Christ but then denied instruction and encouragement. Their ability to recognize their giftedness, like the rest of their spiritual progress, is limited.

4. You have had confusing teaching on the motivational gifts.

Since the same word in English is used to translate the three different Greek words for "gift" in the New Testament, it has led some to suppose that all biblical teaching on gifts should be lumped together.

You may have heard teaching that combines the nine manifestation gifts of 1 Corinthians 12:7–10, the five ministry gifts of Ephesians 4:11, the seven motivational gifts of Romans 12:6–8—and a few others, like celibacy, as well. The result? Confusion!

You may have even taken a test made up of as many as twenty-six "gift" possibilities. Yet, when you were finished, you still felt unsure of your giftedness. We continue to meet people who were so puzzled by such teaching that they had given up the effort to find their own giftedness altogether.

It is important to have clear teaching on the gifts with which we are endowed so that we can identify them and use them for the glory of God and in service to others. It is only when the motivational gifts of Romans 12:6–8 are identified as the gifts that we possess that the Body of Christ can begin to take full advantage of them.

Even when we know about the gifts, however, and have singled out our own, we may not see evidence of their operating in our lives.

OBSTACLES THAT BLOCK THE FLOW OF MOTIVATIONAL GIFTS

1. You may have bondages that hinder the flow of your gifts.

Just as debris in a river can block the flow of the river, so the bondages in our life may block the flow of our God-given motivational gifts.

The most common bondage we see is that of fear. Incapacitating by its very nature, fear prevents our developing the full potential of our gifts.

Bondage generally results from negative childhood conditioning. Unfortunately, not every child is brought up in a positive home atmosphere. Divorce, fighting parents, alcoholism, drug usage, occult practices, mental problems, parents who abuse their children with words or actions, all limit the freedom with which the individual, when grown, will function.

On a survey questionnaire where we ask people to comment on what they were like as children, we'll occasionally get responses like, "I'm sorry, but I could not complete this. Memories of my childhood are too painful."

Happily, a person can be delivered from such bondage with good Christian counseling and ministry.

2. Anger can block the flow of your gift.

Anger is our response to being abused, wounded, or rejected. If the anger is not resolved it is either *expressed* (as in rebellion, retaliation, resentment, hatred, violence, and in some cases even murder) or it is *suppressed* (as in self-pity, self-hatred, depression, and even suicide).

Either way the person winds up in a prison house of his own making, described so graphically in Matthew 5:21–26 where Jesus equates the harboring of anger with murder.

In our experience three steps are necessary to dislodge the obstacle of anger: There need to be 1) complete forgiveness of all who have angered us in any way, 2) deliverance, and 3) inner healing prayer.

3. If you have been trying to be someone other than yourself, that too prevents the natural expression of your motivational gift.

Sometimes other people put pressure on us to conform to a certain image. Or we ourselves may try to imitate someone we admire. Unless this role model happens to have the same motivational gift we do, this can hamper the flow of our own giftedness.

We find that when teenagers take the motivational gifts test they get really excited as they find out who they are and are released to be themselves and follow God's plan for their lives.

4. A poor self-image can hinder the operation of your motivational gift.

Most people have some degree of a self-image problem stemming from the problems and pressures of childhood.

A child is designed by the Creator to be nurtured by two loving parents who will build basic trust and confidence. Not all children are so fortunate. The condition of our fallen race leaves much to be desired; often parents have themselves lacked the nurturing that would have made them whole persons.

But no matter what damage has been done, we can be grateful that we are being transformed into Christ's image as we abide in Him.

5. Irresponsibility can impede the flow of your motivational gift.

Who me? Irresponsible? Only you can check it out. Here is the principle:

"Every one to whom much is given, of him will much be required; and of him to whom men commit much, they will demand the more" (Luke 12:48, RSV).

Those who have been greatly endowed have a greater responsibility for using all that they have to help others. To neglect to use your gifting is to be irresponsible.

As you discover your motivational gift (or gifts) you may find you have not used them well. Do not let that be a source of discouragement or guilt. It is possible that you did not realize that your giftedness was there, let alone know what to do with it. So, relax, read on, discover. Then, you can become responsible.

6. Sin can block or distort the working of your gift.

There's no doubt about it. Sin pollutes. It pollutes every area of our lives and the motivational gifts are no exception.

In fact, the degree to which we are able to use our gift is dependent upon the degree to which we are in the will of God. Or, conversely, the more we entertain sin in our lives, the more the use of our motivational gifts is polluted.

Sin is missing the mark. God has a plan for each life and our goal should be to discover and cooperate with that plan. Sometimes we commit sins of omission because we are not aware of God's will on a matter. Other times we sin deliberately, doing something we know is wrong. But sin is sin whether it's done knowingly or unknowingly.

The purpose of this book is not to discuss sin. But we do exhort you to get rid of known sin in your life (and ask God to reveal to you any unknown sin so you can get rid of that, too) if you want your motivational gifts to flow freely and beautifully through your life to the benefit of others.

THE HOLY SPIRIT EMPOWERS THE GIFTS

You may be doing everything else just right in your life, but if you are not in touch with the power of the Holy Spirit you are missing the great dynamic of the third Person of the Trinity that is freely available to every believer. Paul expressed it this way: ". . . But ever be filled and stimulated with the (Holy) Spirit" (Ephesians 5:18, TAB). It's part of our inheritance. It's ours for the asking.

God the Holy Spirit wants to be released into our lives to become that well of living water, the sap that flows as we abide in the vine. We have observed that the ongoing flow of the Holy Spirit in a person's life invariably increases the pure and effective flow of his motivational gifts.

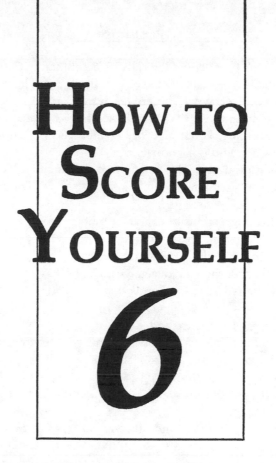

HOW TO SCORE YOURSELF

6

I recall thinking to myself, when I was first introduced to the motivational gifts concept, "Why hasn't someone come up with a self-testing method to help us discover our gifts?" Then I realized that asking the question itself was my primary motivational gift in action. So, I set out to try.

I have always been intrigued with psychological and aptitude tests such as the ones I took in high school and college. I knew something of that nature must be applicable here. I also knew that if indeed God had created seven basic motivational gifts (or what might be called seven basic personality types) then there had to be characteristics consistently found for each. Together Don and I sought unique and strong indicators and designed a testing procedure. We tried our set of testing materials with a number of groups and it worked! People discovered their giftedness.

Four years later, while I was presenting a motivational gifts seminar in Kansas City, Missouri, before a gathering of the Full Gospel Business Men's Fellowship, I learned that a well-known clinical psychologist, Edward Carr, was present. Feelings of inadequacy swept over me and I found myself making apologies for my "just-a-housewife-and-mom" status.

After the meeting Mr. Carr came over to me. "Don't you ever apologize again for what you are teaching," he admonished me. "What you have presented to us tonight is incredible! You've based your findings on the Bible, but it parallels what clinical psychologists have discovered over many years of research, and with the expenditure of vast amounts of money, from a secular investigation into personality traits. It's known as the Cleaver Technique and it divides all people into nine different types. It's amazing how similar they are to the seven gift categories that you have described.

"In fact, two of the nine types could logically be combined with two others, reducing the number to seven, matching precisely the seven biblical gifts. The research of these secular psychologists simply confirms what you are teaching."

I was grateful to know that what we were teaching was not only biblically sound, but also psychologically accurate. What God has created can be empirically discovered and verified, even by those who do not know Him.

For each of the seven motivational gifts we have developed a list of twenty characteristics typical of that person's personality and approach to life. They are based on:

1) The biblical examples of each gift,

2) Some of the initial suggestions of character traits presented by Bill Gothard and Don Pickerell,

3) Insight from the input of our brainstorming group,

4) Our own research over the past twelve years as we have taught thousands of people in many countries and benefited from their verbal and written feedback about characteristics consistent in their lives, and

5) Hundreds of letters of response and suggestions.

We have tried to include only characteristics unique to each gift. In a few cases a trait must of necessity overlap another gift's as well. While each list is reasonably comprehensive, we realize there may be additional characteristics that could be added. But we have attempted to come up with the most indicative qualities so that an effective method of scoring could be developed.

We are indeed wonderfully made and, like snowflakes, no two of us are exactly alike. Even though thousands share your gift, your expression of it will be unique. Even if you are an identical twin you are going to have differences that affect your individual performance.

These differences come from the influence of countless variables in your life. For instance, health is a variable. While for some the event of sickness or injury may thwart giftedness, for others it may be the very thing that challenges them to rise above limitations and use their gifts in an even greater way. Other variables are heredity, education, culture, economics, marital status, location, talents, self-image—well, the list is endless and each one has an impact on your life and the way you use your gift.

This should help give you some feeling for the magnitude of God's plan in creating such unique individuals—even though, amazingly, we all operate primarily influenced by one of the seven motivational gifts.

SCORING

Here's how the scoring is done. As we present and define each characteristic in the following chapters, ask yourself, "How true is this of me?" Your first response will probably be the most accurate. Don't answer the way you'd *like* to be or the way you think you *ought* to be. Be honest! Remember, there are no right or wrong answers. This is simply a self-discovery process. You alone know yourself well enough to be able to score properly.

It is also important to differentiate, when scoring, between learned behavior and the way you naturally act or think. If you are presently employed, be sure that your current duties do not unduly influence your answers. Your job may or may not be using your motivational gifts.

If the characteristic is never true of you, put an "x" (or a check mark) in the box under *never*. Then place a "0" in the points column.

If the characteristic is true of you only on rare occasions, mark under *seldom* and put a "1" in the points column.

If the characteristic is sometimes true of you (up to 49 percent of the time), score under *sometimes* and give yourself a "2" in the points column.

If the characteristic is true of you 50 to 75 percent of the time, score under *usually*, and write a "3" in the points column.

If the characteristic is true of you most of the time, score under *mostly*, and put a "4" in the points column.

If the characteristic is true of you all of the time, score under *always* and place a "5" in the points column.

After you have scored yourself on all twenty characteristics, add up your score on the tally sheet at the end of each testing chapter. It does not matter whether you score high, low, or in the middle. Remember, this is a subjective test. It is the *comparison* of your seven scores that will help you to determine your motivational gifts.

If you were to give yourself a "5" for each of the twenty characteristics of a particular gift you would receive the maximum score of 100.

Now take a look at the profile sheet at the end of this chapter. Take your total for each gift and transfer it to the profile sheet by shading in the appropriate horizontal column from left (0) to right, stopping where your score corresponds to the number at the top of the chart. (A sample profile sheet is on page 203.)

After you have transferred all seven scores you will have a composite profile of yourself. The score that stands out farthest to the right, much like the nose on a person's face, is your primary motivational gift. You will also see at a glance which is your secondary gift, third, and so forth. It is equally important to identify areas where you are the *least* gifted. You need to know this so that you can:

1) recognize your areas of maximum dependence on others,

2) rejoice in those who are gifted in those ways,

3) avoid trying to be what you are not, and

4) say, "No, thank you" with confidence when asked to do things (except of course in a general way or in immediate need, as discussed in chapter four) that are outside the sphere of your giftedness.

On the other hand, discovering your gifts will release you to accept responsibilities that will use your giftedness. It will help you to use your time and energy in pursuits in which you will tend to be successful and also a blessing to others.

Now, move on to *your discovery of your motivational gifts!*

Adult Questionnaire

ADULT MOTIVATIONAL GIFT PROFILE SHEET

Gift	0	10	20	30	40	50	60	70	80	90	100
Perceiver											
Server											
Teacher											
Exhorter											
Giver											
Administrator											
Compassion Person											

NAME _____ #1 GIFT _____

ADDRESS _____ #2 GIFT _____

CITY/ST/ZIP _____ #3 GIFT _____

© *Copyright 1987, Don & Katie Fortune*

PART
2

THE SEVEN GIFTS

CHARACTERISTICS OF THE PERCEIVER

7

We have chosen to call this first of the Romans 12 list, the gift of perception. The King James Version uses the word "prophecy." But since the same word is used in the other two lists in the New Testament it would be easy to confuse it with either the manifestation gift of prophecy or the ministry gift to the church, the prophet.

Also, the word "prophecy" in our current vocabulary has a variety of connotations, both positive and negative. It seemed to us that a fresh new word would eliminate confusion.

The Greek word for "prophecy" in verse six is *propheteia*, related to *prophetes*, which means according to *Strong's Exhaustive Concordance*, "an inspired speaker." One of its root words is *phemi*, meaning "to show or make known one's thoughts, to speak, say or affirm."

According to biblical scholars, the prominent idea of prophecy in the New Testament is not prediction, but "the inspired delivery of warning, exhortation, instruction, judging and making manifest the secrets of the heart."[4]

In the specific context of motivational gifts we see that the word refers to one who is especially sensitive to perceiving the will of God, and then proclaiming it—or, depending upon the Lord's direction, praying for it to be accomplished.

The perceiver, then, is one who readily perceives, prays about, proclaims, and promotes the will of God.

In this chapter we will examine each of twenty characteristics of the perceiver in detail, giving examples from the experience of those with this primary motivational gift.

Now proceed to score yourself as indicated in the previous chapter.

	Never	Seldom	Sometimes	Usually	Mostly	Always	
1. Quickly and accurately identifies good and evil and hates evil.	0	1	2	3	4	5	**POINTS**

The perceiver views people or situations as either *in* the will of God or *out* of the will of God. To him there is no such thing as *sort of* in the will of God or *partly* in the will of God, for in his understanding not to be perfectly in the will of God is to be out of God's will.

Perceivers see life as a matter of choices. They view the option to choose right as imperative: not to choose right is by default choosing wrong. Compromise is not an option.

They have intense hatred for evil. They want to see evil overcome and eliminated, and the Kingdom of God evidenced here on this earth.

A biblical figure with the gift of perception is John the Baptist. From the beginning of his public ministry he exposed evil and identified with and expressed God's hatred of it. He publicly denounced Herod's adulterous relationship with his brother's wife, even when his stand meant prison and death.

Spokesmen for righteousness and just causes are frequently perceivers. Their giftedness equips them to be bold and outspoken without regard for either public esteem or their own advantage.

We asked our perceiver friend Vicki why she spent so much of her free time campaigning against abortion.

"Why," she replied emphatically, "abortion is murder! Murder is wrong! How can anyone observe such an evil in our society and *not* speak out about it?"

Our youngest son, Dan, has the gift of perception. At age ten he was somewhat overweight and becoming concerned about it. One day he asked me what he could do to lose weight. I explained to him that sugar was the biggest culprit and that it would help to cut out desserts and sweets.

Sugar immediately became his "public enemy number one." He determined to rid his diet of this evil once and for all. During the next few months his weight dropped until he was slim and trim. Even when he went to birthday parties he refused to eat ice cream or cake. To this day Dan still refuses to eat sugar, even conscientiously reading the labels on jars and boxes. He has taken his stand against sugar and he will not budge!

	Never	Seldom	Sometimes	Usually	Mostly	Always	
2. Sees everything as either black or white; no gray or indefinite areas.	0	1	2	3	4	5	**POINTS**

Perceivers make decisions easily. They form quick evaluations. They see things as right or wrong, appropriate or inappropriate, true or false. They don't see how there can be anything in between. They tend to answer yes or no. They seldom say maybe. They are people of extremes in feelings, words, and actions.

Most of us think in terms of a scale from black through many shades of gray to white.

We could say, "I'm not doing as well as I might, but at least I'm doing better than I did yesterday." Not so the perceiver. No halfway measures.

Emily Binning, author of *Gordon Takes a Wife,* had been fighting a weight problem most of her life without much permanent success. One day the Lord told her to submit everything she ate to her perceiver husband's approval.

These were his ground rules: She could put anything she wanted on her plate and then ask Gordon what she could eat—a daring thing to submit to the decisions of an uncompromising perceiver! In her book she wrote:

"A couple of nights after this decision, we were invited out to dinner. It was our first experience away from home in submitting my food for Gordon's evaluation. It took quite a bit of whispering back and forth during the meal, during which time I lost a half a potato, one slice of meat, and a roll with butter. Dessert was served: pumpkin pie with whipped cream. I carefully spread the whipped cream over the entire piece before asking Gordon how much I could have, so there would be whipped cream on whatever portion was to be mine! Gordon looked at the pie and said out loud, 'You can't have *any* pie.' "[5]

Gordon saw the situation the way a classical perceiver does: If you are going to do it, let's do it right. (She got her weight down and kept it down.)

	Never	Seldom	Sometimes	Usually	Mostly	Always	
3. Easily perceives the character of individuals and groups.	0	1	2	3	4	5	**POINTS**

It's easy for perceivers to "get the feel" of individuals and groups—not by any outward analysis, but by the intuitive perception that is their gift.

John the Baptist did not need to ask questions of the group of Pharisees that came out to observe him baptizing. "You brood of vipers!" he accosted them (Matthew 3:7, NAS). John knew that the Pharisees had not come to repent but rather to judge and criticize and condemn.

A perceiver can go into a church, a prayer group, a healing service, or any group for that matter, and soon tell how spiritual it really is. He also has keen sensitivity to what is going on in an individual's life.

During a Canadian seminar we met Bea, a mature perceiver. Later she wrote us saying, "I was one of those who scored 100% on the perceiver gift. During a coffee break I was talking with a minister I was acquainted with and began to be aware that there was something more going on in his life than he was expressing. I suddenly perceived that he was going through a mid-life crisis. I don't know how, but I just *knew* it. I didn't say anything, but prayed for him for several days. Two weeks later the minister resigned from his position and confided in me that it was due to a *mid-life* crisis!"

It's not that perceivers know everything about a person; God shows them only what He wants them to see. And always for a purpose, usually so that the perceiver can effectively pray for that person.

4. Encourages repentance that produces good fruit.

	Never	Seldom	Sometimes	Usually	Mostly	Always	POINTS
	0	1	2	3	4	5	

After challenging the spirituality of the Pharisees and Sadducees, John the Baptist went on to say, "Bring forth fruit that is consistent with repentance—let your lives prove your change of heart" (Matthew 3:8, TAB).

John was well aware of the claims of these "religious" individuals to be spiritual leaders, but he was also aware of their hypocrisy. John knew that only a genuine and evident change in their behavior would prove the inward condition of a repentant heart.

We do a lot of personal counseling and have learned to observe the fruit in a person's life in order to help diagnose underlying problems. Evidence of bad fruit means bad roots. We pray for the exposure of the cause of those bad roots, help the person identify all of the hatred and judgment against the one who hurt him, and then help the person repent of it. If there is genuine repentance, his life begins to bear good fruit.

5. Believes the acceptance of difficulties will produce positive personal brokenness.

	Never	Seldom	Sometimes	Usually	Mostly	Always	POINTS
	0	1	2	3	4	5	

Most of us avoid problems. We do not view trials as friends, or see trauma and tragedy as stepping stones to maturity. Not so the perceivers. They rejoice in negative events as being the greatest opportunities to work brokenness into their lives.

By brokenness we mean that experience of once again coming to the end of ourselves where we say, "God, I can't handle this. I can't do anything without You. Help, Lord!"

Perceiver, prophet, and author John Sandford says that two-word cry is the most spiritual prayer a person can utter.

Perceivers welcome the difficulties that press a person into brokenness because they feel it means that God loves them enough to deal with another area of their lives.

It seems God sifts and sifts the perceivers. He wants to do a thorough and deep work in them so they will be tools well fitted for building His Body here on earth.

Years ago I heard Iverna Tompkins say, "God is not letting me get by this year with what He let me get by with last year." She said she often argued with the Lord that "everyone else seems to be getting away with it" and He would gently but firmly tell her that she was not "everyone else"—that He had a plan for her life and it was a narrower way.

Perceivers also rejoice to see evidence of brokenness in others. Have you ever shared a difficult thing you were going through with a perceiver only to have him exclaim, "Praise the Lord! I know God's going to bring forth some great things in your life through this!"

And you say, "Thanks a lot!" That was not what you wanted to hear; you wanted some sympathy. You won't get it from a perceiver! These people know that brokenness not only does them good, it does you good, too.

	Never	Seldom	Sometimes	Usually	Mostly	Always	
6. Has only a few or no close friendships.	0	1	2	3	4	5	POINTS

Often perceivers go through childhood with only one or two good friends—or none at all. Some worry about this, wondering why they don't want to reach out more to kids their own age. Others instinctively know that it's okay—that God made them this way. They feel comfortable in their aloneness.

Most often it's the parents of the perceiver who get overly concerned, feeling that the child should be friendlier, more involved with others.

We faced this with our younger son, Dan, before we understood about gifts. During his primary years Dan seemed to prefer playing alone after school, or just with his older brother, Dave.

"Why don't you invite the boy down the street to come over and play with you, Dan?" we would ask.

"I don't want to."

"But why?"

"He's dishonest. I've seen him steal things from other kids at school."

"Then why not ask the boy up the hill to come over?"

"Not him! He's mean."

"How about Johnny, then?"

"No way. He lies. I don't like to be around him."

And so it would go. Dan couldn't seem to find a friend who lived up to his standards.

Dave was, in so many respects, just the opposite of Dan. Dave always brought friends home after school—usually a bunch. It seemed logical to push Dan into friendships so he "wouldn't feel left out." Then we learned about the motivational gifts and recognized that Dave was an administrator child, naturally drawn to a wide range of broad friendships. Dan, as a perceiver child, would tend to be a loner or have highly selective friendships.

Interestingly, when we put our boys in a Christian school Dan made several close friends within the year. For our perceiver son, this was a more congenial atmosphere in which to develop friendships without compromising values.

Just as the Levites were uniquely set apart from the rest of the twelve tribes of Israel to minister to the Lord in the Temple, so, we believe, perceivers have been called apart to spend much time in prayer, to bring God's Word to the Body of Christ, and to uphold God's highest standards. They will not have the luxury of broad friendships for several reasons:

1) Time for friendships is limited since their call to a ministry of prayer requires a significant time commitment.

2) Broad friendships require a degree of tolerance for people with differing standards and beliefs. Perceivers cannot compromise.

3) God's gifting draws the perceivers to enjoy being "alone with Him."

	Never	Seldom	Sometimes	Usually	Mostly	Always	
7. Views the Bible as the basis for truth, belief, action, and authority.	0	1	2	3	4	5	**POINTS**

Perceivers are in the Word a lot. They love to study the Bible and find that God often speaks to them through specific Scriptures. They believe there isn't any other dependable basis for truth but the Bible.

John the Baptist's call was based on the Word of God. He knew well Isaiah 40:3 and that his was the long-awaited voice of one crying in the wilderness.

Desiring to assure John that He (Jesus) was indeed the Christ, Jesus said to the Baptist's disciples, "Go and tell John what you have seen and heard: the blind are receiving their sight; the lame are walking; the lepers are cleansed; the deaf are hearing; the dead are raised up, and the poor have the good news (the Gospel) preached to them" (Luke 7:22, TAB).

John saw the scriptural evidence in that answer since he knew the prophecies about the Messiah and what he would do.

Perceivers also depend on the Holy Spirit to illuminate the Word. Our friend Steve Lightle, a perceiver/prophet, describes such an experience:

"While I was sitting in a chair, the power of God came into the room. . . . Things began to happen to me spiritually of such a deep nature that I wondered what was going on. For the first time in my life, I had such an intimate and personal time with Jesus, that I could say with Paul, 'I . . . heard inexpressible words, which a man is not permitted to speak' (2 Corinthians 12:4, NAS). During these days, the Lord was taking me mainly through the book of Isaiah. This was where I was reading almost constantly for the six and a half days. The Lord would make everything so real to me. It was an ongoing process of revelation."[6]

	Never	Seldom	Sometimes	Usually	Mostly	Always	
8. Boldly operates on spiritual principles.	0	1	2	3	4	5	**POINTS**

From the Bible perceivers are able to extract principles that they apply to daily life. In fact, they are often very demanding of themselves about this. Children who have this gift are incredibly strict with themselves. They usually develop into the kind of teenagers who don't have to have parental restrictions imposed on them because they are already setting their own high standards.

One parent related how her perceiver teenager keeps her honest: "One day I was talking on the phone to a friend who wanted to borrow our utility trailer. Feeling inwardly irritated because this particular person was always borrowing things, I made up an excuse. 'Sorry, the trailer's being used right now,' I said.

" 'Mom!' my daughter said in a shocked tone of voice after I had hung up the phone. 'The trailer's just sitting there! It's *not* being used. We're supposed to give to those who ask of us and not turn away from those who would borrow from us.'

"She was right," the mother continued. "She had quoted a principle from Matthew 5:42. Feeling reproved by a daughter I had grown to respect for her principled life, I called my friend back and told her the trailer was available."

The perceiver is a person of principle in all aspects of life, the way he runs his home, business, personal relationships. Perceivers are truly the standard-bearers of the Church. They are the ones who hold up God's righteousness and say, "This is what we ought to aim for!" It there weren't any perceivers many of us would settle for less. We *need* these people in the Body of Christ.

While perceiving is my third motivational gift, it often pops up in my life. I find I can't get around it even when the circumstances are to my disadvantage.

For example, two years ago I held a big garage sale—twenty-two years of accumulated stuff to turn into cash to help pay college tuition for our sons. Among the items was a doll I had played with as a child. Having no little girls in our family to pass it on to, I propped up the doll on one of the sale tables with a $10 sign on her. Half the way through the day she had not been sold, so I marked her down to $8. Shortly afterward a woman picked her up and handed her to me saying, "I'll take this doll, but I want to look around a bit more."

"Okay," I said, "I'll hold her for you."

Before I could set the doll down another lady, who had just arrived, said, "I'll give you twenty dollars for that doll."

"I'm sorry," I replied, "but I just told that other lady she could have her."

"I'll give you fifty dollars for her," she urged me.

"But I've given my word to the other lady," I said, by now regretting that I'd done so!

"I'll give you a hundred dollars. I've got to have her."

I realized I was being tested, not by the woman, but by God. One hundred dollars would go a lot further on college bills that eight dollars. I could feel the temptation but I could also feel an even stronger pull on my heart. The Lord reminded me of His words, "Let your Yes be simply Yes, and your No be simply No; anything more than that comes from the evil one" (Matthew 5:37, TAB). The principle was clear.

Even though the second woman explained that this was a collector's item, a Shirley Temple doll worth $125 or more, I knew what I must do. The doll went for eight dollars.

	Never	Seldom	Sometimes	Usually	Mostly	Always	POINTS
9. Is frank, outspoken, and doesn't mince words.	0	1	2	3	4	5	

This characteristic sometimes gets perceivers into trouble. One woman who came to work at the Aglow International office had this gift but didn't know it. She was a fairly new Christian who was always criticizing people and telling them what she thought. It wasn't long before most of the people at the Aglow office were upset with her—as schoolmates and associates had been, all her life.

I started teaching the motivational gift seminar during Carol's third week there. She came up after the very first session and said, "Katie, I know my gift already! For the first time ever I feel I can begin to understand and accept myself," she added, brushing away the tears.

"I've had so much self-hatred because I was always hurting people with my mouth. I didn't know what else to do with what I *saw*," she said, "except to blurt it out. Now I can see that it is wrong to do it that way. I want to grow in my gift so it will help people, not hurt them."

I shared with Carol how perceivers are allowed to *see* many things that are out of God's will, but that God's plan for them is usually to *pray* about it, not to talk about it or confront it.

I saw Carol change into an increasingly sensitive Christian. She has learned how to mitigate her frankness.

We have found that a *mature* perceiver is the most exciting person in the world to be around. You can count on his being honest, up-front, and candid—yet guided by wisdom and love. We love to talk with perceivers. They are so transparent. They never beat around the bush.

John the Baptist again is a good example. He warned of judgment. He told selfish people to share. He told tax collectors to be honest and soldiers not to misuse authority. And so electrifying were his words that thousands flocked to the wilderness to hear him.

10. Is very persuasive in method of speaking.

	Never	Seldom	Sometimes	Usually	Mostly	Always	
	0	1	2	3	4	5	POINTS

Their persuasiveness stems from the fact that perceivers have such strong convictions about everything. Things are either right or wrong and they will speak out accordingly.

Our perceiver son, Dan, sang in the Living Faith Ensemble during his senior year at Kings, a Christian high school. At the beginning of one church concert the mike partners introduced each other to the congregation. Ursula Rueb, Dan's partner, said with a twinkle in her eye, "This is Dan Fortune, and he's *always* right!"

Peals of laughter broke out among the eighteen members of the group who loved Dan but were often also painfully aware of his strong opinions and persuasiveness.

Phil, a perceiver, shared how important he felt it was to be persuasive. "Even in high school I was aware that some of my friends were aimless, with a lack of ambition to do anything constructive with their lives. I would spend hours urging them to make their lives count. Today they are people of influence with a strong Christian witness."

11. Grieves deeply over the sins of others.

	Never	Seldom	Sometimes	Usually	Mostly	Always	
	0	1	2	3	4	5	POINTS

This is a person who will (inwardly and even outwardly) weep when he sees someone involved in serious sin. He knows that sin carries within itself the seeds of destruction. He—feeling the heart of God—would spare the person the inevitable consequences of such sowing, but he also knows that it is only through repentance that it can be so. Thus he prays for the convicting power of the Holy Spirit to bring the person to repentance.

An assistant pastor's wife, a perceiver we will call Nancy, looked up at the end of the service as the senior pastor was leaving the pulpit and heard God clearly speak to her that this man was involved in adultery with a certain woman in the church.

Deeply grieved over the situation, Nancy went home and interceded for them both. For days she wept before God, pleading with Him to change the pastor's heart, to change the woman's heart, to bring them both under conviction of their sin and to stop the affair. After a week of earnest daily prayer the Lord told Nancy He wanted her to go and confront the woman.

"How did you find out?" the startled woman asked.

"God revealed it to me," Nancy replied. "He wants you to end the affair."

"Well, I won't!" the woman snapped back. "Stay out of my life!"

Nancy went back home and for another week she prayed and wept. At the end of the second week the Lord told her to go again and confront the woman. It was not a pleasant prospect, yet Nancy was obedient. Still the woman refused to listen.

At that point, Nancy reported, the burden abruptly lifted from her shoulders. There was still a human grief for the situation but the godly grief and burden was lifted from her. God calls upon perceivers to intercede but the free will of the sinner can still thwart His will.

We would like to report a happy ending to the story but tragically sin took its course: two families were destroyed and many friends and church members wounded and disillusioned, some even falling away in shock and bitterness.

	Never	Seldom	Sometimes	Usually	Mostly	Always	
12. Is eager to see his own blind spots and to help others see theirs too.	0	1	2	3	4	5	**POINTS**

All of us have blind spots. That's what Jesus was talking about when He asked,

"Why do you look at the speck of sawdust in your brother's eye and pay no attention to the plank in your own eye? How can you say to your brother, 'Brother, let me take the speck out of your eye,' when you yourself fail to see the plank in your own eye?" (Luke 6:41–42, NIV).

That plank is our blind spot.

One time my friend Marcia Kruesel was driving me to the Sea-Tac airport when a woman just ahead and to the right of us suddenly started to move over into our lane. Had she continued we would have had a collision. Marcia honked and the woman quickly swerved away. "We were in her blind spot," Marcia said to me.

It's true. There's an area just over the driver's left shoulder that is not visible in the rear-view mirror.

How true this is in life, too, I thought. If we don't sound a warning where there is a blind spot and the person keeps on his predetermined course, not seeing the danger, eventually there will be a collision—some sort of crisis.

When we are ready for God to deal with us in the area of our blind spots, we can do nothing better than find a friend with the gift of perception and request his discernment.

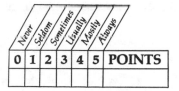

13. Desires above all else to see God's plan worked out in all situations.

	Never	Seldom	Sometimes	Usually	Mostly	Always	POINTS
	0	1	2	3	4	5	

Perceivers discern God's plan, and will never let personal desires get in the way of that plan for themselves or others. When a perceiver counsels another person a characteristic phrase is: "You need to let go of *your* plans and discover what *God's* plan is for your life."

When working with an organization, the perceiver will encourage the individuals in it to sacrifice their own needs and desires for the good of *God's plan* for the group.

Often, perceivers are given insights, visions, and revelations so that they will know God's will on a matter. Simeon was a devout man rigorously observing the Law while he waited for the Messiah. The Holy Spirit revealed to this perceiver that he should not see death before he had seen the Lord's Anointed.

How excited Simeon must have been to be let into the very heart of God's plan! Led by the Holy Spirit, he came into the Temple just as Mary and Joseph brought their Son for His dedication. Recognizing Jesus, Simeon took Him in his arms and praised God saying, "And now, Lord, You are releasing Your servant to depart (leave this world) in peace, according to Your Word. For with my [own] eyes I have seen Your Salvation Which You have ordained and prepared before (in the presence of) all peoples, A Light for revelation to the Gentiles—to disclose what was before unknown—and [to bring] praise and honor and glory to Your people Israel" (Luke 2:29–32, TAB).

14. Strongly promotes the spiritual growth of groups and individuals.

	Never	Seldom	Sometimes	Usually	Mostly	Always	POINTS
	0	1	2	3	4	5	

Perceivers want to see spiritual growth. They view themselves as ever growing and are eager to help others grow, too.

A perceiver/evangelist ministering in Africa trains young men for mature ministry of their own. As he puts it, "It's the way to multiply my ministry. As I help them grow, the Gospel is spread more widely and effectively."

Perceivers view the spiritual growth of groups as the product of changes in individuals. Just as the weakest link in a chain determines the strength of that chain, so they see that in a group the person who is weakest spiritually limits the whole group's effectiveness.

Therefore the perceiver realizes that he has to deal on a one-to-one basis, helping individual members in order to see the whole group become strong.

Kit, a perceiver missionary with Youth With A Mission, wrote to us recently from Montana, "I have enjoyed working with groups during these last years and especially individuals within those groups that needed to grow spiritually. My joy is helping to mature the saints and seeing them operate more effectively in the Body of Christ."

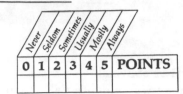

15. Is called to intercession.

This is perhaps the most important characteristic of the perceiver. We have yet to find an adult Christian with the gift of perception who has not been called to intercession. We have found a few who have not yet taken the time to *listen* to discover if they are so called. But the call is there—it's just a matter of *tuning in* to hear it!

Most perceivers are aware of the importance of intercession. They have an innate sense that it is the most important aspect of their life and ministry. They realize that "mountains are moved" and more can be accomplished through prayer than any other way.

One perceiver said, "About ninety percent of my ministry is in intercessory prayer. Only ten percent of the time do I work directly with people. Usually after I've prayed through on a matter I see the results manifested in the situation. Seldom do I have to take any specific action other than prayer."

Another perceiver said candidly, "Perceivers should be slow to speak but quick to pray!"

Good advice. Perceivers "see" many things that are not in God's will. They may be given revelations about other people's problems and needs. If they don't take it to prayer they can become negative criticizers or obnoxious meddlers. God's purpose in giving them insight is so that they can intercede effectively.

Perceivers are key people in prayer groups. They motivate others to pray. They have the most powerful prayer ministries of the seven gifts. (The giver and the shower of compassion are also especially effective in this area—but with different emphases.) Perceivers often fast along with their ministry of intercession.

16. Feels the need to verbalize or dramatize what he "sees."

Hosea is a biblical example. Remember how he took a harlot for his wife, to demonstrate Israel's faithlessness? Hosea heard the Lord say, "Go, take to yourself a wife of harlotry and have children of [her] harlotry, for the land commits great whoredom by departing from the Lord" (Hosea 1:2, TAB).

It was a pretty dramatic move but it got the nation's attention. And when his wife Gomer left Hosea to return to prostitution he went out seeking her, to demonstrate how God will go out of His way to seek those who have turned their backs on Him.

Sometimes perceivers will use the stage as a vehicle for getting across the message of God. We find that these people are often drawn into the field of drama. It enables people with this giftedness to graphically present what God wants said.

A perceiver friend, Diana, said, "During my late teen and young adult years I was involved in drama groups because I loved to dramatize things I felt strongly about. Once I met the Lord, my interest transferred to Christian drama groups."

The perceiver may have a dramatic flair for illustrating God's truth when teaching, preaching, or just talking.

Many Old Testament prophets also had a dramatic flair. Some dressed in sackcloth and ashes when they wanted people to repent. Elisha told leprous Naaman to dip seven times in the Jordan River. Elijah called down fire from heaven. Nathan used a dramatic story of a poor man with only one lamb to touch David's conscience.

In the New Testament John the Baptist dressed in rough garments of camel's hair and ate insects and wild honey. A prophet named Agabus warned Paul of impending imprisonment by taking off Paul's belt, binding his own hands and feet, and saying, "The Holy Spirit says, 'In this way the Jews of Jerusalem will bind the owner of this belt and will hand him over to the Gentiles' " (Acts 21:11, NIV). Jesus rode a donkey into Jerusalem in an enactment of an ancient prophecy.

Never	Seldom	Sometimes	Usually	Mostly	Always	
0	1	2	3	4	5	**POINTS**

17. Tends to be introspective.

Perceivers know the meaning of the Scripture "Search me [thoroughly], O God, and know my heart! Try me, and know my thoughts! And see if there is any wicked or hurtful way in me, and lead me in the way everlasting" (Psalm 139:23–24, TAB).

Getting rid of imperfections is a top priority of perceivers. They want God to bring forth that pure gold in their life, to refine them and make them what He wants them to be. Therefore, they are not afraid to look within and identify those things with which they need to deal. They know the importance of pure motives prompted by the Holy Spirit and not the desires of the flesh.

Howard Pitman describes how he died medically on the operating table and was taken in spirit to the gates of heaven. Thinking his life of "good works" entitled him to come before God with a request, he was shocked to find that God was not pleased with him.

"The sound of His voice came down on me from over the Gates even before the words hit me. The tone of His anger knocked me on my face as God proceeded to tell me just what kind of life I had really lived.... He pointed out that my faith was dead, that my works were not acceptable, and that I had labored in vain....

"All of these years I thought I was doing those works for God! Now He was telling me that what I did, I did for myself. Even as I preached and testified about the saving grace of Jesus Christ, I was doing that only for myself in order that my conscience might be soothed.... This made my priorities out of order and unacceptable."[7]

He had some soul-searching to do! He saw that only what was *prompted by the Spirit* would be of value to God.

Helen, another perceiver from Montana, wrote to us recently: "Introspection has always been a problem in my life. I thought I took myself too seriously. How glad I was to know that this is part of my giftedness—that it's okay to be introspective."

	Never	Seldom	Sometimes	Usually	Mostly	Always	
18. Has strong opinions and convictions.	0	1	2	3	4	5	POINTS

Perceivers have an opinion on just about everything. And if you happen to bring up a subject they have never thought about—guess what? They form an opinion on the spot!

Fortunately perceivers usually seek God's help in forming their convictions; thus the perceiver's opinion often carries with it the ring of truth.

But perceivers don't necessarily present their opinions gently. They can be the proverbial "bull in the china shop" and leave a trail of destruction behind them.

Don ran painfully up against this characteristic ten years ago when he was responsible for a home meeting of twenty-five people. After just a few meetings he could see that five of the women were perceivers. "Lord," I remember hearing him pray, "what are You trying to do to me? Five at once!"

At first, he reports, the sparks used to fly. Each of the five had such strong opinions! Often the opinions did not coincide, and needless to say, there were never any lukewarm discussions. Don was fascinated to watch the Lord at work in the hearts of all five perceivers. The more mature ones tended to be more open to the opinions of others. But there was growth for all of them, and for the rest of the group, as they interacted.

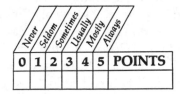

	Never	Seldom	Sometimes	Usually	Mostly	Always	
19. Has strict personal standards.	0	1	2	3	4	5	POINTS

Perceivers are never satisfied with less than their best effort. Unless they are out of fellowship with God, they have impeccable morals. Even teenagers with this gift will seldom compromise their standards. In fact, they are usually more strict with themselves than their parents are with them.

One young man with this gift found out that his older sister had moved in with her boyfriend. At first he was angry because his sister's behavior was reflecting on himself and his family. Then he was angry because it was an offense to God. Then he was angry at Satan for prompting her to immorality. At this point he channeled his anger into prayer and spiritual warfare on her behalf.

While some can live their lives heedless of God and the fact that He is aware of all they do, the perceiver cannot. He is keenly aware of the Lord's constant presence with him. He wants to live in a way that is consistently pleasing to Him.

Perceivers are honest. Integrity is their byword. Carolyn came home from the grocery store one day to discover that the clerk had not charged her for a case of canned goods she had placed on the lower shelf of the grocery cart.

"Never mind," her husband said. "They'll never know it."

"But I'll know," Carolyn replied, her gift going into action. "I'm going back to pay for it."

The grocery store clerk was amazed when Carolyn explained the situation. "You're really honest!" he exclaimed.

"Shouldn't everyone be?" Carolyn asked. "I wouldn't be able to live with myself unless I was."

20. Desires to be obedient to God at all costs.

Never	Seldom	Sometimes	Usually	Mostly	Always	POINTS
0	1	2	3	4	5	

Perceivers recognize the importance of obedience. The opposite, in their estimation, is rebellion—a sin described in the Old Testament "as the sin of witchcraft" (1 Samuel 15:23, KJV).

One perceiver did a study of obedience in the Bible. "I became aware," she said, "that being obedient to God (1 Peter 1:14) also meant that I was to be respectful to and obedient to others. Starting with Jesus, I am not only to obey Him in everything he tells me to do (James 1:22), I must also bring every thought into obedience to Him (2 Corinthians 10:5). Then I saw that I must be obedient to secular rulers (Titus 3:1), to leaders (2 Corinthians 2:9), to my parents (Colossians 3:20), to my husband (Ephesians 5:22), and even to my employer (Ephesians, 6:5–8). It's a big order, but with His strength I can do it.

"Jesus is my pattern. He was obedient to God in all things, even to His death on the cross."

We often urge parents of young perceiver children to teach these children to be obedient to *them* so that as they mature they can also be obedient to *God*. We speak from experience. Dan, our perceiver child, was not at all easy to discipline. While he wanted to obey us, his own will and stubbornness would sometimes get in the way.

Fortunately when Don and I got married we found that we agreed on discipline. We also believed the warning, "Spare the rod and spoil the child" (see Proverbs 13:24). We read a powerful little pamphlet presenting the Christian perspective on discipline, *Children, Fun or Frenzy?*, and promptly went to the local lumber store. We bought a 36-inch dowel, cut it in half, and strategically placed the two 18-inch rods for quick access when needed.

It worked! The children soon learned that we did indeed wield the rod of authority. After a spanking for disobedient behavior we would scoop them up in our arms, love them, explain why they were being disciplined in that instance, and then forgive them. It was clear that this approach made them feel loved and secure.

In fact, one day when David was three he brought the rod to us saying, "Spank me, I did something wrong." He had broken something he'd been told not to touch and he knew he'd feel better after being disciplined. He did.

Dan was not so eager to be disciplined. Perceiver children are typically strong-willed and hard-headed. They are a challenge to parents and must be taught obedience or their gift will remain polluted for the rest of their lives.

Dan always tried to justify his actions. He would argue with us. Often we had to send Dan to his room after a spanking while Dave quickly repented, asked for forgiveness, and went merrily on his way to play. We remained consistent with Dan and eventually he began to be obedient without arguing. He became a delightful child—internalizing the learned discipline, developing into a youngster of high standards. He grew close to the Lord and grew in his desire to be obedient to Him.

Today Dan understands why we had to discipline him more than we did his brother, and appreciates it. "I would never have been able to obey my heavenly Father," Dan says, "if I had not learned to obey my earthly father." Dan is now a missions major and has already taken out a year to serve in the Philippines under missionary-evangelist Rod McDougal. "God said to go and so I went," Dan says.

NOW SCORE

Transfer your scores to the perceiver scoring sheet on page 61. Add all twenty numbers and record in the total box. Then transfer that total to the profile sheet on page 44.

Remember, there are no right or wrong answers. This is a subjective self-discovery test. Do not try to compare your scores with anyone else's scores. What is important is the comparison of *all seven* of your *own* scores, revealing your personal profile.*

---

* Additional sets of the seven scoring sheets along with the profile sheet are available from the authors in 8½ x 11" size. Scoring sheets are also available in a randomly arranged form that allows identification of the gifts only after the testing is completed and in sets designed for youth, for children, for secular users, and in seven foreign languages. See the back of the book for details.

THE GIFT OF PERCEPTION

	Never	Seldom	Sometimes	Usually	Mostly	Always	POINTS
	0	1	2	3	4	5	
1.							
2.							
3.							
4.							
5.							
6.							
7.							
8.							
9.							
10.							
11.							
12.							
13.							
14.							
15.							
16.							
17.							
18.							
19.							
20.							
						TOTAL	

Characteristics:

1. Quickly and accurately identifies good and evil and hates evil.
2. Sees everything as either black or white; no gray or indefinite areas.
3. Easily perceives the character of individuals and groups.
4. Encourages repentance that produces good fruit.
5. Believes the acceptance of difficulties will produce positive personal brokenness.
6. Has only a few or no close friendships.
7. Views the Bible as the basis for truth, belief, action, and authority.
8. Boldly operates on spiritual principles.
9. Is frank, outspoken, and doesn't mince words.
10. Is very persuasive in method of speaking.
11. Grieves deeply over the sins of others.
12. Is eager to see his own blind spots and to help others see theirs too.
13. Desires above all else to see God's plan worked out in all situations.
14. Strongly promotes the spiritual growth of groups and individuals.
15. Is called to intercession.
16. Feels the need to verbalize or dramatize what he "sees."
17. Tends to be introspective.
18. Has strong opinions and convictions.
19. Has strict personal standards.
20. Desires to be obedient to God at all costs.

PROBLEMS OF THE PERCEIVER

8

Each one of the seven motivational gifts has its own set of problems.

We have found it helpful for people to know that along with their gift there will be specific challenges. One woman said to us, "It's a relief to know that my problems are typical for my gift. I thought I was the only one in the world wrestling with these things. Now I have hope and direction."

Without problems there would be no opportunity for spiritual growth!

As you take an honest look at the problem areas:

1. You will be relieved that you are not alone.

2. Your identification of the problems will assist you in discovering specific solutions.

3. You will know better how to pray for God's help and grace in overcoming the problems.

The scoring is the same as it was for the twenty positive characteristics, but you will *not* fill out a negative profile on yourself! You'll just use the negative scores to see how your maturity level is coming along. The scale goes something like this:

    0 to 5 points = mature
    6 to 10 points = growing in grace
   11 to 15 points = average
   16 to 20 points = immature
   21 to 25 points = needs help!

We made initial tests on various people eight to ten years ago and again more recently. Often, the negative score was significantly reduced, although they typically still had higher negative scores in their primary gift compared to their negative scoring in the other gifts (those scores improved as well). We can all heed Paul's exhortation in Philippians to "work out" our own salvation with fear (awe) and trembling.

Here are the five typical problem areas of the perceiver:

	Never	Seldom	Sometimes	Usually	Mostly	Always	
	0	1	2	3	4	5	POINTS
1. Tends to be judgmental and blunt.							

Perceivers have what one of them calls a severe case of foot-in-the-mouth disease.

Jonah is the biblical example here. God told Jonah to go preach repentance to Nineveh. Jonah didn't like the assignment because he knew they were wicked and he couldn't imagine how God could forgive them. So he took off in the opposite direction.

You know the story. God appointed special transportation to get him to the right beach at the right time. Jonah decided he'd better get on to Nineveh where he did preach on the need for repentance. And, the people repented.

Well, Jonah hadn't counted on that. He had already judged these people in his own heart and decided they deserved God's punishment. You see, he had a critical spirit. He never got around to praying for Nineveh. Instead he went up on the hillside and waited for judgment to fall. When it didn't, he got angry and God had to deal with Jonah's judgment of others.

Perceivers will find that God will deal firmly, even sternly, in their lives if they don't learn to pray more and criticize less. Prayer is the safeguard that prevents a perceiver from developing a critical attitude. Perceivers are called to intercessory prayer. *There are no exceptions!*

A lady in Kansas City came up to me after a seminar and said in a huff, "Well, I'm a perceiver according to the testing, but, I'm not an intercessor."

"Have you been called to intercede?" I asked.

"Well, I don't really know," she replied, "but I don't have time for that. I find I can get things done so much faster if I go right to the person and confront them with what they're doing wrong."

"You can get the job done faster than God?" I marveled.

"As a matter of fact, sometimes I can. He takes so long."

I thought to myself, *This is sheer ego!*

"You must always start with prayer," I urged her, "and only go to someone if the Lord tells you to. If you're not careful you could become a critical person that nobody is going to like."

A couple of her friends overheard. "She's already that way," they confided later. "Lots of people can't stand her *now!*"

Well, the Lord dealt with her that night. She couldn't sleep for a long time. The next morning she said to me, "Katie, last night God told me that He had called me to intercession a long time ago, but that I'd been refusing to listen. I realized I've been making a mess of things."

Since then she's grown as an intercessor and has become sensitive rather than blunt. People love her now.

If you discover that you have the gift of perception and you have not yet heeded the call to intercession, watch out! God won't let you off the hook.

We like to share this with perceivers: While in the natural world the shortest distance between two points is a straight line, that's not true in the spiritual world. The shortest distance between you and another person (especially a problem person) is a line of prayer straight up to God, trusting God to deal with the situation and work out the solution to the problem.

You see, no one likes to be told by someone else that he should change. But when you give the problem to God, He can speak directly to the person's heart. He can surmount walls of resistance that we can't get past.

The only time a perceiver should confront someone is after praying about it, giving it to God, and receiving a direct instruction to do so. Even then, unless God first softens the person's heart, the confrontation may not be received. But the perceiver's job is not to change others; he is only to deliver the message. It's the Holy Spirit's job to do the convicting and changing.

	Never	Seldom	Sometimes	Usually	Mostly	Always	
2. Forgets to praise partial progress due to goal consciousness.	0	1	2	3	4	5	POINTS

The perceiver's desire is always to get himself and others to that place of perfectly following the will of God. He focuses on the fact that Jesus said we are to "be perfect."

When counseling, for instance, the perceiver may be so eager for the counselee to come to perfection in Christ that he expects too much. He pressures the person to change—faster than he is able.

The perceiver needs to learn how to look at a step of progress as being valid in itself. He needs to be able to say, "Hey, I'm really glad that you took this step this week. That's good! Now, let's work on the next step."

Lem, a perceiver husband and father, came to us for advice. He complained that his wife was just not making progress spiritually.

We spoke to his wife. Hers was a different story. She was upset because Lem was always expecting her to be spiritual in the same way he was, which meant to spend lots of time in prayer, fast often, and follow Lem's rigid rules for the family. She was also frustrated because he was critical of the children to the point that they felt he didn't love them. She said Lem never praised the spiritual efforts of any of them.

Since his wife had the gift of administration we explained to Lem that he could not expect her to think and act just like him, that she was never going to be one to fast and pray a lot, but that she was able to see the unique differences in their children and allow them to develop at their own rate.

Lem has taken some of the pressure off and is allowing the progress of the family members to take its course more naturally. He is also learning to compliment and encourage his wife and children along the way.

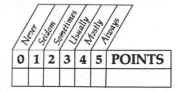

3. **Is pushy in trying to get others and groups to mature spiritually.**

There's nothing wrong in wanting people to mature spiritually; the problem is the pushiness.

Jill was thrilled when her husband finally made a commitment of his life to Jesus. But a polluted perceiver gift caused her to try to push him into spiritual growth. She would insist that he be at church every time the doors opened. She laid out "the right books" for him to read. And she let him know every time he did something that wasn't "Christian."

Of course it backfired. He dug in his heels and refused to have anything more to do with "that religious stuff."

Jill was deflated and discouraged. But an older woman in her church saw what she'd been doing and gave her some helpful counsel. "Look, Jill," her friend said, "you need to pray more for your husband and talk less. Let him make his own discoveries and decisions."

As soon as Jill stopped pushing, her husband started attending the men's early morning prayer meeting. Today he's as mature a Christian as Jill could wish for.

4. **Is intolerant of opinions and views that differ from his own.**

Perceivers are always convinced that their views are right—and most often they are. But sometimes truth has various facets to it. The perceiver may see one facet of a truth while those with different motivational gifts see other facets. Get all the facets together and you see the whole. Perceivers need to learn to value an encompassing perspective.

We came across an extreme case of this intolerance when we were asked to counsel a couple having serious marriage problems. We'll call them Sam and Sue. Sam was an opinionated perceiver and Sue an intimidated person with a strong gift of compassion.

As soon as they sat down Sam said, "I want you to know that Sue is the one who needs help. There's nothing wrong with me. She's the problem." Obviously *he* was more of a problem!

Then he proceeded to tell us what was wrong with her and how we were to fix it. At that point we wondered why they'd even come for counseling since he had all the answers! According to him a wife was to have no ideas of her own but was to be in an unquestioning servant's role to her husband. He was upset because Sue had recently dared to question his orders.

When we tried to suggest that his view of the marriage relationship was unbalanced, he came back with, "But I *know* I am right. The Bible says so! Sue is being rebellious and she must obey me!"

We never saw them again.

	Never	Seldom	Sometimes	Usually	Mostly	Always	
	0	1	2	3	4	5	POINTS

5. Struggles with self-image problems.

Since perceivers have such an inner drive to do what is right, and since they are introspective and readily aware of their own shortcomings, they are quick to judge themselves inadequate.

Of all the motivational gifts, these people seem most relieved when they discover that the things they've wrestled with internally are indicative of divinely ordained giftedness rather than a testimony to shortcomings and failures. It is not at all unusual for a perceiver to come to us at the close of a seminar to tell us how thrilled he is to know that who and what he is are part of God's plan.

We often hear comments from perceivers like, "I always thought I was a misfit, but now I see that God has made me see things the way I do."

One time we noticed tears welling up in the eyes of an older woman (she was seventy-three) while we were teaching on the gift of perception. "If only I had heard this fifty years ago," she told us afterward. "I have lived all my life with a torturing awareness of what was wrong in people and situations. But I didn't know what to do with it, so I criticized. Then I criticized myself for being critical. All my life I've wanted to be different. Now I see that God gave me perception for a reason—so that I could pray for people."

Three weeks later we returned to do another seminar. At the first coffee break this woman came over to us with joy written all over her face.

"These three weeks have been the best in my whole life!" she exclaimed. "Every day I'm interceding for the needs that God is showing to me. It's wonderful. I'm seeing so many answers to prayer. And, I like myself now. I'm so glad I learned about my giftedness while I still have some of my life left to live."

We wish that every perceiver could say that. So many are bound up in self-condemnation and self-rejection because they don't understand about their giftedness.

If you know any perceivers, please share this good news with them!

Typical problem areas of the gift of perception:

1. Tends to be judgmental and blunt.
2. Forgets to praise partial progress due to goal consciousness.
3. Is pushy in trying to get others and groups to mature spiritually.
4. Is intolerant of opinions and views that differ from his own.
5. Struggles with self-image problems.

	Never	Seldom	Sometimes	Usually	Mostly	Always	POINTS
	0	1	2	3	4	5	
1.							
2.							
3.							
4.							
5.							TOTAL

BIBLICAL
PERCEIVERS

9

We have been fascinated to discover the motivational gifts of biblical characters. Recognizing the specific giftedness of these biblical personalities has made the reading of Scripture come alive for us. We find ourselves saying things like, "Oh, that's why David did that" or "So that's what motivated Barnabas." They are no longer one-dimensional historical figures who lived 'way back when, but rather real people that we can relate to and appreciate with a new depth.

Identifying their motivational gifts helps us to see why God chose them for their particular tasks. He gifted them (knowing them from before the foundation of the world, Ephesians 1:4) in accordance with His purpose for each life. We see a wide spectrum of giftedness, all the way from Jonah's stubborn critical spirit—a manifestation of a polluted gift of perception—to John, the beloved disciple's faithful and loving detailing of the life of Jesus—a manifestation of a mature gift of compassion.

For some biblical characters there is such a wealth of recorded information that we can see the person's gift in full breadth of action. For others, the details are limited: We get only a glimpse of their gifts. And for some we can make only an educated guess. But all through the Bible now we see living people with distinct needs, desires, motivations, and abilities.

We have written seven chapters highlighting biblical characters as examples of the seven motivational gifts. This chapter will deal with the perceiver.

We'd like to challenge you (our gifts of teaching and exhorting are coming through here) to read for yourself the following Scriptures about biblical perceivers:

John the Baptist— Matthew 21:32; Luke 3:2–20; 7:18–29
Anna—Luke 2:36–38
Mary—Matthew, 1–2; Mark 6:3; Luke 1:26–56; John 2:1–5; Acts 1:14
Ananias—Acts 9:10–17; 22:12–16
Hosea—Hosea 1–14
Jeremiah—Jeremiah 1–52
Isaiah—Isaiah 1–66
Jonah—Jonah 1–4

See how many perceiver characteristics you can find in these biblical characters as you read these passages. You'll be amazed! And the person will become far more understandable to you.

To get you started we are printing out the first Scripture here for you to work on. We've used the Amplified Bible which captures more nuances from the original Greek.

The right-hand column is for your comments. Simply jot down the number of the characteristic, or describe it if you prefer. If the characteristic is from the problem list, identify it with a minus (−) before the number.

Some characteristics will be obvious, others only implied. Ask the Holy Spirit to guide you in this discovery process—to give you eyes to see with, and help you read between the lines. You will have fun!

Scripture: Luke 3:2–3, 7–20 (TAB)	*Your Comments:*
2 In the high priesthood of Annas and Caiaphas, the Word of God [concerning the attainment through Christ of salvation in the Kingdom of God], came to John, the son of Zechariah, in the wilderness (desert).	
3 And he went into all the country round about the Jordan, preaching a baptism of repentance (that is, of hearty amending of their ways with abhorrence for past wrongdoing) unto the forgiveness of sin.	
7 So he said to the crowds that came out to be baptized by him, You offspring of vipers! Who secretly warned you to flee from the coming wrath?	
8 Bear fruits that are deserving and consistent with your repentance	

—[that is,] conduct worthy of a
heart changed and abhorring sin.
And do not begin to say to yourselves, We have Abraham as our
father; for I tell you God is able
from these stones to raise up
descendants for Abraham.

9 Even now the ax is laid to the
root of the trees, so that every
tree that does not bear good fruit
is cut down and cast into the fire.

10 And the multitudes asked him,
Then what shall we do?

11 And he replied to them, He who
has two tunics (undergarments), let
him share with him who has none; and
he who has food, let him do the same
way.

12 Even tax collectors came to be
baptized, and they said to him,
Teacher, what shall we do?

13 And he said to them, Exact and
collect no more than the fixed
amount appointed you.

14 Those serving as soldiers also
asked him, And we, what shall we do?
And he replied to them, Never demand
or enforce by terrifying people or
by accusing wrongfully, and always
be satisfied with your rations
(supplies) and with your allowance
(wages).

15 As the people were in suspense
and waiting expectantly, and everybody
reasoned and questioned in their
hearts concerning John whether he

perhaps might be the Christ, the
Messiah, the Anointed One.

16   John answered them all by saying,
I baptize you with water, but
He Who is mightier than I is coming,
the strap of Whose sandals I am not
fit to unfasten; He will baptize you
with the Holy Spirit and with fire.

17   His winnowing shovel (fork) is
in His hand, to thoroughly clear and
cleanse His [threshing] floor, and
to gather the wheat and store it in
His granary, but the chaff He will
burn with fire that cannot be
extinguished.

18   So, with many other (various)
appeals and admonitions, he
preached the good news (the Gospel)
to the people.

19   But Herod the tetrarch, who had
been (repeatedly) told his fault and
reproved with rebuke producing
conviction, by John for [having]
Herodias, his brother's wife, and
for all the wicked things that Herod
had done,

20   Added this to them all, that he
shut up John in prison.

Now that you've gotten to know John the Baptist, perceiver, we'll share what we found:

Scripture: Luke 3:2–3, 7–20 (TAB)

Our Comments:

2   In the high priesthood of Annas
and Caiaphas, the Word of God
[concerning the attainment through
Christ of salvation in the Kingdom
of God], came to John, the son of
Zechariah, in the wilderness
(desert).

#13   desires God's plan
#15   received revelation through
intercession

Our Comments:

3   And he went into all the country round about the Jordan, preaching a baptism of repentance (that is, of hearty amending of their ways with abhorrence for past wrongdoing) unto the forgiveness of sin.

#1   identifies evil
#3   sizes up character
#4   encourages repentance
#9   frank, outspoken
#11 grieves over sins
#20 obedient to God

7   So he said to the crowds that came out to be baptized by him, You offspring of vipers! Who secretly warned you to flee from the coming wrath?

#1, 3, 4, & 9   (as above)
#12 sees blind spots
#16 dramatizes
#18 strong opinions

8   Bear fruits that are deserving and consistent with your repentance —[that is,] conduct worthy of a heart changed and abhorring sin. And do not begin to say to yourselves, We have Abraham as our father; for I tell you God is able from these stones to raise up descendants for Abraham.

#4   wants evidence of repentance
#8   boldly operates on spiritual principles
#9   frank, blunt
#10 speaks persuasively
#12 reveals blind spots
#16 dramatizes
#18 strong opinions

9   Even now the ax is laid to the root of the trees, so that every tree that does not bear good fruit is cut down and cast into the fire.

#4, 8, 9, 10, 16, 18 (as above)

10   And the multitudes asked him, Then what shall we do?

#10 evidence of John's persuasiveness

11   And he replied to them, He who has two tunics (undergarments), let him share with him who has none; and he who has food, let him do the same way.

#2   no gray areas
#4   demands fruit
#8   spiritual principles
#14 promotes growth

12   Even tax collectors came to be baptized, and they said to him, Teacher, what shall we do?

#10 evidence of persuasiveness

13   And he said to them, Exact and collect no more than the fixed amount appointed you.

#2   black & white standard
#8   spiritual principles

Our Comments:

14 Those serving as soldiers also asked him, And we, what shall we do? And he replied to them, Never demand or enforce by terrifying people or by accusing wrongfully, and always be satisfied with your rations (supplies) and with your allowance (wages).

#1   identifies evil
#2   black and white standard
#3   perceives character
#4   demands fruit
#9   frank, outspoken
#10 persuasive
#14 promotes growth
#18 strong opinions

15 As the people were in suspense and waiting expectantly, and everybody reasoned and questioned in their hearts concerning John whether he perhaps might be the Christ, the Messiah, the Anointed One,

(evidences operation of all of the above characteristics in the response of the listeners)

16 John answered them all by saying, I baptize you with water, but He Who is mightier than I is coming, the strap of Whose sandals I am not fit to unfasten; He will baptize you with the Holy Spirit and with fire.

#13 focus on God's plan
#14 promotes growth of others
#20 obedience to God's (lesser) plan for him

17 His winnowing shovel (fork) is in His hand, to thoroughly clear and cleanse His [threshing] floor, and to gather the wheat and store it in His granary, but the chaff He will burn with fire that cannot be extinguished.

#1   good and evil identified
#2   black & white division
#9   frank, outspoken
#13 desires God's plan
#20 obedient to God by revealing His plan

18 So, with many other (various) appeals and admonitions, he preached the good news (the Gospel) to the people.

#4   encourages repentance
#10 persuasive
#13 wants God's plan
#20 obedience to call

19 But Herod the tetrarch, who had been (repeatedly) told his fault and reproved with rebuke producing conviction, by John for [having] Herodias, his brother's wife, and for all the wicked things that Herod had done,

#1   identified Herod's evil
#3   perceived his character
#4   called for repentance
#9   frank, outspoken
#18 strong convictions
#20 obeyed God

20 Added this to them all, that he shut up John in prison.

#2 uncompromising

#10 evidence of John's persuasiveness

We may have listed some perceiver qualities that you did not discover, and you probably detected others that we missed. But you can see that John is a magnificent example of this motivational gift!

CHARACTERISTICS
OF THE
SERVER

10

The second of the seven gifts listed in Romans 12:6–8 is the gift we call server. The King James Version uses the word "ministry," the New International Version—as well as most other modern versions—uses the word "service," and The Amplified Bible the words "practical service." The Greek word is *diakonia* which conveys the idea of doing practical things in order to be of service to others.

The server receives joy in helping, assisting, carrying out instructions, being of use in a wide variety of ways. As you consider each characteristic, score yourself, then transfer your scores to the final page of the chapter and tally the points for recording on your profile sheet.

1. Easily recognizes practical needs and is quick to meet them.

	Never	Seldom	Sometimes	Usually	Mostly	Always	
	0	1	2	3	4	5	**POINTS**

A server can spot a need a mile away. It's as though he has built-in radar geared to others' necessities, and high motivation to do something about those needs.

You can spot these servers easily at a church potluck dinner. Check who's regularly out in the kitchen making the preparations, or setting up tables and chairs, or doing the cleanup afterward.

All our married life our home has been a center for youth meetings, Bible study groups, and potlucks. We used to wonder why some of the women quickly migrated to the kitchen to help out while others stayed in the living room to chat. Now we know it's the natural inclination of servers to help in that way. And the server men are the ones who put away the folding chairs, push the furniture back into place, and pick up the Styrofoam cups still sitting around the room. The important thing is that servers enjoy doing it.

Iverna Tompkins, author of *How to be Happy in No Man's Land*, was the main speaker at a convention where I was doing a workshop on the motivational gifts. I was seated to her left at the closing banquet and her secretary, Shirley Green, to her right. As we started to eat Iverna commented, "Cool in here, isn't it?" Shirley excused herself, went to the cloak room, retrieved Iverna's shawl, returned, and placed it around her shoulders. A servant's heart! The need was so obvious to her.

How sensitive! I thought. It had never dawned on me that Iverna's casual remark was an expression of practical need.

2. Especially enjoys manual projects, jobs, and functions.

Never	Seldom	Sometimes	Usually	Mostly	Always	POINTS
0	1	2	3	4	5	

Of all the motivational gifts it is the servers who have the greatest dexterity—the ability to work well with their hands. That's why we call them the hands of the body. They can do just about anything that involves manual skill: artistic endeavors, fixing things, carpentry, plumbing, electrical work, sewing, cooking, gardening.

Five server men from our church recently volunteered to take a week off from their jobs and go to Guatemala to do repairs on a children's orphanage. They loved every minute of it and got twice as much done as those with any other gift could have.

We find that servers often are not interested in college. They prefer trade schools, beauty schools, art schools, and other technical training.

An item in Dear Abby a few years ago was so appropriate that we've shared it at all our motivational gift seminars.

College Dropout
Son's choice upsets mother

DEAR ABBY: Our middle son, Greg (made-up name), is our problem. He is a very intelligent young man of 19 who went to college for one year just to please us, then he quit.

"Why waste your money and my time?" he asked.

His grades were above average and he could have continued. His reason for quitting? He likes to work with his hands. He is now going to a trade school, and we are so disappointed in him.

I'm not putting down people who work with their hands, but it seems to me that a man works with his hands only because he isn't smart enough to work with his mind. Greg's father and grandfather are physicians, and both Greg's brothers are lawyers.

Please put something in your column stating that a college degree is absolutely necessary these days. After Greg graduates from college, he can do anything he chooses, but we want him to finish college first. Thank you.

—Greg's Mother

DEAR MOTHER: College is not for everybody. If Greg likes to work with his hands, that's what he should do. It's not true that those who work with their hands aren't smart enough to work with their minds. Handwork done well requires as much skill, talent and brains as a profession.[8]

To which we say, "Amen, Abby!"

In addition to "Mother's" intellectual snobbery, it is probable that the other men in the family were gifted differently—teachers, exhorters, and administrators, perhaps. To insist that a server follow in their footsteps is sheer folly. Not only would Greg not have done well in such pursuits, but he would also have been constantly frustrated and probably resentful that his parents pushed him into a career for which he was not suited.

3. Keeps everything in meticulous order.

Never	Seldom	Sometimes	Usually	Mostly	Always	
0	1	2	3	4	5	**POINTS**

Servers cannot stand clutter, dirt, or disorganization. Women with this gift often dust every day. There are no dirty dishes left in their sinks, their laundry is folded and put away the day it is washed, the beds are made before nine A.M. You can drop in on them at any time of the day and the house will be ready for company.

Men with the serving gift keep their closets in order, their socks never get thrown in the shirt drawer, you can always see the top of their desk, and every tool is hanging on the right hook on the pegboard. What's more, the lawn is mowed on schedule and weeds don't have a chance to grow in the flowerbeds.

We stayed in a home in Scotland where the lady was a classic server. When we ate meals in the big family kitchen she would clear the table after each course, quickly wash the dishes and place them in a drainer before serving the next course!

4. Is a detail person with a good memory.

Never	Seldom	Sometimes	Usually	Mostly	Always	
0	1	2	3	4	5	**POINTS**

Servers have a computer-type memory for details. They can remember where they filed away an article they clipped out of the newspaper three years ago. They remember that you like cream in your coffee, but not sugar. They remember all the birthdays on both sides of the family (and remember to send cards), and they can relate an episode from the thirteenth chapter of the book they read last week with amazing accuracy.

I was so grateful during the years I was an international vice-president of Women's Aglow Fellowship International for secretaries who were servers. They could actually find things in the files! I could look for hours without locating something. (The most difficult were things I had filed myself.)

When I was in charge of television production one of the tasks was to circulate our videotaped programs to cable and UHF stations. With dozens of stations using our thirteen-week sets it was a challenge to keep track of them. Lois McGrew was wonderful. She kept such detailed accounts that we always knew where every tape was, where it was going next, and when it would come back to us. I could not have survived without her.

5. Enjoys showing hospitality.

Never	Seldom	Sometimes	Usually	Mostly	Always	POINTS
0	1	2	3	4	5	

When the pastor announces that a place is needed for the visiting missionary, it will likely be the servers who offer their homes first. They love to entertain people.

They look for opportunities to invite others over for dinner or dessert, and they do a terrific job of making their guests feel welcome.

There's a couple in our area we are sure must both be servers. When they got married Alice said, "John, let's build a big house so we can entertain lots of people." John, being an excellent carpenter, obliged by building a house with nine bedrooms. They had only two sons but all the rooms were often filled.

At one point the Wikenes became acquainted with the singing Cameron family from Scotland and became headquarters for them whenever they came to Seattle. There were three Cameron men, and each had a family group. Usually just one of the families came at a time, but one year all seventeen of the clan came at once. Alice and John put them up in style.

The families stayed for three weeks and Alice thought it would be nice to make a new dress for each of the women and girls, which she did in her "spare time." She was also holding down a full-time job. "I've never had such a good time in my life," Alice confided to me. "I just love having company!"

6. Will stay with something until it is completed.

Never	Seldom	Sometimes	Usually	Mostly	Always	POINTS
0	1	2	3	4	5	

Servers finish what they start. They have wonderful stick-to-it-iveness. When they say they will do something they will do it. The only thing that produces frustration is when you give them something to do in too short a time. You see, they not only want to finish a task, they want to do it well.

My friend Claudia has all the earmarks of a mature server. She serves on our church's women's council and usually volunteers for registrar responsibility for retreats and conferences. Within a day or two—and usually 'way ahead of schedule—she has all the forms and sign-up sheets designed, printed, and ready to go. She follows through on every detail during the registration process, then patiently keeps all the necessary records in incredibly neat order.

7. Has a hard time saying no to requests for help.

	Never	Seldom	Sometimes	Usually	Mostly	Always	
	0	1	2	3	4	5	**POINTS**

Because servers are naturally geared to be helpful, and because they know that they are good at it, it is difficult for them to turn down a request for help. As a result they tend to get over-involved. Even a simple question like, "Do you know what to use for a clogged drain?" will elicit a response like, "Let me come over and look at it." Before he has time to think, the server is under the person's sink with wrench in hand and the drain apart.

I was teaching the motivational gift seminar at an Aglow convention in San Diego when a woman came up to me during the morning coffee break looking as though she had the weight of the world on her shoulders. "What's the matter?" I asked.

"I scored ninety-five on server," she replied, "and it's true. I can't say no to anyone. Would you believe I'm currently on twenty committees between church, PTA, community groups, Cub Scouts, Campfire Girls, and Aglow?"

I nodded, indicating I could well believe it.

"I'm exhausted. I can't even get my housework done."

"How many of those committees did the Lord tell you to serve on?" I inquired.

"Oh!" she exclaimed, looking surprised. "I never thought to ask the Lord about any of them."

"I suggest you do," I said. "We can be out of His will by doing too much, as easily as by doing too little."

At the lunch break she returned. "I asked Him," she said, her face beaming. "He said five. And He showed me which ones. I'm going home and resigning from the other fifteen. And I'm never going to say yes again without praying first."

That's good advice for all servers. Learn to check with the Lord so you won't get overloaded. It *is* okay to say no.

8. Is more interested in meeting the needs of others than own needs.

	Never	Seldom	Sometimes	Usually	Mostly	Always	
	0	1	2	3	4	5	**POINTS**

Servers are such caring people. When we were in New Zealand we stayed for a week with a lovely Christian family. Two of the Eynons' four girls were still at home, Greta, eighteen, and Aly, sixteen.

We were struck by how much Greta seemed to enjoy preparing meals. "Mum," she'd say, "let me fix the dinner. You spend time with the Fortunes." She'd put on a beautiful meal and when her mother would get up to clear the table Greta would say to her, "No, you stay there and talk, I'll take care of the dishes."

Aly would take a few dishes to the kitchen, then say, "Please excuse me but I've got to run. I'm setting up the school's talent show and we've got a meeting tonight."

A similar scene would take place each evening with Greta serving dinner and doing the dishes and Aly running off to organize something else. Their parents worried about the situation. They felt that Aly was running out on domestic responsibilities while Greta was overly conscientious around the house. They wished Greta would have more outside interests.

We were able to help them to see that Greta was a server and Aly an administrator. It was predictable that Aly's interests would lean toward group involvement while Greta's giftedness would cause her to focus on meeting other people's needs even to the neglect of her own. We encouraged the parents to let Greta concentrate on the domestic needs of the family for the time being, for that was bringing her joy.

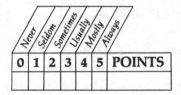

9. Enjoys working on immediate goals rather than long-range goals.

Never	Seldom	Sometimes	Usually	Mostly	Always	POINTS
0	1	2	3	4	5	

Servers prefer short-term projects. They like something that takes two hours better than something that takes two weeks, and prefer a two-week or two-month project to a two-year project. They enjoy something they can get their teeth into and finish in a foreseeable amount of time. They leave long-range goals to the administrators.

A server would enjoy providing food for the family of a woman who is temporarily in the hospital, but would not necessarily want to take on that kind of service on an ongoing basis. He or she would be glad to work one day a week at the food bank, but would not want to manage the project.

Martha saw the immediate goal: Jesus needed a meal. Mary saw the long-range goal, her need to learn from Him.

Stephen was appointed a deacon, with responsibility for providing for widows, while the apostles saw to the long-range spread of the Gospel.

If you have a server child here's a formula for getting him to be productive. Never give a server child a list of fifteen jobs to do on a Saturday. It would look overwhelming to him. Instead, give him one job to do. When it is completed, show your appreciation and then ask if he'd like to help with another job. He'll continue this process all day.

10. Shows love for others in deeds and actions more than words.

Never	Seldom	Sometimes	Usually	Mostly	Always	POINTS
0	1	2	3	4	5	

Servers believe actions speak louder than words. They express their love by what they do.

One server said to us, "It's easy to say, 'I love you,' but the other person may never really know if you mean it. I believe that when I do something for someone he *knows* how I feel."

One day when I was working at Aglow International I found a freshly baked loaf of bread on my desk. It was tied attractively with a bow and a few silk flowers. A little note attached to it read: "Dear Katie, I'm not very good with words but I hope this loaf of home-baked bread will say that I like you and would like to get to know you better. Love, Lorene."

What a joy to be the object of her love in action!

One woman complained to me that her husband never said the words "I love you."

I knew her husband and had observed many ways in which he showed his love. "But he's a server," I reminded her. "Think how often he takes you out for dinner so you won't have to cook. He buys you unbirthday presents. He makes you all kinds of things in his workshop. He fixes things that break. He helps you clean house. I wish my husband did half as much!"

The woman had to admit she was blessed to have a server husband.

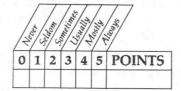

	Never	Seldom	Sometimes	Usually	Mostly	Always	
	0	1	2	3	4	5	**POINTS**

11. Needs to feel appreciated.

It's not that servers serve in order to be praised, but appreciation assures them that they've done well. It builds up a positive self-image in them. It is the culmination of their joy in serving.

In the early days of *Aglow* magazine we were entirely a volunteer staff.

I remember when *Guideposts* editor Len LeSourd visited our Aglow Publications editorial offices in Edmonds, Washington. As we introduced him to our various department heads he was impressed with their enthusiasm. "It's good you could hire such dedicated people," Len commented. "It's impossible to run a publishing house with volunteers. You can't count on them."

"Then it's nice to know we're doing the impossible!" I told him.

"You mean you do have volunteers on your staff?" he asked.

"I mean our staff is *all* volunteers."

"I can't believe it!" he said with astonishment.

"But it's true," I replied. "We have sixty-five workers, and none of them is paid. Some give as much as three or four days a week. We probably have less absenteeism than the average business—and when one of them does have to miss a day for some reason he or she arranges for a substitute from our volunteer substitute list."

"Incredible!" he said. "How is it possible?"

"Well," I said, "we pray in each new staff member. Also, we find that a lot of our volunteers have the motivational gift of serving. We've learned to express appreciation to them regularly for what they do. They know they are important, needed, and valued."

	Never	Seldom	Sometimes	Usually	Mostly	Always	
12. Tends to do more than asked to do.	0	1	2	3	4	5	**POINTS**

Servers so enjoy the doing that they often don't want to stop.

When Berta gave birth to twins the family had five children under the age of six. Her server mother-in-law told her she would be glad to keep the baby books for each of the five up to date. Berta was delighted because she'd had time only to throw items into a box.

As the years passed Berta continued to channel photos, drawings, and miscellaneous mementoes to her mother-in-law. Then, when her oldest child graduated from high school, his grandmother presented him with his completed book. Not only were the usual milestones recorded, there were detailed accounts of his growing up. She had chronicled every event, both great and seemingly insignificant, with photos, quips, comments, candid descriptions, and quotes. The book had been extended to almost one hundred pages of "this is your life" in incredible detail.

What a gift! The son was delighted. Everyone in the family was amazed. The kids knew that Grandma always did more than expected, but this was something else. She assured them that a similar chronicle was in process for each of the others, to be received on his or her graduation day.

	Never	Seldom	Sometimes	Usually	Mostly	Always	
13. Feels greatest joy in doing something that is helpful.	0	1	2	3	4	5	**POINTS**

Don's mother was a classic server. Every time she came to our home for dinner the first thing she would ask as she came in the kitchen door was, "What can I do to help you?"

Now I do just fine in the kitchen if people leave me alone to concentrate. So my usual answer to her was, "Nothing, thanks, I've got everything under control."

One Thanksgiving she arrived a whole hour early. I had been working on the dinner since eight that morning and had timed everything to finish just on schedule. "I came early to see if I could help you," she offered.

"Thanks anyway," I responded. "Everything's under way."

I could tell she was disappointed as she sat down at the kitchen table to watch me work. She began to talk and the distraction was more than I could handle. "Why don't you go and chat with Don awhile?" I suggested.

She found Don deeply engrossed in the Thanksgiving Day football game on TV. The boys were also watching the game.

Meanwhile in the kitchen the Lord spoke to me: *Katie, you are being selfish.*

"How?" I asked with astonishment.

You're so busy functioning in your gift that you are not making room for your mother-in-law's gift.

The words cut deeply into my heart. I *was* being selfish. She wanted to help and I wouldn't let her. That was downright unkind of me. I repented and realized I needed to do something about it. I called into the rec room. "Mother, I could use your help now!"

She was there in a flash, her face bright.

"Could you make the tossed salad?" I asked.

"I'd love to."

She chatted merrily as she tore up bits of lettuce. It distracted me as usual, but I knew that was okay, too. I needed to learn to cook and carry on a conversation at the same time.

After that I always set something aside for my mother-in-law to do when she came for dinner. I can't say I ever learned to love having her help me but I learned to adapt to it and our relationship improved. Learning to give place to her gift blessed me, too.

	Never	Seldom	Sometimes	Usually	Mostly	Always	
14. Does not want to lead others or projects.	0	1	2	3	4	5	**POINTS**

Servers are not leaders; they are followers. God made them that way. If a leadership position is forced on them they are frustrated.

It is tempting to turn leadership over to servers. Because they do such a good job at whatever they do, it may seem that they are the natural ones to take charge. But when this happens, they lose their joy. They've been placed in a situation for which they are not equipped. The result is frustration for them, and probably (eventually) frustration for those they try to lead.

Our friend Glenn Koontz, who originally introduced us to the concept of motivational gifts, is a server. He is gifted with his hands and developed hand-tooled parts and equipment that sold very well. Soon Glenn's business outgrew his backyard facility and he moved to larger industrial quarters, continuing to grow until he had eighteen employees.

Now Glenn found himself in a supervisory position as head of his own company. His frustration grew in proportion to the company's growth. As he would observe the work of the people he hired he realized he could do the jobs faster and better, but his time was no longer available for that. So he put into practice what he had learned about the gifts and hired a foreman who had the gift of administration and left the supervisory work to him. Result? Glenn's frustration disappeared. A wise man indeed.

	Never	Seldom	Sometimes	Usually	Mostly	Always	
	0	1	2	3	4	5	**POINTS**
15. Has a high energy level.							

Servers have one speed: *fast forward.*

They seem to have boundless energy. First Peter 4:11 urges them to serve "with the strength which God furnishes abundantly." And indeed servers seem to have unusual endurance and often get by with less sleep than the average person.

We can only surmise that God has endowed servers with all this energy because they are the doers and there's so much that needs to be done.

Don's mother was such a prime example of this high energy level. She worked until forced retirement at sixty-five, then got involved in all kinds of activities through her church.

Even at eighty (she would never admit her age) she would leave us huffing and puffing in a shopping mall trying to keep up with her. We'd often lose her only to find her a dozen counters ahead of us. After two hours of this we'd suggest that we find somewhere to sit down and take a coffee break. "You can't be tired already!" she'd exclaim.

16. Cannot stand to be around clutter.

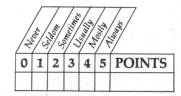

Never	Seldom	Sometimes	Usually	Mostly	Always	
0	1	2	3	4	5	POINTS

We've heard servers say things like, "I can't leave the office until my desk is clear." Or: "It's only after I have the house picked up that I can sit down and watch television." Or: "I can't stand to go over to my neighbor's house. I feel like I want to dig in and put things away, but I don't think she'd appreciate it."

Servers are the ones who straighten crooked picture frames on your walls.

This trait can be seen even in server children. One pastor shared how his two-year-old grandson gave evidence of his giftedness whenever he went to another child's home to play. Finding the other's room in disarray he would always proceed to tidy it up, line up all the toys, and only *then* relax and play.

Never	Seldom	Sometimes	Usually	Mostly	Always	
0	1	2	3	4	5	POINTS

17. Tends to be a perfectionist.

Whatever servers do they want to do well. They want things to be just right and are willing to work toward that end.

For other gifts perfectionism could be a sign of abnormal behavior. But the server has been created a perfectionist for God's purposes. Someone in the Body of Christ needs to exhibit this trait in a positive and balanced way.

Our friend Dr. David Stewart of Everett, Washington, is a heart surgeon with the motivational gift of serving. His work requires precision. Fortunate the patient whose surgeon is a perfectionist.

My brother-in-law Bob is a perfectionist server, too. The other day he was building some stools in his garage-workshop. "I've got to go to town to get some screws," he announced. (They live out in the country.) "Would you believe with all the screws I have on hand [he must have 3000] I don't have the right ones? I could get by with what I have—but I want the stools to look perfect."

18. **Views serving to be of primary importance in life.**

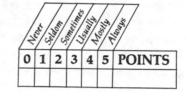

Never	Seldom	Sometimes	Usually	Mostly	Always	
0	1	2	3	4	5	POINTS

One server said to us as he was stacking up the chairs after a meeting at church, "I just can't understand why the other men don't chip in and help."

Serving seems to the server to be the essence of Christianity. To him, the rest is mere words. Certainly Jesus' example and teaching on the importance of having a servant's heart reinforces his conviction that serving is the greatest activity of all.

But servers need to be careful not to insist that others feel the same way. Each gift thinks its type of functioning is the most important of all.

19. **Prefers doing a job to delegating it.**

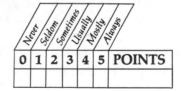

Never	Seldom	Sometimes	Usually	Mostly	Always	
0	1	2	3	4	5	POINTS

Not only do servers prefer to do the job themselves, they also have a sense of guilt when they don't. One man said, "I find it very hard to delegate messy or menial types of work to my kids. I generally end up doing those jobs myself."

Don recalls growing up with a server mother. "She would give me a job to do," he says, "and when she would see that I was doing it too slowly, or with difficulty, she would take the job back and do it herself. I guess I learned that I could get out of various responsibilities that way. But, unfortunately, there were a lot of skills I should have learned at home that I'm now having to learn as an adult. I wish my mother had delegated more to me during those growing-up years."

20. **Supports others who are in leadership.**

Never	Seldom	Sometimes	Usually	Mostly	Always	
0	1	2	3	4	5	POINTS

Servers make wonderful secretaries, vice-presidents, or committee members. They have incredible loyalty to those they serve under. It is not unusual for a server to burn the midnight oil to bring a project to culmination. Servers want to see those they support succeed.

A large accounting firm in downtown Seattle invited me to teach the motivational gifts seminar to their employees. The entire staff were Christians and wanted to utilize their giftedness more effectively within the business context. It was amazing how many of the group were already functioning in areas that made good use of their gifts. Of the four owners, three had the gift of administration. Very appropriate.

Two weeks later Don Kurth, one of the owners, called me to find out what motivational gift would be most suitable for the secretary-receptionist position they needed to fill. "Find a server," I said, "and you will find the best possible secretary. She will be supportive of the leadership, loyal, detailed, accurate, and a joy to work with."

They interviewed three women for the job. When one turned out to be a server with a secondary gift of exhortation, she was hired.

A month later Don called us to report, "We took your advice and hired a server. She's the best secretary-receptionist we've ever had. She's all you said she'd be and more. And her secondary gift of exhortation gives her the friendly, people-oriented qualities that the receptionist part of the job requires. She's perfect for the position."

AN EXCEPTION TO THE RULE

Here's a good place to point out an important exception to the rule that people will function best in the motivational gift(s) that God has given them. Here it is: *When God calls you to do a job outside the sphere of your motivational gift He will also give you an anointing that will enable you to do the job.* The anointing supersedes the giftedness.

We continue to emphasize that this teaching on motivational gifts is not designed to put you in a box labeled *All I Can Do*. Be led by the Holy Spirit in everything. Be open to a special call from God—and the subsequent provision—at any time in your life.

For a biblical example of this, consider Moses.

If you were God and wanted to deliver several million people from slavery, you would probably choose someone with the gift of administration. He'd organize the exodus in super-efficient fashion.

But that's not what God did. He called a server, Moses, to do the job. How do we know which gift Moses had, and which he lacked?

First of all, what was Moses' response when God called him?

"But Moses said to God, 'Who am I, that I should . . . bring the sons of Israel out of Egypt?' " (Exodus 3:11, NAS).

Now if Moses had been a natural leader he would have been excited about the prospect: "Great, Lord! When can we get started?" But as a server Moses had no desire for leadership. He had no confidence in his own ability to tackle the job.

Secondly, Moses was not so much giving an excuse as stating a fact when he went on, "O Lord, I am not eloquent or a man of words . . . for I am slow of speech, and have a heavy and awkward tongue" (Exodus 4:10, TAB).

Moses was well aware of his own limitations. His natural capabilities all worked *against* his succeeding at the task to which God was calling him. The server usually has little capacity for speaking in front of a group.

But God had a solution to the problem. "He said, Is there not Aaron your brother, the Levite? I know he can speak well. . . . He shall speak for you to the people, acting as a mouthpiece for you" (Exodus 4:14–16, TAB).

Undoubtedly Aaron had one of the "speaking gifts."

Thirdly, the people were unable to recognize any natural leadership qualities in Moses. They did not always follow him eagerly as evidenced by their constant murmuring and complaining. They grumbled that Moses had "brought us out into this wilderness to kill this whole assembly with hunger" (Exodus 16:3, TAB).

Now an administrator with a charismatic personality would have been able to rally their wholehearted allegiance. One need only remember the tragedy at Jonestown where hundreds of men, women, and children drank Kool-Aid laced with deadly cyanide at Jim Jones' instruction, to realize how compelling a smooth-talking, clever leader can be. Moses was none of that.

Fourthly, Moses, like so many servers, tried to do the job all by himself. It was his administrator father-in-law, Jethro, who bailed him out of the predicament.

"Moses sat to judge the people, and the people stood about Moses from the morning until the evening.

"Now when Moses' father-in-law saw all that he was doing for the people, he said . . . 'Why do you alone sit as judge?' " (Exodus 18:13–14, NAS).

It never dawned on Moses that there might be a better way to organize the handling of all the cases that were brought to him. But Jethro saw it immediately.

" 'You will surely wear out, both yourself and these people who are with you, for the task is too heavy for you; you cannot do it alone' " (Exodus 18:18, NAS).

Jethro told Moses to instruct the people clearly about God's statutes and laws and then to select godly men and delegate the cases to them. He laid out a specific organizational plan with leaders over thousands, hundreds, fifties, and tens—the plan upon which the judicial system of the United States is based—leaving only the most difficult cases for Moses himself.

" 'And . . . let it be that every major dispute they will bring to you, but every minor dispute they themselves will judge. So it will be easier for you, and they will bear the burden with you' " (Exodus 18:22, NAS).

Fifthly, a good administrator would have led the children of Israel from the land of Goshen to the Promised Land in eleven days—the time it takes to walk between those two places. The administrator, operating in his own strength, would have gotten the job done too quickly. For God not only wanted to get the children of Israel out of Egypt, He also wanted to get Egypt out of the children of Israel. That took forty years—two generations!

Their ancestors had been living in a pagan culture for four hundred years—that's twenty generations. Ungodly aspects of the Egyptian culture had rubbed off on them over the years. Moses, being a server, simply followed God and His timing. God needed obedience more than ability. But God also gave Moses an anointing to be able to do the job.

There may be times in your life when God calls you to do some task and your first response is, "Lord, You know I am not gifted in that area." No matter. God will equip and anoint you for the job; you'll be able to do with His help that which you'd never be able to do on your own.

Don't ever use the knowledge of your motivational gift(s) as an excuse to not do what God calls you to do. Remember, *the anointing supersedes your giftedness.*

THE GIFT OF SERVING

	Never	Seldom	Sometimes	Usually	Mostly	Always	POINTS
	0	1	2	3	4	5	
1.							
2.							
3.							
4.							
5.							
6.							
7.							
8.							
9.							
10.							
11.							
12.							
13.							
14.							
15.							
16.							
17.							
18.							
19.							
20.							
							TOTAL

Characteristics:

1. Easily recognizes practical needs and is quick to meet them.
2. Especially enjoys manual projects, jobs, and functions.
3. Keeps everything in meticulous order.
4. Is a detail person with a good memory.
5. Enjoys showing hospitality.
6. Will stay with something until it is completed.
7. Has a hard time saying no to requests for help.
8. Is more interested in meeting the needs of others than own needs.
9. Enjoys working on immediate goals rather than long-range goals.
10. Shows love for others in deeds and actions more than words.
11. Needs to feel appreciated.
12. Tends to do more than asked to do.
13. Feels greatest joy in doing something that is helpful.
14. Does not want to lead others or projects.
15. Has a high energy level.
16. Cannot stand to be around clutter.
17. Tends to be a perfectionist.
18. Views serving to be of primary importance in life.
19. Prefers doing a job to delegating it.
20. Supports others who are in leadership.

Copyright © 1987, Don & Katie Fortune

88

PROBLEMS OF THE SERVER

11

The server, like each recipient of motivational gifts, has his own typical problem areas. Remember, you are to score these five characteristics just to discover any areas where you may need improvement or growth. *They do not go onto your profile sheet.*

1. Is critical of others who do not help out with obvious needs.

	Never	Seldom	Sometimes	Usually	Mostly	Always	
	0	1	2	3	4	5	**POINTS**

The classic example is Martha, the sister of Mary and Lazarus. In Luke 10:38–42 we see Mary sitting at Jesus' feet listening to His teaching. Meanwhile, back in the kitchen, Martha is preparing food to serve their hungry guests. To her, Mary's obliviousness to a practical need is incomprehensible.

"But Martha (overoccupied and too busy) was distracted about much serving; and she came up to Him and said, Lord, is it nothing to You that my sister has left me to serve alone? Tell her then to help me—to lend a hand and do her part along with me" Luke 10:40, TAB).

To Martha, getting that meal ready is the most important thing in the world. Jesus loves the server gift in her, of course, but also identifies the server's problem and speaks kindly correction. It is always a temptation for servers to feel put upon by those who ignore "obvious" needs.

89

Our church meets in a school gymnasium. Our services usually run to about 12:30, and we must be entirely out of the area by 1:00 since another group rents the space then.

Several servers regularly take down the platform, put away the PA system, fold up the chairs, etc. Other people stand around to fellowship, oblivious to the activity around them. Sometimes, when time is especially short, an announcement is made, requesting additional help to get the job done.

"Why should we have to ask for it?" we overheard one server say. "Can't people see what needs to be done?"

"How can they be here every Sunday," another agreed, "and never lend a hand?"

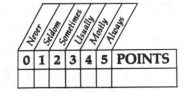

2. May neglect own family's needs by being too busy helping others.

Never	Seldom	Sometimes	Usually	Mostly	Always	
0	1	2	3	4	5	POINTS

The typical example is that of the server husband who so enjoys helping out the neighbors that he never has time to fix things around his own house.

Then there's the wife who does so much volunteer work that soon the laundry is stacking up; dinners are getting later.

Betty, a server, wrote us: "I'm *always* behind at home because I'm so involved doing things for others. When I'm baking the kids ask, 'Who is that for?' They're surprised when I say, 'For us.' They're used to its being for someone else."

Because servers can so easily get overextended they need to be sure of their priorities.

One server (we'll call him Jack) loved to do volunteer work at the church. So, when the new building project started he threw himself into it. Soon it was a hit-and-run situation. He'd hit the house after work, grab a quick bite, and run to the church to work until it was time to retire in the evening.

"Jack," his wife pleaded, "I never see you anymore! The kids hardly know they have a father. I know the building project is worthwhile, but you *do* have a family."

Jack's priorities had gotten out of order. They should be 1) God, 2) family, 3) job, and only then 4) church. In his eagerness to serve Jack had them 1) God, 2) job, 3) church, and 4) family if there was any time left over.

Although written about a woman, Proverbs 31:16 is good advice for all, especially the servers:

"She considers a new field before she buys or accepts it—expanding prudently [and not courting neglect of her present duties by assuming others] . . ." (TAB).

3. May become pushy or interfering in eagerness to help.

Never	Seldom	Sometimes	Usually	Mostly	Always	
0	1	2	3	4	5	POINTS

Servers can sometimes "help" where help is not wanted.

One time we had a server stay at our home for two weeks who wanted to be helpful all the time. She would become restless if her hands were not busy, so she'd do things without asking.

Sometimes she was truly helpful, but other times she just made more work for us. When we'd be gone she'd empty the dishwasher and put the contents away in places we'd never think to look. Months later we were still finding dishes and pans in the most surprising places.

A lady from one of our motivational gift seminars shared this example with us. It seems that there was a server in her church who noticed that one of the Sunday school rooms needed painting. She went to the pastor about it and he assured her that the deacons would take care of it. After several weeks when nothing seemed to be happening she decided to take matters into her own hands.

She went to the local paint store, bought supplies, and painted the whole room.

Later she discovered that the deacons had decided to remodel that room, knock out one wall to enlarge it, and build floor-to-ceiling cupboards on another wall. As the paint that she had used was a dark color, on the remaining walls they had to put on two extra coats of the lighter paint the deacons had chosen.

4. Finds it hard to accept being served by others.

Never	Seldom	Sometimes	Usually	Mostly	Always	POINTS
0	1	2	3	4	5	

Because servers so love to do the serving they can feel awkward when someone else serves them. But the fact is that they need to learn to receive as well as give. Otherwise they rob others of the joy of serving.

Barbara told us she really loved doing things for others but that she felt unworthy and uneasy when someone did something for her. "I would immediately look for something to do for them," she recalled, "like bake them a batch of cookies or take them flowers. Then I'd feel better."

Then Barbara's church started a "secret pal" program. "Mine kept doing all these wonderful things for me and I couldn't find out who it was. I was terribly frustrated until I realized this might be the Lord's way of showing me that I needed to be willing to be served, too."

5. Is easily hurt when unappreciated.

Never	Seldom	Sometimes	Usually	Mostly	Always	POINTS
0	1	2	3	4	5	

The need for appreciation is so deeply built into the server that some hurt is almost inevitable.

Gloria wrote to say, "I love to be appreciated. I'm highly motivated to do more when people are grateful. But frankly, it really hurts me when I put myself out to help someone and they never even say, 'Thanks.' That seems to be happening a lot lately. What should I do? Should I just quit helping those people who don't seem to appreciate my efforts?"

"Dear Gloria," we responded. "First of all, check your motives. Are you helping others just to get their thanks? We know that your gift motivates you to be helpful, but you need to learn how to be helpful without expecting any thanks. We find it's important to look to the Lord for appreciation. He always gives it even when others don't. Let His love and appreciation be enough for you, and then if a person thanks you too, that's the frosting on the cake! Keep on serving!"

If you know any servers, appreciate them. They'll love you for it.

	Never	Seldom	Sometimes	Usually	Mostly	Always	POINTS
	0	1	2	3	4	5	
1.							
2.							
3.							
4.							
5.							
TOTAL							

Typical problem areas of the gift of serving:

1. Is critical of others who do not help out with obvious needs.
2. May neglect own family's needs by being too busy helping others.
3. May become pushy or interfering in eagerness to help.
4. Finds it hard to accept being served by others.
5. Is easily hurt when unappreciated.

BIBLICAL SERVERS

12

It's a little harder to identify servers in the Bible since their ministries are apt to be behind the scenes, not the kind of thing that is usually recorded for posterity. But we do have a very clear example in Martha.

Poor Martha, she has had an unfair share of detractors. How we wish more had been recorded about her, and especially about Jesus' responses to the normal functioning of her motivational gift of serving. Had we been there in person on any of the occasions when Jesus visited her home, we're sure we would have heard the Lord say something like, "Martha, dear Martha, thank you for that marvelous meal. I want you to know that I appreciate all your work and effort."

Maybe as you ponder the following scene, the setting, and the fact that Martha was a server, you will see how much her actions demonstrate her gift.

Scripture: Luke 10:38–42
John 12:2 (TAB)

Your Comments:

Luke 10

38 Now while they were on their way, it occurred that Jesus entered a certain village, and a woman named Martha received and welcomed Him into her house.

94

39 And she had a sister named Mary, who seated herself at the Lord's feet and was listening to His teaching.

40 But Martha (overoccupied and too busy) was distracted about much serving; and she came up to Him and said, Lord, is it nothing to You that my sister has left me to serve alone? Tell her then to help me— to lend a hand and do her part along with me.

41 But the Lord replied to her by saying, Martha, Martha, you are anxious and troubled about many things;

42 There is need of (but a few things, or) only one. Mary has chosen the good portion—that which is to advantage—which shall not be taken away from her.

John 12

2 So they made Him a supper, and Martha served, but Lazarus was one of those at the table with Him.

Please note that Jesus never criticized or called to account Martha's gift of serving in its appropriate form. In fact, we read again and again about Martha showing hospitality to Jesus. But when negative characteristic #1, "Critical of others who do not help out with obvious needs," came to the surface Jesus addressed the problem.

Martha had become a fusser. She couldn't see the forest for the trees. Her focus was so much on the meal preparation (no packaged foods or TV dinners then!) that she missed the priceless privilege to sit at the Master's feet and learn.

Scripture: Luke 10:38–42
John 12:2 (TAB)

Our Comments:

Luke 10

38 Now while they were on their way, it occurred that Jesus entered a certain village, and a woman named Martha received and welcomed Him

#5 showed hospitality
#10 showed love with actions

Our Comments:

into her house.

39 And she had a sister named Mary, who seated herself at the Lord's feet and was listening to His teaching.

40 But Martha (overoccupied and too busy) was distracted about much serving; and she came up to Him and said, Lord, is it nothing to You that my sister has left me to serve alone? Tell her then to help me— to lend a hand and do her part along with me.

#1	recognized practical need
#12	did more than needed
#17	perfectionist
#18	sees serving as all-important
#-1	critical of Mary

41 But the Lord replied to her by saying, Martha, Martha, you are anxious and troubled about many things;

#12	overextended
#17	perfectionist
#-5	feels unappreciated

42 There is need of (but a few things, or) only one. Mary has chosen the good portion—that which is to advantage—which shall not be taken away from her.

#4	details got in way
#-2	too busy

John 12

2 So they made Him a supper, and Martha served, but Lazarus was one of those at the table with Him.

#5	showed hospitality
#10	showed love, with actions

Perhaps one of the reasons Jesus went so often to the home of Mary, Martha, and Lazarus was because Martha's gift made Him feel so at home. Jesus had no place to call His own, but we can easily imagine that this was the nearest place he had to an earthly home.

Now read about some other biblical servers (including another reference for Martha). See how many motivational-gift characteristics you can see in each of them:

Martha—John 11:1–40
Phoebe—Romans 16:1–2
Stephen—Acts 6:1–15; 7:1–60
Philip (the deacon)—John 1:43–45; 6:5–7; 12:21–22; 14:8; Acts 6:5; 8:5–40; 21:8–9
Onesimus—Philemon; Colossians 4:9
Peter's mother-in-law—Matthew 8:14–15
Jacob—Genesis 25–30

CHARACTERISTICS OF THE TEACHER

13

The third motivational gift listed in Romans 12:6–8 is the gift of teaching. The Greek word here for a person who teaches is *didasko* which means, simply, "to teach or to give instruction."

The person with this gift then should be functioning—at least to some degree—in the area of teaching others. Actually we were tempted to use the word "researcher" because we found that many with this gift were especially drawn into fields of research and may or may not be overtly involved with the function of teaching. Or, they may do their teaching through writing (papers, articles, dissertations, books) rather than in person.

But we found that the majority of people with this gift were also involved in some form of in-person teaching too, so "teacher" stands.

Proceed through the following twenty characteristics of the teacher, scoring as you go, then transfer the total to your profile sheet.

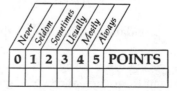

Never	Seldom	Sometimes	Usually	Mostly	Always	
0	1	2	3	4	5	**POINTS**

1. Presents truth in a logical, systematic way.

Looking back over school days you can always tell the teachers who had this gift because their lectures were in outline form: points 1, 2, 3, a, b, c. The procedures were systematic. It was easy to take notes.

Derek Prince, renowned author and scholar, is a classic example of a person with the

97

motivational gift of teaching. We have file folders full of notes taken at his lectures. The notes are rich in facts, Scriptures, and conclusions, all nicely organized by virtue of the fact that Derek speaks that way. It's easy to look up information from these notes since they are so logically arranged.

We will find that exhorters are actually the most interesting and popular teachers, but they may teach for an hour and make only one significant point. You'll have hardly any notes—and those not in any particular sequence.

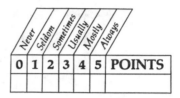

2. Validates truth by checking out the facts.

A family in our church recently got a ferret for a pet. He's an animal who seems to be actively looking for something all the time—in corners, under chairs, in jackets. The word "ferret" has come to mean *to search out*, and that is what the teacher is doing all the time, ferreting out the truth.

Teachers want to be sure that what they believe and accept is based on fact. This was the case with doubting Thomas. Being motivated by his teaching gift he did not want to trust what he heard about Jesus' resurrection and so it was natural for him to respond:

". . . Unless I shall see in His hands the imprint of the nails, and put my finger into the place of the nails, and put my hands into His side, I will not believe" (John 20:25, NAS).

However, when Jesus did appear to him eight days later, Thomas could only respond, "My Lord and my God!" (verse 28).

If you have the motivational gift of teaching you have probably been called a "doubting Thomas" from time to time. Count it an honor. You were designed by God to investigate the facts and you are doing a good enough job of it that others are noticing it. That's great!

Don calls teachers "spiritual detectives." Perhaps that's why so many teachers love to read mystery stories. They are armchair detectives at heart.

3. Loves to study and do research.

Since this is my secondary gift I can relate thoroughly to this characteristic. I love to research!

When our boys were pre-school ages I wanted to be at home, but there were spare hours in my day. So I began to do freelance writing of junior high Sunday school materials for both the David C. Cook Company and Union Gospel Press. They would send me the assignments and I would get out my commentaries and concordances and begin to research the Scripture. I'd often spend up to twenty hours on one lesson.

"Why do you spend so much time on that research?" Don would ask. "Couldn't you cut it down a bit?"

The thought horrified me. What if I didn't look into the subject thoroughly enough and wound up writing something inaccurate! I could visualize thousands of Sunday school teachers passing on my marred material to trusting students. The errors would be multiplied in vast numbers of innocent minds, and I'd be responsible. My research had to be *complete.* Besides, I loved doing it.

Because of their love of study and research, teachers also like to have a large personal library of research books.

Dick Mills, a popular speaker with the motivational gift of teaching (and the ministry gift of prophet), has an almost insatiable love for books, especially versions of the Bible (he regularly quotes from twenty-five translations.) He can't pass a Christian bookstore without slipping inside to see if they have any new research books.

One day his wife, Betty, observed that Dick's books had filled all the available spaces around the house and were now spilling over to her kitchen counters. Before long they were appearing on the dresser, then the nightstands, then stacked up in corners. That was it!

"Dick," she announced, "I can't stand it. I can't even clean house without having to move stacks of books. Either they go or I go!"

Well, Dick didn't want to lose his wife, but neither did he want to lose his books. He went to the local lumber store and soon a new addition appeared on their house. You guessed it. He built on a library.

	Never	Seldom	Sometimes	Usually	Mostly	Always	
	0	1	2	3	4	5	POINTS

4. Enjoys word studies.

Teachers are fascinated with words. They like to investigate the root meanings, and the Greek or Hebrew counterparts. They see words as the building blocks of communication. They want to use words well, and correctly.

They will often check out a word in a reference like W. E. Vine's *An Expository Dictionary of New Testament Words* to determine the precise meaning of the Greek original. They also enjoy topical studies with aids like *Nave's Topical Bible* or *Harper's Topical Concordance.*

Sometimes the study of just one word will lead the teacher into hours of pursuit as one insight leads to another.

When Dick Mills teaches he often will take a single verse of Scripture and spend time explaining the facets of meaning of each major word in it, quoting a variety of authorities. The verse comes alive.

5. Prefers to use biblical illustrations rather than life illustrations.

	Never	Seldom	Sometimes	Usually	Mostly	Always	
	0	1	2	3	4	5	POINTS

The Bible is the ultimate authority to the teacher. Even if he does not understand a particular verse, he believes that it is his own lack of knowledge, not the Scripture passage, that is the problem. It is a source of new understanding yet to be discovered.

Teachers quote liberally from the Bible, often using stories, parables, or characters to prove or illustrate a point. They can trust this source.

Life illustrations are another matter; they are by their very nature subjective. They are not, in the teacher's estimation, a reliable rock upon which to build.

A teacher may use personal anecdotes to enhance a point, but only *after* the point is well illustrated by Scripture.

I find that this is my tendency. For instance, when I developed a teaching on the subject of anger I first studied what the Bible had to say about it in these passages:

Jesus teaches about it in Matthew 5:21–26.

Paul warns against it in Ephesians 4:26–27.

It was Cain's main problem in Genesis 4:1–12.

It was Jonah's problem in Jonah 4:1–9.

Only then did I add to this what I had learned experientially about anger through the counseling I had done.

6. Gets upset when Scripture is used out of context.

Never	Seldom	Sometimes	Usually	Mostly	Always	
0	1	2	3	4	5	POINTS

Wow! Does this unpardonable action ever drive the teacher up the wall! To him it is like fingernails across a chalkboard. He is so concerned for the integrity of teaching—be it spoken or written—that he cannot help but lose confidence in the person who proof-texts a point with disregard of the true sense of a passage.

One popular traveling teacher was the rave of many in conferences and camps in recent years. He was clever and dramatic in his presentations, keeping his audiences captivated for the most part, except for those with the motivational gift of teaching. When others would leave a session saying, "Wasn't that wonderful!" the teachers would reply, "Not really."

The problem was that the speaker, being blessed with the motivational gift of exhortation, would set out to prove a point and tag on several Scriptures to give it validity. The point itself was usually well-taken but the Scriptures quoted in that context might not be at all what the biblical writer meant by them. It would have been better to have used no Scriptures at all than to use ones lifted out of context. We noticed that those with the teaching gift quit going to his meetings.

The teacher views *misuse* as *abuse*.

7. Feels concerned that truth be established in every situation.

Never	Seldom	Sometimes	Usually	Mostly	Always	
0	1	2	3	4	5	POINTS

Whether it's in business, education, religion, human relationships, or any other area of life, teachers want truth to prevail. It is the foundation, the anchor, the framework within which they can securely work.

Characteristics of the Teacher

The Berean believers must have had many people with the motivational gift of teaching among them for they checked out carefully what Paul said every day to be sure that it lined up with the truth of the Old Testament Scriptures (see Acts 17:11).

Aquila and Priscilla, both teachers by motivational gift, welcomed Apollos who was also a teacher. But they could see that he was operating on limited knowledge of the Gospel and were quick to instruct him "more perfectly in the way of the Lord" (Acts 18:26). With truth fully established in him, Apollos was then able to go to Greece and confound the intellectuals of that day.

	Never	Seldom	Sometimes	Usually	Mostly	Always	
8. Is more objective than subjective.	0	1	2	3	4	5	**POINTS**

In general men tend to be more objective, women more subjective. There are, of course, exceptions. But when a man has the motivational gift of teaching we see the most objective type of person of all. Such men often become research scientists, business analysts, or judges.

Women with the motivational gift of teaching go into similar fields. And it is not unusual for them to hear a shrouded compliment like, "For a woman you are amazingly objective."

Teachers look at life with a certain detachment. They participate, but without their emotions getting in the way. This works as a sort of insulation factor that keeps them from being hurt or emotionally wounded.

Eighteen-year-old Erin, the third of four sisters, attended one of our seminars in her Baptist church. At one point she came to us to share some interesting insights.

"It's been invaluable to discover that my motivational gift is teaching," she told us. "I've always wondered why I could be so detached and objective. Now I see why.

"My parents fight like cats and dogs," she went on. "They love each other, but the fights get pretty bad. My two older sisters couldn't handle it and they both left home when they were sixteen. They're still working through a lot of emotional damage. Now I see that they both have the gift of compassion. They've felt the tension and hurt much more than I ever have.

"My viewpoint has been, if they want to fight that's their business, but I'm not going to waste my time listening to it. So I just go into my bedroom and read a good book."

	Never	Seldom	Sometimes	Usually	Mostly	Always	
9. Easily develops and uses a large vocabulary.	0	1	2	3	4	5	**POINTS**

Teachers use words well and are fond of learning new ones. Even as children they enjoy word games—Scrabble, Boggle, crossword puzzles. They are good communicators, often commanding in their speech and sometimes eloquent.

Several years ago I was one of the speakers at the Billy Graham Writers' Conference in

Calgary, Canada. The banquet speaker was Philip Yancey, author of many books including *Where Is God When It Hurts.* His speech was marvelous. Eloquent! Polished! As an editor I mused that it would be almost possible to take a transcript of what he said and print it without any editing at all.

Later that evening I was talking with Philip. "Your speech was magnificent," I told him. "How long did it take you to prepare it?" I assumed he had worked on it for weeks.

"Well," he confided, "to tell you the truth I put it together on the flight up here this morning. Basically I just jotted some notes on the back of an envelope."

As we talked a bit more I realized that he spoke eloquently *all* the time. Even his casual conversation was polished and impressive. Obviously his motivational gift was that of teacher.

10. Emphasizes facts and the accuracy of words.

	Never	Seldom	Sometimes	Usually	Mostly	Always	POINTS
	0	1	2	3	4	5	

Teachers are not so interested in opinions; they want facts. Facts are the building blocks of their lives. This coupled with their ability to use words well and accurately, and their exceptional objectivity, all work together to make them gifted in editorial work. They make great copy editors. Like the homing pigeon they readily find their target: misspelled words, improper grammar, or inadequate vocabulary.

My Aunt Aleda was one so gifted, much to my dismay as a child. Through my mother's urging I wrote to Aunt Aleda regularly. But she always returned my letters—edited! She'd circle misspelled words and tell me to look them up. She'd correct my grammar, even diagramming sentences to reinforce what I was obviously not learning adequately in school. Needless to say I did not relish the returned epistles. But looking back now, I'm glad she took the time and interest to use her giftedness for my benefit.

In Japan our missionary friend Noel Morris is likewise gifted. Coupled with the detailedness of his serving gift his teaching gift makes him meticulous in editing skills. While his main ministry is managing the largest Christian tape loan library in Japan, he helps to support himself and his wife by editing English manuscripts written by Japanese.

11. Checks out the source of knowledge of others who teach.

	Never	Seldom	Sometimes	Usually	Mostly	Always	POINTS
	0	1	2	3	4	5	

Whenever we teach a motivational gift seminar it is the teachers who come up to us at the close of the session to say, "Now where did you get all this information?" This has happened so often that now we usually include an explanation in the presentation itself.

Teachers are the ones most apt to ask: who, what, where, when and how come? In a young person this can come across as rude or impudent.

Such was the case with the fourteen-year-old grandson of friends of ours who were living in Munich, Germany. They had invited their grandson to come and live with them for a while and go to a German school. They had not bargained for an adolescent with the motivational gift of teaching nor did they recognize this as the cause of his incessant questioning.

"He must ask five hundred questions a day," Vi bemoaned. "Some that are none of his business."

"He follows me around asking why I do this and why I do that," Jim said. "And the worst is that he's learned more German that we have, so he's always correcting us."

When we had the opportunity to meet the boy our suspicions were confirmed. He was a teacher.

We were able to share with Vi and Jim that this was a giftedness that needed to be channeled, not squelched. Just the simple awareness of their grandson's gift took a lot of pressure off the situation.

12. Prefers teaching believers to engaging in evangelism.

When it comes to evangelism the teacher keeps a low profile. He will lead people to Jesus Christ, but usually in circumstances where he's already built a bridge of relationship or friendship.

Aggressive types of evangelism are not appealing to the teacher. He is definitely not drawn to street witnessing or door-to-door evangelism. But he's glad that others make these efforts. And, once new people have been won to the Lord, the teacher will spend endless hours joyfully teaching the new converts.

Julie Wayner, author of *His Gentle Voice*, is just such a teacher. She confided, "I'd almost rather die than go out door-to-door evangelizing. But give me a group of new believers and I'll commit all the time necessary to train them in the Word of God."

We saw her put this into action some years ago as she faithfully taught the Bible to a group of women (mostly new believers) for six years. I was privileged to continue teaching the group when Julie moved to Michigan and was greatly impressed with the maturity of their faith and the extent of their Bible knowledge.

How fortunate it is that not every Christian is geared primarily to evangelism, for without people to teach the newly evangelized, the Body of Christ would not mature.

13. Feels Bible study is foundational to the operation of all the gifts.

Teachers cannot imagine anything more important than studying the Bible. They believe it is the foundation upon which all the gifts operate.

Their thinking goes something like this:

How can the perceiver perceive accurately unless he has a solid understanding of the Bible?

How can the server serve well if he is not acquainted with the biblical reasons for service?

How can the teacher teach unless he has studied the Scriptures thoroughly?

How can the exhorter exhort effectively unless he knows the biblical basis for his exhortation?

How can the giver give properly if he is not aware of the biblical guidelines for giving?

How can the administrator be an effective leader unless he understands God's will as revealed in the Word?

How can the compassionate person minister God's love if he does not encounter that love in the Bible?

"Nothing," says the teacher, "is more foundational than studying the Bible!"

14. Solves problems by starting with scriptural principles.

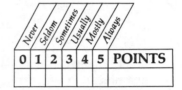

	Never	Seldom	Sometimes	Usually	Mostly	Always	POINTS
	0	1	2	3	4	5	

Teachers believe that there is an answer to every problem in God's Word, if not in actual example or principle, at least by implication.

In her book Julie Wayner describes the problems and challenges she faced as she set out to become a missionary to China. With the closing of that nation to the West, her love for a young man committed to the South American mission field, and his subsequent engagement to another woman, she turned at each point to the Bible to give her the principles by which to make decisions.

Julie told us, "I always looked first for the biblical principles that fit the situation. Then secondly for the leading of the Holy Spirit, and thirdly for the juxtaposition of circumstances. If, for any reason, the other two guidelines (as best I could interpret them) did not line up with the first, then I always chose to abide by the biblical principles."

	Never	Seldom	Sometimes	Usually	Mostly	Always	POINTS
	0	1	2	3	4	5	

15. Is intellectually sharp.

These are the ones you don't want to invite over to play Trivial Pursuit. They'll win for sure.

The fact is that God has gifted these, the "mind" of the Body of Christ, with what they need to be successful in their sphere—a high IQ. They are often brilliant. They were good students in school, loved to study, were self-motivated, and often came home with straight A's.

The teacher's mind can be likened to a thirsty sponge, soaking up everything it can. As a result he's a prolific reader, drawn to books filled with facts and accurate information. He has a good memory, especially for dates and history.

When we went to New Zealand eight years ago we traveled around the South Island with our dear friends Rita and Len Restall. Len is a schoolmaster with the motivational gift of teaching. His reservoir of information constantly amazed us. Everywhere we went Len would spontaneously spill out rich and interesting history about each New Zealand town.

Len was like a living, walking, and talking encyclopedia. Whenever we brought up a new subject it was like pressing a computer button: out would come his amazing contribution of vast amounts of information to enhance our understanding.

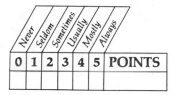

16. Is self-disciplined.

Mix a good dose of seriousness with a lot of objectivity, add a love for truth and a keen mind, and you have the ingredients for self-discipline.

Teachers can set goals and stick to them, set parameters and work effectively within them, and project time schedules and abide by them.

One woman with this gift was amazing to watch in action. Her life was so self-regulated that fellow workers could set their watches by the moment she walked in the office: always at 8:30 A.M., never 8:29 or 8:31. She also exited at 4:30 on the nose! But while some chuckled at this, her punctuality set a good example of putting in a good day's work for a day's wages.

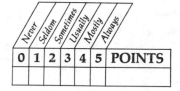

17. Is emotionally self-controlled.

Of all the motivational gifts this is the one that grants the greatest emotional equilibrium. Some people have emotional ups and downs that track like the pathway of a roller-coaster ride. Others have smoother patterns of ups and downs with only occasional jolting bumps. But the teacher's graph of mood swings looks more like a horizontal line.

Teachers are highly analytical. They believe reasonable choices can resolve potentially volatile situations. When someone's upset, they may advise, "Calm down. You can, you know."

At one of our Prayer Counseling Training sessions we staged a little melodrama to illustrate just that point:

The scene is a home. Wife is stirring the pot, looking again and again at her watch. Furious looks flash across her face. Finally husband comes in the door, obviously late again. He offers a weak excuse and his wife goes into a tirade of complaints about his inconsiderateness. He retaliates with complaints about her temper. The argument escalates, wife becoming all but hysterical with rage.

"Get *control* of yourself," husband demands.

"I *can't*!" she screams.

Brrrrrring. The telephone pierces the commotion.

Wife picks up the receiver. "Hellooo," she calmly coos into the phone. "Why Charlotte, how good to hear from you. No, I wasn't doing a thing. Yes, we're both fine. How about you?"

On and on she goes. Completely in control.

The point is: It's not that she *can't* control her emotions when arguing with her husband, she *won't*. It's a matter of choice.

18. Has only a select circle of friends.

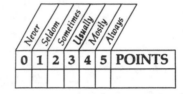

Never	Seldom	Sometimes	Usually	Mostly	Always	POINTS
0	1	2	3	4	5	

Common interests seem to be the prerequisite for the development of close relationships. Teachers are seldom drawn into superficial friendships. They tend to be aloof or uneasy in unstructured social situations and they hate meaningless chitchat. They prefer friends with whom they can discuss ideas and concepts. Sometimes they are loners. More often they are comfortable with just a few close friends.

Teachers often tell us, "Some interaction with people is okay, but, quite frankly, I'd just as soon curl up with a good book." Books are often their "best friends."

Our niece, Gayle Hansen, is that way. We spent summers at our cabin on Puget Sound right next door to my sister's cabin. From the time Gayle was old enough to read we noticed that she often preferred being inside, even on nice days, with her nose in a book, to playing outside with the other kids. We often wondered why this attractive girl seemed so antisocial. When we gave her the motivational gift test (in her teens) we were not surprised that she came out teacher.

Recently she visited us from California. "I'm still a bookworm, Aunt Katie," she said. "I don't go out much. I like to tuck my son into bed early and spend the rest of the evening with a good book."

19. Has strong convictions and opinions based on investigation of facts.

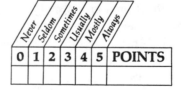

Never	Seldom	Sometimes	Usually	Mostly	Always	POINTS
0	1	2	3	4	5	

Teachers have so many areas of interest. They willingly drop what they are doing to investigate a new area of knowledge.

Eadie and Jim Goodboy are both teachers by motivational gift. It is always interesting to visit them in their home, which is loaded with books of every description. We'll be talking and happen to bring up a new subject. Invariably it triggers something in them.

"Just a minute," Jim will say. "I think I have a book that gets into that." He'll quickly retrieve a book from the shelf and flip to the relevant reference.

Or: "I read something about that just the other day," Eadie will say.

Before long the dining room table will be loaded with open books, all contributing to the development of new opinions and convictions.

	Never	Seldom	Sometimes	Usually	Mostly	Always	
	0	1	2	3	4	5	POINTS

20. Believes truth has the intrinsic power to produce change.

When teachers teach they present the truth without necessarily explaining to their listeners how to apply that truth to their lives. Teachers believe the application of truth is the job of the Holy Spirit.

"You will know the truth, and the truth will set you free" (John 8:32, NIV) is a favorite verse of teachers. They assume that others will respond to truth in the same way that they do—as energizing and liberating.

Teachers are even able to teach truth they themselves have not yet appropriated. One summer I worked as a counselor at a private girls' camp on the beautiful wooded shores of Lake Winnipesaukee in New Hampshire. One of my responsibilities was to teach swimming, for which I was provided an instruction manual.

All went well until I got to the lesson on the breast stroke. I had been a reasonably good swimmer all my life, but this was one stroke I was never able to master. I memorized the directions, then walked out on the dock and instructed the girls, step by step. They did it! And I couldn't do it myself. No matter. The instructions worked. Later I slipped into the water myself and, following what I had taught, swam my first breast stroke.

Most with other gifts would have practiced before class. But the teacher has confidence that whatever is truth will be effective.

THE GIFT OF TEACHING

Characteristics:

	Never	Seldom	Sometimes	Usually	Mostly	Always	POINTS
	0	1	2	3	4	5	
1. Presents truth in a logical, systematic way.							
2. Validates truth by checking out the facts.							
3. Loves to study and do research.							
4. Enjoys word studies.							
5. Prefers to use biblical illustrations rather than life illustrations.							
6. Gets upset when Scripture is used out of context.							
7. Feels concerned that truth be established in every situation.							
8. Is more objective than subjective.							
9. Easily develops and uses a large vocabulary.							
10. Emphasizes facts and the accuracy of words.							
11. Checks out the source of knowledge of others who teach.							
12. Prefers teaching believers to engaging in evangelism.							
13. Feels Bible study is foundational to the operation of all the gifts.							
14. Solves problems by starting with scriptural principles.							
15. Is intellectually sharp.							
16. Is self-disciplined.							
17. Is emotionally self-controlled.							
18. Has only a select circle of friends.							
19. Has strong convictions and opinions based on investigation of facts.							
20. Believes truth has the intrinsic power to produce change.							TOTAL

PROBLEMS OF THE TEACHER

14

The teacher's problem areas are unique to the teacher gift. But in identifying the problems the teacher will believe that the solutions cannot be far away. (And so it is with each of the motivational gifts—the solutions to the problem areas will come as we see the need for change and cooperate with the work of the Holy Spirit in bringing us into maturity.)

1. Tends to neglect the practical application of truth.

Never	Seldom	Sometimes	Usually	Mostly	Always	
0	1	2	3	4	5	POINTS

Because teachers believe that their job is to communicate truth and let people make their own use of it, they usually do not give much in the way of practical suggestions. This frustrates exhorters especially. (They focus on the actual application of teaching.) It can also frustrate those with other gifts.

The listener may say, "So we've heard lots of facts, now what do we do with them?" The teacher responds, "You've got a mind. You figure it out."

But not all minds work with the degree of logic that the teacher's mind does. Many need specific directions—steps one, two, three. A teacher needs to learn how to give at least some measure of practical application to his hearers.

I have the benefit of living with an exhorter. Don keeps me accountable. He's helped me see the need to give practical application when I teach and make my teaching more interesting with anecdotes and illustrations.

We've noticed that when public speakers become known for their style of teaching they tend to draw specialized audiences. Teachers draw other teachers and those interested in gaining knowledge in general. Exhorters draw other exhorters and those interested in gaining practical, life-related knowledge. But if they learn to use both the solid presentation of facts and the practical application of those facts, they will appeal to everyone.

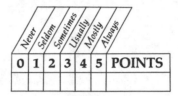

2. Is slow to accept viewpoints of others.

The "know-it-all" attitude can be a real pitfall for the person with the motivational gift of teaching. Of course they do know a lot. But no one knows *everything*.

George, now a professor at a university, told us, "I was always dubious about the teaching of other Christians. If they spoke on something I had researched myself and knew was true, that was fine. But if the subject was new I would go home and check out all the Scriptures for myself."

Shawn, who is now attending law school, said he grew up loving to study and learn. But his dedication to this along with his desire to be right caused some strains in his relationships with peers. "They often called me 'Professor Shawn' or 'Mr. Information Booth'—neither meant as a compliment. But as I've learned to be more accepting of others, I've learned to respect their viewpoints, too."

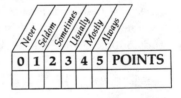

3. Tends to develop pride in intellectual ability.

Pride is probably the number one problem for those with the motivational gift of teaching. It was Lucifer's problem and it changed him from an angel of God into Satan. We know that pride brings downfall. Listen to what Proverbs has to say about it:

"When pride comes, then comes disgrace, but with humility comes wisdom" (Proverbs 11:2, NIV).

"Pride goes before destruction, a haughty spirit before a fall" (Proverbs 16:18, NIV).

"A man's pride brings him low, but a man of lowly spirit gains honor" (Proverbs 29:23, NIV).

In 1 Corinthians 8:1 Paul says that knowledge puffs up, but love builds up. The greatest qualities a teacher can seek are humility and love. These will neutralize the pride problem.

One who scored very high on teaching wrote to us: "I have always enjoyed learning new things. I couldn't understand why others didn't pursue learning like I did. I thought they were lazy or unmotivated. I am ashamed to admit that this led me to think I was better than most people. At the seminar I was helped to value the other gifts and the people who so beautifully demonstrate them."

Teachers can indeed develop a superiority complex. The problem is that intellectually they usually are superior. But they need to be careful not to lean on human knowledge and reasoning rather than on the Holy Spirit. The primary tool of the teacher is his mind, but Proverbs 3:5 warns us not to lean on our own understanding.

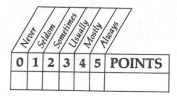

4. Tends to be legalistic and dogmatic.

Never	Seldom	Sometimes	Usually	Mostly	Always	
0	1	2	3	4	5	**POINTS**

This trait can show up even in children.

Becky, today a young mother, shared how inflexible she used to be. "Even when I played games I insisted that we play strictly by the rules. If someone suggested we take shortcuts in Monopoly I'd tell them to play it right or not at all. Now I see that I was much too legalistic, but at the time I just thought I was being right."

Being right is so important to the teacher that he easily becomes argumentative. The feeling may be "I alone am right and everyone else is wrong." Such lack of checks and balances can expose the teacher to deception. (Perhaps that's why some get off into cults.) God's truth is not exclusive; it can be verified by many.

Have you ever been involved in a good group discussion where each person is openly interacting? And then a polluted teacher gift comes along and blurts out, "Well, I happen to *know* that the truth of the matter is. . . ." No one can end a good discussion faster.

Never	Seldom	Sometimes	Usually	Mostly	Always	
0	1	2	3	4	5	**POINTS**

5. Is easily sidetracked by new interests.

Teachers are interested in so many things! Their prolific reading takes them into all kinds of areas. Their research extends to endless subjects. Focusing is not always easy.

We know one man who admits that when he picks up an encyclopedia he seldom gets right to the subject at hand. Just flipping through the pages sends him off on many tangents. "I'll be looking up 'transistors' and on the way I come across 'tape recorders.' Well, I always wanted to know how they came into being so I spend fifteen minutes there. Then I happen to see 'technology.' Another quarter hour goes by. Then I stop at 'television.' Fascinating! After a good look at 'theater' and 'thermometer' and 'thermostat' and 'tide' and 'tornado' I've almost forgotten what I wanted to know in the first place."

Josh, an avid reader, admits that many of the hundreds of books he owns have never been finished. "I've got bookmarks in scores of them," he confesses.

Kathleen hopes she will have a long retirement because she has so many incomplete projects. "I start things, but then if something else comes along that seems more interesting I'll set the first project aside. My attic and closets are full of them."

If you know anyone with the motivational gift of teaching, be patient with them. As the saying goes: God isn't finished with them yet!

Typical problem areas of the gift of teaching:

1. Tends to neglect the practical application of truth.
2. Is slow to accept viewpoints of others.
3. Tends to develop pride in intellectual ability.
4. Tends to be legalistic and dogmatic.
5. Is easily sidetracked by new interests.

POINTS	Never	Seldom	Sometimes	Usually	Mostly	Always
	0	1	2	3	4	5
1.						
2.						
3.						
4.						
5.						
TOTAL						

BIBLICAL TEACHERS

15

Teachers have a highly visible ministry. However, biblical teachers often have another "public" gift as well, such as perceiver or exhorter, and it not always easy to tell which is the primary one. Also, they may have the motivational gift of teaching but the ministry gift of pastor or prophet. To compound matters they may flow in certain manifestation gifts more than others. How we wish we could ask the writers of the Bible for more information!

Thus, we may identify a biblical character as having a certain gift, while you with equal logic feel that another gift predominates.

We feel, however, that Apollos is a clear example of someone with the motivational gift of teaching. In fact, he's what we call a classic example. It is probable that he also was called of God to the ministry gift of teaching. As you look at the following Scripture passage you will see his giftedness in many aspects of his actions.

Scripture: Acts 18:24–28
1 Corinthians 3:6 (TAB)

Your Comments:

Acts 18

24 Meanwhile there was a Jew named Apollos, a native of Alexandria, who came to Ephesus. He was a cultured and eloquent man, well versed and mighty in the Scriptures.

25 He had been instructed in the way of the Lord, and burning with spiritual zeal, he spoke and taught diligently and accurately the things concerning Jesus, though he was acquainted only with the baptism of John.

26 He began to speak freely—fearlessly and boldly—in the synagogue; but when Priscilla and Aquila heard him, they took him with them and expounded to him the way of God more definitely and accurately.

27 And when [Apollos] wished to cross to Achaia [most of Greece], the brethren wrote to the disciples there, urging and encouraging them to accept and welcome him heartily. When he arrived, he proved a great help to those who through grace—God's unmerited favor and mercy—had believed (adhered to, trusted in and relied on [Christ as Lord and Savior]).

28 For with great power he refuted the Jews in public [discussions], showing and proving by the Scriptures that Jesus is the Christ, the Messiah.

1 Corinthians 3

6 I planted, Apollos watered, but God [all the while] was making it grow, and [He] gave the increase.

What a focus Apollos had on knowing the truth! He was a keen student of the Scriptures and an eloquent speaker. He was drawn to Greece, the intellectual capital of the world, where he used his gift to great effect refuting the Jews in public debate, and proving that Jesus was the promised Messiah. His was the most appropriate gift for the task.

Scripture: Acts 18:24–28
1 Corinthians 3:6 (TAB)

Our Comments:

Acts 18

24 Meanwhile there was a Jew named Apollos, a native of Alexandria, who came to Ephesus. He was a cultured and eloquent man, well versed and mighty in the Scriptures.

#1 logical, cultured
#3 well versed in Scriptures
#9 eloquent vocabulary
#15 intellectually sharp

25 He had been instructed in the way of the Lord, and burning with spiritual zeal, he spoke and taught diligently and accurately the things concerning Jesus, though he was acquainted only with the baptism of John.

#1 logical
#2 accurate facts
#3 student, researcher
#5 biblical focus
#13 teaching focus
#16 diligent

26 He began to speak freely— fearlessly and boldly—in the synagogue; but when Priscilla and Aquila heard him, they took him with them and expounded to him the way of God more definitely and accurately.

#7 open to new truth
#9 speaks impressively
#19 strong convictions

27 And when [Apollos] wished to cross to Achaia [most of Greece], the brethren wrote to the disciples there, urging and encouraging them to accept and welcome him heartily. When he arrived, he proved a great help to those who through grace— God's unmerited favor and mercy— had believed (adhered to, trusted in and relied on [Christ as Lord and Savior]).

#12 helps fellow believers
#15 aimed at Greek culture
#19 took along convictions based on facts

28 For with great power he refuted the Jews in public [discussions], showing and proving by the Scriptures that Jesus is the Christ, the Messiah.

#1 proved truth of Gospel
#9 speaks impressively
#13 used biblical base
#15 used intellect
#19 strong convictions

1 Corinthians 3

6 I planted, Apollos watered, but
God [all the while] was making it
grow, and [He] gave the increase.

#12   taught believers
#20   truth produces change

How valuable the teaching gift is! How important a role it plays in the lives of those who would take the Gospel into all the world.

Take time to read about some of the other New Testament teachers:

Aquila and Priscilla—Acts 18:1–3, 24–28; Romans 16:3–5; 1 Corinthians 16:19; 2 Timothy 4:19

Timothy—1 and 2 Timothy; Acts 16:1–3; 1 Corinthians 4:17; 16:10–11

Thomas—John 20:24–28

Luke—Gospel of Luke and Acts

It is very likely that Aquila and Priscilla were a husband/wife team who had the same motivational gift.

Thomas, famous for his doubting, was simply exercising his teaching gift in wanting to know the facts.

Luke wrote the most systematic account of the life of Jesus and the history of the early church (Luke and Acts). His being a medical doctor is also compatible with his gift of teacher.

CHARACTERISTICS OF THE EXHORTER

16

The teacher aims for your head; the exhorter aims for your heart. It is not so much the content that the exhorter wants to impart as how that content can be made effective in peoples' lives.

Every one of the gifts can teach, but the exhorter makes the most interesting and palatable teacher. All of his efforts are geared toward edifying and encouraging other people. We could have called this person the encourager. In fact, the Greek word *paraklesis* means "a calling to one's side to aid" denoting both exhortation and encouragement.

As you proceed through the scoring in this chapter (as for all the gifts) remember to score the way you really are, not the way you would like to be.

Even if you do not turn out to be an exhorter you can benefit from observing how they operate. We can all learn qualities of life and action from those who exhibit the other motivational gifts.

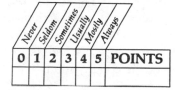

1. Loves to encourage others to live victoriously.

	Never	Seldom	Sometimes	Usually	Mostly	Always	
	0	1	2	3	4	5	POINTS

The exhorter wants everyone to have a full, meaningful life. Exhorters are builders, not of buildings but of people. They want to help people live up to their full potential. Their greatest joy is being an instrument to help another to live victoriously.

The pastor of a church we went to some years ago is an exhorter. His sermons were always vibrant, uplifting, and positive. We always left his services encouraged and strengthened. He made people feel expectant and hopeful about their abilities; an I-can-do-it-with-the-Lord's-help type of confidence emerged in many lives.

One young man came out of Bible school eager to become an evangelist. In his first church Martin kept trying to preach soulwinning sermons, but instead he drew in wayward believers who wanted to get their lives right with the Lord. The same thing happened in his second church. Believers were strengthened. Lives were changed. People learned how to overcome problems. Everyone was built up.

"Then I learned about the motivational gifts," he recalls. "I saw that I was not an evangelist at all. I was an exhorter with a teaching ministry. I was gifted to pastor and build up the flock. They, in turn could evangelize among nonbelievers and bring them into the church. God had gifted me to edify the believers. What a release it was to go ahead and be what God meant me to be!"

2. Wants a visible response when teaching or speaking.

Never	Seldom	Sometimes	Usually	Mostly	Always	
0	1	2	3	4	5	POINTS

Interaction with his hearers is essential for the exhorter. He watches the expressions on people's faces, listens for reactions, analyzes body language. He needs to know that he's really communicating. Perhaps the most frustrating experience for the exhorter is to share something of value with a person and then find out he wasn't listening.

Since Don is equipped with this gift he can relate to this: "I find I do much better with an enthusiastic and responsive audience. The more people respond the more I feel God's anointing. Lack of response makes me feel flustered. I feel that if they don't want to hear what I'm saying I might as well not say it."

On our third trip to Great Britain we went 'way up north in Scotland to teach at an evening service at the church connected with Faith Bible School in Peterhead. It was cold and windy when we arrived. The wind came right off the ocean, and they don't heat their buildings as we do. They are a hardy bunch.

We had always heard that the Scottish were reserved. But the chill in the room seemed to be coming from both the weather *and* the church members. The first half hour that we spoke was misery for Don. "They didn't laugh at my puns," he recalls. "Their expressions seemed frozen. I didn't think I'd last an hour.

"Then suddenly I began to see reactions and responses. They were warming up to us. They had sized us up and had accepted us. What a relief! I felt I could have shared all night (but good sense had me stop on schedule). Afterward we had wonderful warm fellowship with the members of the congregation."

3. Prefers to apply truth rather than research it.

Research is not the exhorter's cup of tea. He avoids it if at all possible. "Why reinvent the wheel?" he'll ask. "If someone else has put together materials on a subject, let's use what's available." It's putting truth to work that he's interested in.

Pat King, an exhorter author and mother of ten who writes at least a book a year, has learned the value of utilizing the research abilities of teachers. When she was preparing to write her book *How Do You Find the Time?* she arranged for her teacher friend Eadie Goodboy to put five hundred hours of research into the field of time management.

"Why should I spend all those hours doing what would be drudgery for me when Eadie, with her beautiful gift of teaching, loves it?" Pat explained. "Together we made a great team, each doing what we do best. She loves the research and I love taking the facts and writing about them in practical ways."

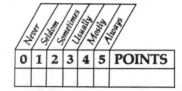

4. Prefers systems of information that have practical application.

Notice that Pat King wrote a "how-to" book. Exhorters enjoy that kind of writing. They are "how-to" people.

They also like to read books that focus on practical application. They prefer sermons that reveal how to apply Christian principles to everyday life. Conversely they do not like abstract books or sermons.

Exhorters love to hear other exhorters teach. "Wow! What great teaching," they will say when someone emphasizes the practicality of a principle. On the other hand, they will not be too thrilled at teaching for teaching's sake. Too much *fact* and not enough *act* is, in their estimation, like overloading circuits that have no outlet.

Betty, a Presbyterian friend who loves to teach the Bible to other women, wrote to us, "I try to create Bible studies that help my classes understand how to apply Scripture in the areas where they need help." Her classes are thriving.

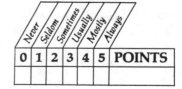

5. Loves to prescribe precise steps of action to aid personal growth.

Exhorters love to give specific steps for people to follow. They know how to instruct others to get from point A to point C in the best possible way. It's all part of their incredible ability to give constructive and helpful advice.

The Seven Gifts

One of the most visible examples of an exhorter in action is Bill Gothard. Anyone who has taken his Basic Youth Conflicts course is aware of the specific steps prescribed for every subject he teaches. The giant notebook that is part of the course is a practical reference manual for spiritual growth. It is probable that his broad popularity is at least in part due to his very workable approach.

Lorraine, an excellent exhorter counselor, regularly outlines definite steps of action for those she counsels. One young woman had come to her because of a strained relationship with her husband. At the close of the session Lorraine wrote out this simple prescription:

1. Apologize to your husband for *your* wrong attitudes.
2. Cook him his favorite dinner tonight.
3. Shower him with hugs and kisses.
4. Don't criticize anything he says for one week.

The day before her next appointment the young woman called Lorraine to cancel. "I don't need it!" she said excitedly. "The four steps worked so well that it's almost like we're on our second honeymoon."

"I love being worked right out of my job," Lorraine adds. "I wish all my counselees would follow my advice that well."

	Never	Seldom	Sometimes	Usually	Mostly	Always	
	0	1	2	3	4	5	POINTS

6. Focuses on working with people.

Exhorters are people people. They are not interested in working with things or systems or abstract ideas. They love to be around people, doing things with people or for them.

Ken took a job as a night watchman because it was the only one available. Being an outgoing person he didn't expect to enjoy it, but he was not prepared for the negative impact it would have on him.

His hours were midnight to eight A.M. When he got home his wife was at work and the kids were in school, and by the time they got home he'd be sleeping. He was all alone at work, all alone at home.

After a few months the isolation began to get to him. He started talking to himself just to have "someone to talk to." He became depressed. He lived for the weekends when he could interact with family and friends.

Ken learned about the motivational gifts and found that he was an exhorter, a people person. He began to pray earnestly for a new job. When he found work as a supervisor in a cannery, "it was like coming back to life again," Ken recalls. "What a joy it was working with *people*. I thanked the Lord every day for that job."

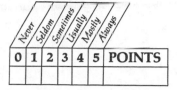

7. Encourages others to develop in their personal ministries.

Exhorters want everyone to develop a full and fruitful ministry. They understand well the concept of the Body of Christ with each member functioning to the benefit of the others. They want this ideal realized in practice.

A pastor who is an exhorter will eagerly develop lay leadership and ministries. He will sense that everyone needs to be involved in ministry. Ephesians 4:11–13 will be a favorite Scripture, especially the part that talks about *all* the saints doing the work of the ministry.

We have taught in a number of churches where the exhorter pastor has invited us specifically to help members of the congregation find their giftedness. He will make photocopies of the profile sheets for his files so that he can begin to know people's gifts, encourage them in them, and utilize them effectively within the life of the church.

Sometimes we get a call to come back a few years later to do another seminar because, as one pastor said, "There are quite a few new people now and they need to function in their giftedness too."

It's been fun for me to watch Don's exhorter gift in action over the years. Whether leading home meetings, serving as a church elder and staff member, teaching, counseling, or just talking with others, Don is always encouraging people to move out into the ministry God has for them. "Don't sit on your hands like I once did," he'll say. "Get involved. Use the gifts God has given you."

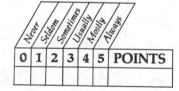

8. Finds truth in experience and then validates it with Scripture.

Life is so full of lessons and insights to exhorters. That's where they primarily learn. Then they check the Bible to see what it has to say on the subject. They're always glad to find "it's in the Bible, too."

Exhorters discover truth by finding out experientially that something "works." To them there is no more solid basis for truth. If someone hits them and they don't hit back, and this neutralizes the other person's anger and brings him to repentance, then "turning the other cheek" is a valid way of life. They may have discovered this truth in practice long before they read Jesus' teaching on it.

An exhorter might be walking by a river and see a large, stately tree. "Ah ha!" thinks the exhorter. "A Christian should be like that tree . . . strong . . . radiating life . . . drawing from the River of Life, Jesus." The next day his eye happens to fall on the third verse of Psalm 1:

"He is like a tree planted by streams of water, which yields its fruit in season and whose leaf does not wither. Whatever he does prospers" (NIV).

"Wow!" he exclaims. "How true that is."

	Never	Seldom	Sometimes	Usually	Mostly	Always	POINTS
9. Loves to do personal counseling.	0	1	2	3	4	5	

Of all the seven motivational gifts, this is the one most gifted in and frequently drawn to counseling. Exhorters are naturals for it. We have talked with dozens of exhorters who tell us that even in their high school days other students sought them out for counsel. People sense their ability, their caring concern, their interest in helping, and their approachability.

One of the most helpful qualities of the counselor is to be able to be transparent about his own problems and how he has worked through (or is working through) them. The counselee easily identifies with such a person: "Well, if he's been through this and overcome it, maybe I can, too."

Exhorters have this ability. They are the first ones to admit that they are not perfect . . . but just another person "on the way." It is easy for them to admit their sins and sorrows, their pains and pitfalls.

Jamie Buckingham, pastor of a church in Melbourne, Florida, and author of many books, is a prime example of this wonderful transparency. His exhorter gift especially comes through in his book *Risky Living.* So many assume pastors are somehow perfect, but here Jamie lays bare his struggles and faults and helps the reader to draw upon the resources of the greatest Counselor of all, Jesus Christ.

	Never	Seldom	Sometimes	Usually	Mostly	Always	POINTS
10. Will discontinue personal counseling if no effort to change is seen.	0	1	2	3	4	5	

While exhorters are not prone to quitting, there is one situation that will make them give up and move on. If a counselee refuses to implement his advice the exhorter may say something like:

"I cannot counsel you any further until you have put into action those things we've already agreed on." (or)

"If you cannot follow my advice I cannot help you." (or)

"Look, both your time and my time are being wasted until you are ready to change."

Exhorters realize that their success rests not so much on how much they know, or how experienced they are, but rather on how far the counselee is willing to act on the advice given. Without such action the exhorter will feel that his efforts are like shoveling against the tide—useless. Exhorters want to make their time and effort count, so they will move on to someone who will act on their advice.

	Never	Seldom	Sometimes	Usually	Mostly	Always	
	0	1	2	3	4	5	POINTS
11. Is fluent in communication.							

Exhorters are the mouth of the body, with the greatest facility in speech of any of the gifts. One of our biblical examples, Peter, was a fluent communicator. Perhaps that's why he was so often the spokesman for the disciples.

Lynn Severance, a gifted elementary teacher, says that communication has always been important to her. "I grew up feeling I had a lot to say and to contribute," she recalls, "but since this was not particularly encouraged in my home, I never felt confident to come forth with it. Now as a teacher, my exhorter gift and especially my communication skills have been released—words roll out as naturally as breath. It's so good not to be burying my gift under a bushel."

Another exhorter friend told us, "My greatest joy has always been to express encouragement to others. If I had no voice I'd probably write prolific letters."

It is not surprising that many exhorters become teachers, or preachers, or counselors, or supervisors—even radio announcers or TV hosts—fields that require giftedness of speech.

	Never	Seldom	Sometimes	Usually	Mostly	Always	
	0	1	2	3	4	5	POINTS
12. Views trials as opportunities to produce personal growth.							

Exhorters unquestioningly believe Romans 8:28: "All things work together for good to them that love God, to them who are the called according to his purpose" (KJV).

They also refuse to accept the word *impossible*, preferring to believe what the angel said: "For with God nothing shall be impossible" (Luke 1:37, KJV); and Jesus' words: ". . . If ye have faith as a grain of mustard seed . . . nothing shall be impossible unto you" (Matthew 17:20, KJV).

Exhorters see opportunities, not obstacles. Challenges, not trials. Possibilities, not problems.

For years I worked closely with Marion Shelton, my dear exhorter friend, at Aglow International. We've shared many joys and sorrows together, many high points and low points. But whenever a problem or trial faced us I could count on Marion's saying, "Hallelujah! God is giving us another opportunity to be overcomers."

She kept us focused on the solution rather than the problem. What a blessing that was! What encouragement to get our eyes back on Jesus and to seek out what He wanted us to do.

Whenever Marion heard anyone grumbling or criticizing she'd whisper, "Attitude check. Testing . . . one, two, three, four." Then we'd know it was time to talk to the Lord, not to others or about others.

13. Accepts people as they are without judging them.

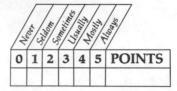

	Never	Seldom	Sometimes	Usually	Mostly	Always	
	0	1	2	3	4	5	POINTS

While perceivers see people as either *in* the will of God or *out* of the will of God—with nothing in between—exhorters are just the opposite. They don't see extremes at all—only a vast gray area where everyone is somewhere along the way. No one has arrived. No one is a complete failure. But everyone is at that point in his life where a few well-chosen steps will bring him that much closer to God's will.

Therefore the exhorter does not see any need to judge people for where they are—or are not—but rather sees the need to help them take those steps in the right direction. It is this non-judgmentalism that enables him to help people so much.

Have you ever been around a judgmental person? He doesn't have to say a word. It emanates from him. It erects a silent barrier between you. You close yourself off from him. It is difficult to receive anything at all from such a person, especially advice or admonition.

But an exhorter accepts you as you are. Imperfect? Yes, but a fellow traveler along life's way. A pastor from Portland says that the three basic ingredients for a mature Christian are to be loving, forgiving, and accepting. Exhorters are good at all three. It's easy to open up to someone like that.

14. Is greatly loved because of his positive attitude.

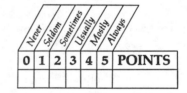

	Never	Seldom	Sometimes	Usually	Mostly	Always	
	0	1	2	3	4	5	POINTS

There is an old song that goes, "Accentuate the positive, eliminate the negative, latch on to the affirmative, and don't mess with Mister In-Between." It must have been written by an exhorter. They are so positive!

Because of this other people like to be around them. Someone has said you draw more bees with honey than with vinegar. So the exhorter draws people to him, just by being optimistic and positive.

One pastor from the Bible Belt says some Christians look as though they've been baptized in lemon juice. Not so exhorters. They radiate the joy of the Lord.

When we were traveling around the South Island of New Zealand with Rita and Len Restall (she was then the Aglow National President) we got to see the fruit of the ministry of a mature exhorter. For years Rita had ministered to women throughout her beautiful country. She had poured out her love and encouragement to them and helped them to develop chapters and train leaders.

Every place we went women greeted Rita with love and honor. They adored her—it showed on their faces and was demonstrated with words and actions. We could not help but think of that marvelous passage about the virtuous woman (the Amplified says "capable, intelligent and virtuous") in Proverbs 31, especially verse 28: "Her children rise up and call her blessed." Rita was like a spiritual mother to many of the women. And verse 31:

"Give her the fruit of her hands, and let her own works praise her in the gates of the city!" Rita's fruit was made evident by the abundance of love the women had for her.

15. Prefers to witness with life rather than verbal witnessing.

While exhorters can witness verbally (and they do), they believe they must *live* the Christian life in order to be credible. "We need to walk our talk," one exhorter said candidly. To them faith must be demonstrated in practical ways in daily life. They love the book of James, especially these verses from chapter two:

But someone will say, "You have faith; I have deeds."
Show me your faith without deeds, and I will show you my faith by what I do.
You foolish man, do you want evidence that faith without deeds is useless?
You see that his [Abraham's] faith and his actions were working together, and his faith was made complete by what he did.
As the body without the spirit is dead, so faith without deeds is dead.

Verses 18, 20, 22, 26, NIV

Exhorters believe that it is not enough to know the *logos*—the written Word—but that it is essential to live the *rhema*—the living word of God. The truth of the Bible must become flesh—in them, here and now. One exhorter says, "I can only teach or witness to that which I've appropriated in my *own* life. If my life is witness, then others will want what I've found—Jesus Christ."

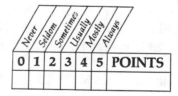

16. Makes decisions easily.

Decision-making comes naturally and easily to most exhorters. For them life is too short to be indecisive. They are action people. They make their decisions based on what they know at the time. "Let's decide and get on with it," their thinking goes. If more information is needed, they figure it will come.

"If I'm wrong in a decision," Belinda says, "God will correct me. I'm confident in that. I don't mind being corrected. It's better to move ahead and get something accomplished, even if I have to make adjustments later on, than to be paralyzed by indecision."

Since exhorters are such practical people and so life-related in all that they do, we find that their decisions are usually right on target.

	Never	Seldom	Sometimes	Usually	Mostly	Always	
	0	1	2	3	4	5	POINTS

17. Always completes what is started.

Similar to the serving gift the exhorter does not like unfinished work or incompleted projects. He finishes the letters he starts, works overtime to complete assignments at the office, or burns the midnight oil to complete a Bible study assignment.

Barb McGriff was in an art class I was taking. She was new at painting but enthusiastic about learning. She and her husband, Mark, are *both* exhorters—something we come across very rarely.

Each week our instructor demonstrated how to paint a new subject. Most of us would not get our pictures done and would just leave them until the next week. Not Barb. She always took her unfinished painting home and usually worked on it that evening until it was completed.

"Why don't you come early next week and finish it up?" I asked her one day.

"Oh, I couldn't wait that long," she insisted. "Once I see the picture taking shape I can't wait to see it finished. Besides, I don't like to leave anything half-done."

We've also noted that exhorters need only *one* bookmark. They never read more than one book at one time.

	Never	Seldom	Sometimes	Usually	Mostly	Always	
	0	1	2	3	4	5	POINTS

18. Wants to clear up problems with others quickly.

Exhorters do not like strained relationships. They go immediately to the other person to find out what's wrong. If necessary, they will even take the blame in order to build the bridge to a right relationship.

"This characteristic shows up in my life so often," wrote Kathy from Canada. "I can't stand having anyone angry at me. So, even if I am not the one who caused the problem, I'll take the step to clear up the situation. I'll say, 'I'm sorry,' to get the air cleared. It feels so great to have relationships right again."

She went on to say, "I love to encourage others to clear up such situations as quickly as possible, too."

	Never	Seldom	Sometimes	Usually	Mostly	Always	
	0	1	2	3	4	5	POINTS

19. Expects a lot of self and others.

Don feels that very few people, including himself, live up to their potential. "I expect a lot of myself," he says, "and I guess that keeps me motivated to accomplish more. God has equipped all of us so abundantly. Often we don't recognize this.

"If we set low goals, that's all we'll ever accomplish. If we set higher goals, we'll grow. Often I can see potential in others that they don't see themselves. I enjoy encouraging them to stretch."

Each of us has a comfort zone, an area within which we can operate without being challenged. It's easy just to stay there. The exhorter doesn't believe that's God's perfect will for us. He believes God wants us to venture out into the unknown and do things we didn't think we could.

"There's so much that needs to be done in the Kingdom of God," Don says. "The Gospel needs to be shared at home and abroad, support ministries are needed everywhere, the hurting need to be helped, the hungry need to be fed. Whenever anyone says to me, 'Well, I don't know what I could possibly do,' I say, 'Okay, let me tell you. . . .' "

Don admits there was a time when he was just a pew-warmer. No more! His only regret now is that there are so few hours in a day. "I want to make the hours I have count," he often tells people. "You have the same twenty-four hours that I have. You can make them count too. (Oops, I'm sounding like an exhorter—but I'm proud to be one!)"

	Never	Seldom	Sometimes	Usually	Mostly	Always	
20. Needs a "sounding board" for bouncing off ideas and thoughts.	0	1	2	3	4	5	**POINTS**

When Don and I were first married I discovered that one of my roles as a wife was to be his sounding board. Don would bounce ideas off me. I would listen, analyze, then give him my opinion. That's not what he wanted. He wanted me to just listen.

You see, exhorters often think with their mouths. They like to verbalize a thought aloud so they can hear how it sounds. It's as though they're trying an idea on for size—to see if it fits. They can then do their own analyzing. A sounding board is basically passive. So, I've learned there is a reason why God created me with one mouth and two ears! I've learned to listen.

While it's common for a married exhorter to use his mate for a sounding board, sometimes it is a close friend. Singles rely on friends, relatives, classmates, teachers, and sometimes whoever is available at the moment.

THE GIFT OF EXHORTATION

Characteristics:

	Never	Seldom	Sometimes	Usually	Mostly	Always	POINTS
	0	1	2	3	4	5	
1.							
2.							
3.							
4.							
5.							
6.							
7.							
8.							
9.							
10.							
11.							
12.							
13.							
14.							
15.							
16.							
17.							
18.							
19.							
20.							
						TOTAL	

1. Loves to encourage others to live victoriously.
2. Wants a visible response when teaching or speaking.
3. Prefers to apply truth rather than research it.
4. Prefers systems of information that have practical application.
5. Loves to prescribe precise steps of action to aid personal growth.
6. Focuses on working with people.
7. Encourages others to develop in their personal ministries.
8. Finds truth in experience and then validates it with Scripture.
9. Loves to do personal counseling.
10. Will discontinue personal counseling if no effort to change is seen.
11. Is fluent in communication.
12. Views trials as opportunities to produce personal growth.
13. Accepts people as they are without judging them.
14. Is greatly loved because of his positive attitude.
15. Prefers to witness with life rather than verbal witnessing.
16. Makes decisions easily.
17. Always completes what is started.
18. Wants to clear up problems with others quickly.
19. Expects a lot of self and others.
20. Needs a "sounding board" for bouncing off ideas and thoughts.

PROBLEMS OF THE EXHORTER

17

Exhorters tend to have a "mouth problem." Since God has made them the mouth of the Body of Christ they use it a lot, either for good—encouraging others—or in negative ways as we will examine now.

Consider your scoring prayerfully to see if there are areas in which you need some growth. None of us has arrived. Even Paul, in the later years of his ministry, realized that he needed to "press on to the goal of the high calling in Jesus Christ."

1. Tends to interrupt others in eagerness to give opinions or advice.

Never	Seldom	Sometimes	Usually	Mostly	Always	POINTS
0	1	2	3	4	5	

Exhorters have much to say. And, normally, that is not a problem. But when there is an ongoing interchange of conversation, or any kind of structured meeting going on, the exhorter's tendency to interrupt can be a source of frustration for the others.

When I was serving on a Christian board there was one member, an exhorter, who was known for her excellent ability to build up people. But in the board meetings she was also known for interrupting.

One day I had tried a number of times to say something but she had repeatedly interrupted me. My frustration level rose.

"You've interrupted me five times," I burst out at last. "Please let me finish what I'm saying."

"I haven't interrupted you." she protested.

"Yes, you have," I insisted.

"You're kidding," she said with a look on her face that made me realize that she didn't realize how often she jumped in to speak before others were finished.

"You *do* interrupt a lot," another member confirmed.

"I don't believe it," she replied. "I'll tell you what," she said to me. "Next time I interrupt anyone, poke me in the side. If I'm doing it I really want to know."

"Okay," I said, hoping her ribs could take it.

During the remaining four hours of the board meeting I poked her fifteen times.

"I'm amazed," she said, still shocked at the revelation. "I had no idea I was interrupting that much. I really want to overcome that habit."

She made excellent progress once she recognized the problem.

2. Will use Scriptures out of context in order to make a point.

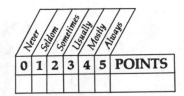

The exhorter believes it is the *point* he is making that is important. In his mind verifying it with Scripture is secondary. Of those who hear the exhorter, many will not bother to check out the proof text. Not so the teachers and the perceivers. They'll check it out and if the Scripture has been used out of context they may reject the point, or even the one who made the point. They may even try to correct the exhorter.

Exhorters are adaptable. So, if their error is pointed out to them they'll say, "Okay, if that Scripture doesn't fit I'll find another one that does."

Exhorters usually have a good sense of humor, too. We'd like to share some of their on-purpose out-of-context antics:

An exhorter who started a Christian diet class used as her motto: "He must increase, but I must decrease" (John 3:30, KJV).

An exhorter Christian dentist tells his patients that his favorite Scripture is, "Open wide your mouth and I will fill it" (Psalm 81:10b, NIV).

An exhorter mom painted the following Scripture in giant letters across one wall of a church nursery in Seattle: "We shall not all sleep, but we shall all be changed" (1 Corinthians 15:51, KJV).

3. May be "cut-and-dried" in prescribing steps of action.

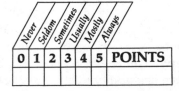

Because those with the motivational gift of exhortation are so good at giving advice they can easily fall into the trap of giving "pat" answers. They may counsel three people in a row with the same basic problem and, after prayer, prescribe the same steps of action. The people are helped. Then along comes the fourth person. Same problem. This time the exhorter doesn't bother to pray about what advice to give since the same counsel worked for the previous three cases. But this time it is not what the Holy Spirit wanted administered. The advice is ineffective.

It is very important for the exhorter to consistently rely on the Holy Spirit—the Counselor—for wisdom and guidance in giving advice. Otherwise he can develop a cocky I-know-what-to-do-in-every-situation mentality.

	Never	Seldom	Sometimes	Usually	Mostly	Always	POINTS
	0	1	2	3	4	5	

4. Is outspokenly opinionated.

An exhorter is always glad to tell you what he thinks. He is not as rigidly opinionated as the perceiver or the teacher, but on matters of life application he has strong opinions. That, coupled with the well-oiled jaw, makes his opinions spill out readily.

He can also be gossipy, bossy, overtalkative, and feisty. Actually, as one exhorter put it, "My mouth often runs ahead of my mind."

Peggy tells about taking care of her ten-year-old exhorter granddaughter for a week. "Things went pretty well the first couple of days," she recalls. "I enjoyed Margaret's chattering. But by the third day I was wishing she didn't talk so much. The fourth day I thought, Does this child do anything but exercise her mouth. On the fifth day, after hearing her go on and on, I blurted out, 'Stop, Margaret! Stop talking! I can't stand to hear another word.'

"Poor child. She looked so bewildered. Her reply brought me up short, I can tell you. Made me realize that she's very appropriately my namesake:

" 'But Grandma,' she objected, 'you talk a lot too!' "

The exhorter's bossiness stems from the desire to give advice. Exhorters rather enjoy telling others what to do. Someone once said, "Don't answer questions that haven't been asked and don't give advice that hasn't been asked for." The exhorter could benefit from that wisdom.

Perhaps the most effective prayer for the overly talkative exhorter would be, "Lord, put a guard over my mouth." Jesus warns that we are responsible for every idle word that we speak.

	Never	Seldom	Sometimes	Usually	Mostly	Always	POINTS
	0	1	2	3	4	5	

5. Can become overly self-confident.

In today's world self-confidence is a sought-after quality. But like the foolish man who built his house upon the sand it makes a bad foundation. Our basic confidence must be in the Lord. Then, with sober appreciation for the gifts and abilities He has given to us, we can begin to build godly self-confidence.

Joleen confessed to us that she was once an over-confident exhorter. "I figured I had an answer for just about everything," she confided. "I passed out advice like some doctors pass out pills. There were no problems, just challenges.

"I was crushed when I began to see the results of some of my meddling. Sometimes my advice was completely wrong for the person, or got in the way of God's dealing with him. God really humbled me and helped me to build my confidence in Him."

She acknowledged that the battle wasn't over—that there was still a struggle with a know-it-all attitude. But she was grateful that she had learned to recognize it and deal with it appropriately.

If you run into any exhorters you will usually be blessed by them. But if one is still a victim of torrents of verbalization, feel free to ask: "Please say that in twenty-five words or less!"

Typical problem areas of the gift of exhortation:

1. Tends to interrupt others in eagerness to give opinions or advice.
2. Will use Scriptures out of context in order to make a point.
3. May be "cut and dried" in prescribing steps of action.
4. Is outspokenly opinionated.
5. Can become overly self-confident.

POINTS	Never	Seldom	Sometimes	Usually	Mostly	Always	
	0	1	2	3	4	5	
1.							
2.							
3.							
4.							
5.							
TOTAL							

BIBLICAL EXHORTERS

18

$\mathbf{W}$here would we be without exhorters? We know how much they are needed today, and it was the same in biblical days. It's one thing to become a Christian and quite another to live the Christian life. Exhorters have been gifted to encourage believers to appropriate the grace of God in their Christian walk.

Barnabas is a good illustration of the gift of exhortation. Even his name means "son of encouragement." Take a look at what the book of Acts has to say about him and we think you'll be struck by his exhorter characteristics.

Scripture: Acts 4:36, 11:22–26 (TAB)   *Your Comments:*

Acts 4

36 Now Joseph, a Levite and native of Cyprus who was surnamed Barnabas by the apostles (special messengers), which interpreted means, Son of Encouragement. . .

Acts 11

22 The rumors of this came to the ears of the church (assembly) in Jerusalem, and they sent Barnabas to Antioch.

134

Your Comments:

23 When he arrived and saw what grace (favor) God was bestowing upon them, he was full of joy; and he continuously exhorted—warned, urged and encouraged—them all to cleave unto and remain faithful and devoted to the Lord with [resolute and steady] purpose of heart.

24 For he was a good man [good in himself and also at once for the good and the advantage of other people], full of and controlled by the Holy Spirit and full of faith [that is, of his belief that Jesus is the Messiah, through Whom we obtain eternal salvation]. And a large company was added to the Lord.

25 [Barbabas] went on to Tarsus to hunt for Saul.

26 And when he had found him, he brought him back to Antioch. For a whole year they assembled together with and were guests of the church, and instructed a large number of people; and in Antioch the disciples were first called Christians.

The fact that Barnabas was full of joy indicates that he was functioning in his proper sphere, for joy is the byproduct of operating in one's motivational gift.

Note also that Barnabas *went after* Saul. Others in the body of believers were not yet ready to trust this one who had persecuted the church so viciously, but Barnabas could see the potential in Saul and most assuredly contributed to his becoming the mighty Paul that we encounter later.

Scripture: Acts 4:36, 11:22–26, (TAB)

Our Comments:

Acts 4

36 Now Joseph, a Levite and native of Cyprus who was surnamed Barnabas by the apostles (special messengers), which interpreted means, Son of Encouragement.

#1 name: encouragement

Our Comments:

Acts 11

22 The rumors of this came to the ears of the church (assembly) in Jerusalem, and they sent Barnabas to Antioch.

#1   sent him to encourage

23 When he arrived and saw what grace (favor) God was bestowing upon them, he was full of joy; and he continuously exhorted—warned, urged and encouraged—them all to cleave unto and remain faithful and devoted to the Lord with [resolute and steady] purpose of heart.

#1   he exhorted faithfulness
#4   practical faith
#7   encourages ministry
#9   counseled group
#13   non-judgmental
#14   positive, joyful
#19   expects a lot of others

24 For he was a good man [good in himself and also at once for the good and the advantage of other people], full of and controlled by the Holy Spirit and full of faith [that is, of his belief that Jesus is the Messiah, through Whom we obtain eternal salvation]. And a large company was added to the Lord.

#2   got visible response
#6   focus on people
#7   encouraged development
#13   accepting
#14   loved by others
#15   life a witness
#17   completed what he started

25 [Barnabas] went on to Tarsus to hunt for Saul.

#13   accepting

26 And when he had found him, he brought him back to Antioch. For a whole year they assembled together with and were guests of the church, and instructed a large number of people; and in Antioch the disciples were first called Christians.

#1   taught how to live
#3   helped apply truth
#4   taught practically
#6   focus on people
#11   communicated
#17   completed teaching job

Some of the apostles had more than one strong motivational gift. Paul was one of those. While we think his primary gift was giving, we also see a strong secondary gift of exhortation as well as perceiving and teaching. We see Paul giving practical advice and encouragement—often! There are too many references to Paul to list here, but as you read about him, or read his writings, observe his gifts in action.

Peter, being the mouthpiece for the disciples, obviously had great facility of speech. We believe Peter too was an exhorter. Consider these passages: Acts 2:14–41; 3:1–4:21.

Also read about:

Silas—Acts 15:22–40; 16:25, 29; 17:4, 10–15; 1 Peter 5:12

Titus—2 Corinthians 2:13; 7:6, 13–14; 8:6–23; 12:18; Galatians 2:1, 3; 2 Timothy 4:10; Titus

Aaron—Exodus, Leviticus, Numbers

CHARACTERISTICS OF THE GIVER

19

Of all the seven motivational gifts this is the one least likely to be identified by the one who has it. Part of the reason may be that the giver's "left hand" does not know when his "right hand" gives alms (Matthew 6:3). Another may be the giver's "all-around" personality. The giver shares several traits of the server, can be a leader or a follower, and like the perceiver and the teacher has a love for the Word of God. But when it comes to the use of resources, the giver is unique.

The Greek word is *metadidomi* (distinct from *didomi*, to give) meaning "to give over, share, or impart." It is to be done with *haplotetes*—simplicity, sincerity, and liberality.

As you score this gift be sure to distinguish between learned behavior and innate tendencies. For instance, you may have been raised and trained by your parents and your church to be generous and to tithe. But has that always been your joyful *inward motivation*? You may need to reflect on your childhood in order to score accurately.

1. Gives freely of money, possessions, time, energy, and love.

Never	Seldom	Sometimes	Usually	Mostly	Always	
0	1	2	3	4	5	POINTS

Notice that givers give far more than just money. If they have money they will give generously of it, but they also give of anything else they possess. They give comprehensively. They give with abandonment. And, in the more mature stages of givers' lives, they give with absolutely no strings attached and no ulterior motives. They simply become channels for the Lord to use for the distribution of His resources, for they are convinced everything belongs to Him.

Sharon, a young homemaker whose gift of giving was yearning for a way to express itself, was well aware of the family's tight budget. It had been a joint decision that she not go to work but be free to be a full-time mother.

One day she had a bright idea. "Honey," she asked her husband, "could we afford twenty-two cents a day, five days a week, for a special project?"

"Well, sure," he replied, "that's only about five dollars a month."

Sharon was delighted. She bought the first five postage stamps and launched her project. Each day she took one name from her Christmas card list and spent time praying for the person (or couple or family), asking the Lord to bless them and guide them. Often, as she prayed, the Lord would quicken a verse of Scripture for them.

Then Sharon wrote a letter, expressing her love for the person, enclosing the Scripture in the form of a simple bookmark using her calligraphy skills.

What a blessing it must have been to be on her Christmas card list, to be the recipient of such a gift of herself at a totally unexpected time of year!

We recently came across this very appropriate quotation: "The best gift cannot be bought or sold. It is giving a part of oneself."

2. Loves to give without others knowing about it.

Never	Seldom	Sometimes	Usually	Mostly	Always	POINTS
0	1	2	3	4	5	

Jesus had a lot to say about not broadcasting our good deeds.

"Be careful not to do your 'acts of righteousness' before men, to be seen by them. . . . So when you give to the needy, do not announce it with trumpets." Giving is to be secret. "Then your Father, who sees what is done in secret, will reward you" (Matthew 6:1, 2–4, NIV).

Givers do not want acclaim or credit. They just want to please their heavenly Father. That joy is reward enough for them. Often they will go to great lengths to assure that others do not find out about their gifts.

While I was editor of *Aglow* magazine we received a book manuscript by Joanne Sekowsky titled *A Christian Roadmap for Women Traveling Alone.* We felt it would be an excellent resource for singles, but we did not have the one thousand dollar advance the printer required, so we put it on hold.

Penny (a fictitious name) heard about it and came by my office, shutting the door behind her. "Here's a check for one thousand dollars," she said. "That book needs to get out."

"This is wonderful. Thank you," I said gratefully.

"Just one thing," Penny insisted. "No one else is to know about this. It's between the Lord and me."

	Never	Seldom	Sometimes	Usually	Mostly	Always	
	0	1	2	3	4	5	POINTS

3. Wants to feel a part of the ministries to which he contributes.

Givers give to ministries that they believe in—ones that are effectively sharing the Gospel. Therefore they not only give monetarily, they also get involved in other ways. They will pray for the ministry, they will write letters of encouragement, send "care" packages, and sometimes they will show up in person to assist in the work.

Weldon, a pastor with a mature gift of giving, had been supporting a ministry in the Philippines. He not only wrote regularly himself, he also encouraged members of his congregation to do so. The children of the missionary were well remembered at Christmas and on birthdays.

Then the Holy Spirit began nudging Weldon about going to help personally. He did, assisting in preaching, ministering to the poor, and teaching leaders. Afterward he said, "It was the best thing that ever happened to me."

	Never	Seldom	Sometimes	Usually	Mostly	Always	
	0	1	2	3	4	5	POINTS

4. Intercedes for needs and the salvation of souls.

It is not unusual for givers to be awakened in the middle of the night with a "burden" for someone.

A man with this gift asked a returning missionary, "What was happening to you three weeks ago, on May 6th to be exact?"

"May 6th!" the missionary exclaimed. "Why, that was the day there was an attempted robbery of our compound. But for some reason the thief dropped everything and fled—we don't know why."

"Oh, that explains it," Graham said.

"Explains what?"

"Well, I was awakened out of a deep sleep and sensed great danger for you and the others," Graham explained. "So I prayed for you, for maybe an hour, until the burden lifted. If I'm calculating right, our night is your day, so it all fits. I'm glad the Lord awakened me."

Givers often keep lists of people who need to receive salvation. They will intercede faithfully until with joy they can check a name off the list. When you ask a group to pray for the salvation of your relative or neighbor, the givers will follow through on your request. Others may mean to, but soon forget. Not so the giver. Above all he wants people to come into the Kingdom of God.

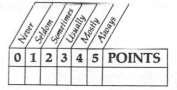

5. Feels delighted when his gift is an answer to specific prayer.

Never	Seldom	Sometimes	Usually	Mostly	Always	POINTS
0	1	2	3	4	5	

Since givers know that the highest and best use of their gift is when they are being led to give by the Holy Spirit, they are especially thrilled when someone says, "How did you know I needed this? It's an answer to prayer."

One time we happened to be right in the middle of such an incident. Annie had come into an inheritance and had $700 she wanted to give to someone who really needed it. She attended a meeting where a missionary couple spoke. Afterward Annie slipped into a chair beside us.

"Do you think they could use $700?" she asked. "As I listened to them I felt God was telling me to give it to them. But I don't know if they really need it."

"Oh, they do," we assured her. "In fact, we happen to know that they have been raising money to buy video equipment and are exactly $700 short of their goal."

"Isn't that great!" Annie exclaimed, hurrying off to present the missionaries with a check. We don't know who was blessed the most, the recipients or the giver. Annie left the meeting still exclaiming, "Isn't God good!"

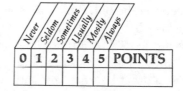

6. Wants gift to be of high quality or craftsmanship.

Never	Seldom	Sometimes	Usually	Mostly	Always	POINTS
0	1	2	3	4	5	

When givers give they give the very best. They are generous, even lavish. They want their gifts to be the highest quality they can afford. If they cannot afford to buy a gift they will make one—with great thoughtfulness and skill.

JoAnn had been attending the Tuesday morning Bible study at our home. She had noticed that my Amplified Bible was falling apart. It was a hardback edition that had seen ten years of extensive use. Whenever I turned to the middle of the New Testament, Ephesians fell out. I'd just stuff it back in place and go on. Soon Galatians began falling out too. I put up with it because it was my favorite Bible and had all my markings and marginal notes.

One afternoon JoAnn arrived at our front door. "Here," she said, thrusting a package into my hands, "this is for you." And she walked off.

I opened it up. It was a beautiful new leatherbound Amplified Bible, the most expensive and durable edition available. JoAnn had gone out and purchased the very best for me. I have used that Bible for fourteen years and guess what? None of the pages has ever fallen out.

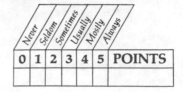

	Never	Seldom	Sometimes	Usually	Mostly	Always	
	0	1	2	3	4	5	**POINTS**

7. Gives only by the leading of the Holy Spirit.

You can't talk a mature giver into giving. They will resist pressure appeals. They give only as the Holy Spirit leads them.

About ten years ago we were getting ready go overseas to teach the motivational gift seminar. We had just revised the materials and had taken them to Barb, a professional typist, so we would have a neat master copy to take with us for duplication purposes. We'd put off picking up the typing, though, because our bank account was down so low we couldn't pay for it.

The day before our departure we decided that I should drive over to Barb's and ask if we could take the work now and pay her when we got back. When I arrived I found Barb in pain. Her back had gone out and she was unable to find a comfortable position.

"Let me pray for you," I offered.

"Thank you," she moaned. "Maybe it will help."

I prayed for her lower back to be adjusted and for the Lord to take away all her pain.

"Hey!" she exclaimed. "It's gone! The pain is gone!" She got up and bent in all directions to be sure. "The Lord sent you at just the right time."

Then Barb handed me the bill. But across the bill had been written, "Paid in full."

"What's this?" I asked.

"Oh, that," Barb replied. "The Lord told me this morning that I needed to have a part in your ministry. It's something I can do to help."

"Barb," I said, "you don't know how much this blesses me."

As I drove home I praised the Lord all the way. "Thank You, Lord, that You spoke to one of Your givers on our behalf."

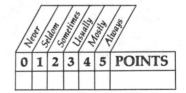

	Never	Seldom	Sometimes	Usually	Mostly	Always	
	0	1	2	3	4	5	**POINTS**

8. Gives to support and bless others or to advance a ministry.

When givers select a ministry to advance with financial support they check it out thoroughly to be sure 1) it gets the Gospel out effectively, and 2) overhead and administrative expenses are not taking too much of a chunk out of the donations.

Sometimes the giver wants to be an anonymous source of blessing for those who have genuine needs.

A man in a small town in Montana is just such a giver. His business is doing well and the more he gives the more it seems to prosper. One day in church his attention was drawn to a young girl with badly protruding teeth. Her mother is a widow and their meager budget did not allow for braces.

The man went to the local orthodontist, gave him three thousand dollars and said, "Call in this girl and see that she gets her teeth straightened. If there are additional costs, let me know. But please, don't tell them, or anyone else, where the money has come from. Just tell them it's the Lord's provision."

Over the next few years this giver had the joy of seeing the girl's bright smile blossom with metal as her teeth came into proper alignment. He was personally blessed in blessing her.

	Never	Seldom	Sometimes	Usually	Mostly	Always	
9. Views hospitality as an opportunity to give.	0	1	2	3	4	5	**POINTS**

Like the server, the giver loves to practice hospitality. Outwardly this characteristic looks the same for both. But the inner viewpoint differs. The server sees hospitality as a chance to serve; the giver sees it as an expression of giving.

I stayed in the home of a giver one time when I was speaking in far northern British Columbia. Charlotte had done everything she could think of to make my stay comfortable. She fixed a lovely dinner, then throughout the rest of the evening kept trying to give me something else to eat—another dessert, another cup of coffee, fruit, mints, nuts.

In addition it seemed that hardly a half hour went by that she did not bring me a gift. "Here's a lipstick I think would look good with your coloring," she told me. A cosmetics distributor, she'd looked through her supplies until she found just the right shade for a red-head.

Later she brought me a special cleansing spray for glasses. "I think you'll find this useful," she said hopefully.

Then came some perfume, a box of powder, a pen, pictures of her house and her cat. I felt a bit embarrassed accepting so many gifts but I knew she was loving the opportunity to give.

"We don't get many guests 'way up here," she explained. "I so seldom get to entertain."

Her stored-up desire to practice hospitality was unleashed and I was the beneficiary!

	Never	Seldom	Sometimes	Usually	Mostly	Always	
10. Handles finances with wisdom and frugality.	0	1	2	3	4	5	**POINTS**

Givers are good at handling money. The best, as a matter of fact. They're careful, cautious, even a little tight with their own spending. They do not squander money.

One couple were in financial difficulty, getting deeper in debt as bills piled up. They went to a church elder for advice. After listening to them awhile he told the husband, "It seems to me that your wife has natural ability with finances. Why don't you turn the responsibility over to her for six months and see if she can't solve the problem?"

"I never thought of doing that," the husband said. "I always assumed it was the husband's responsibility to handle the money. But I'm not good at it, so I'd love to give it to her."

The wife, a classic giver, immediately established a budget, began making partial payments to creditors, and cut out all spending except for absolute necessities. No more restaurant lunches for her husband or school cafeteria meals for the kids. Brown bag would have to do. No more clothes purchases for anyone. She stretched the food budget by clipping coupons and by getting fruits, vegetables, and bread at the church's food bank.

By the end of the six months they were almost in the black. "Honey," her grateful husband said, "I'm delegating the family finances to you *permanently*."

Givers make great treasurers too for any kind of group. They are excellent to have on financial committees, and make fastidious bookkeepers and accountants.

11. Quickly volunteers to help where a need is seen.

Never	Seldom	Sometimes	Usually	Mostly	Always	POINTS
0	1	2	3	4	5	

Here's another characteristic that the giver has in common with the server. The server, however, is apt to jump in first to meet a need while the giver comes alongside to help once someone else has identified the need.

Announce a church work party some Saturday and it will be the servers and the givers who show up with greatest enthusiasm. They'll work all day and come back again if the job isn't finished.

Ask for volunteers for any worthwhile cause and guess which gifts will respond first.

If someone is sick or hospitalized the servers and the givers will be taking in meals even before someone thinks to organize such acts of kindness.

12. Seeks confirmation on the amount to give.

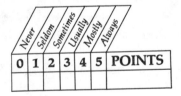

Never	Seldom	Sometimes	Usually	Mostly	Always	POINTS
0	1	2	3	4	5	

Steve Lightle shared with us that he and his wife, Judy, always pray about the amount of money they give above their basic tithe to others or other ministries. "We find that at least eighty percent of the time Judy and I feel we should give exactly the same amount," Steve said. "It's so good to have such confirmation."

Steve gave a specific example. "Recently while I was spending time in prayer the Lord kept bringing to my mind a special friend of ours in Israel who has a very vital ministry. After praying for him awhile, the Lord laid it on my heart to give him a specific amount of money. What was unusual was that the amount was not in round numbers like fifty, one hundred, or two hundred. It was specifically two hundred and forty dollars.

"I told Judy that the Lord was saying to send our friend some money and asked her to pray about it and see what amount it should be. A bit later Judy called to me, 'Steve, I believe the Lord wants us to send two hundred and forty dollars.'

" 'Thank You, Lord,' I said, 'that's confirmation!' And I quickly got the check off to our dear friend in Israel.

"We received a letter back. He was overjoyed. Our gift was a specific answer to prayer. He had been in need of an essential piece of equipment costing four hundred dollars. He'd been given two hundred dollars toward it and been praying for the other two hundred and forty dollars so that he could pay a tithe on the four hundred dollars. Our gift had been *exactly* what he had needed. 'Nobody knew about my need,' he said, 'but God.' "

13. Has strong belief in tithing and in giving in addition to tithing.

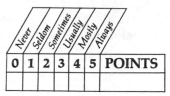

Never	Seldom	Sometimes	Usually	Mostly	Always	
0	1	2	3	4	5	POINTS

The person with the motivational gift of giving would never think of withholding part of his tithe. To him that would be robbing God. He believes that everything he has, money, home, car, and all other possessions, belongs to the Lord. He sees himself as a steward of God's resources. The tithe is only the foundational aspect of his giving. Givers give beyond that, often up to twenty or thirty percent of their income or more.

In a book about one famous giver, inventor-manufacturer Robert Gilmour LeTourneau, the biographer writes, "In the matter of giving R. G. LeTourneau considers himself merely a steward of the money God has placed at his disposal. His oft-repeated statement is that he gives away ninety percent of his earnings to the Lord's work."[9] At the time the biography was written, twenty-eight years before LeTourneau died, he had already donated twelve million dollars to missions and other Christian work.

14. Focuses on sharing the Gospel.

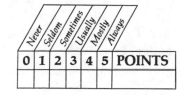

Never	Seldom	Sometimes	Usually	Mostly	Always	
0	1	2	3	4	5	POINTS

Givers are naturally evangelistic. We've found that even as children (providing they knew the Lord themselves) givers attempted to lead other children to Jesus.

Jerry Raaf, a Canadian Armed Forces chaplain, recalled how strong his desire to share the Gospel had been all his life. Even as a five-year-old he would try to tell his little friends about Jesus. They didn't always want to hear and would run home. But that did not discourage Jerry.

One day his parents searched for him and finally found him out in the chicken yard. He had locked the gate so the chickens couldn't get away and was preaching his heart out to his captive audience.

Giver-evangelist Rod McDougal has held fifty-seven "miracle crusades" throughout the Philippines during the past four years. (We've known Rod and his wife, Trena, since they were leaders in the Jesus People movement in Seattle in the sixties.) After we participated in one of his city-wide crusades in Iriga City and saw with our own eyes between seven hundred and two thousand people come to the Lord each evening, we said to Rod, "Why don't you report this in your newsletter? You only speak of a few hundred being reached."

"Those who have not been here cannot believe it," Rod explained. "Some are skeptical even of the numbers we do use; they think we must be exaggerating. It's hard to believe ourselves. But the harvest fields are white here. It's a joy to help with a harvest that's so plentiful."

15. Believes God is the Source of his supply.

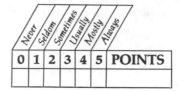

	Never	Seldom	Sometimes	Usually	Mostly	Always	POINTS
	0	1	2	3	4	5	

Since, from the giver's viewpoint, everything belongs to God, the Christian's job is simply to distribute money and resources wherever He directs. Therefore, if the supply runs out (he reasons), it is God's responsibility to replenish that supply. Meanwhile, the giver is content to get by with whatever he has or, as the case may be, has not. Like Paul, the giver knows how to be abased or to abound.

Givers love the Scripture "But my God shall supply all your need according to his riches in glory by Christ Jesus" (Philippians 4:19, KJV). They have every confidence that if they are being obedient to God's direction in their life, He will indeed take care of their needs.

There is a seeming paradox. On the one hand givers seem most capable of all the gifts of earning a good living, while at the same time they are the ones most likely to live by faith.

Perhaps the most outstanding example of such faith that we know of is George Mueller who lived in England more than a hundred years ago. Starting with one children's home he never asked anyone but God to supply his financial needs, knowing without a doubt that He was the source of supply for the work he was called to do. God met those needs by prompting people from many walks of life to bring or send resources. Eventually five children's homes were built at Ashley Down, caring for 2,050 orphans at a time.

Today the work continues in Mueller's tradition, and still conducts no financial campaigns, but trusts God for its support.

16. Is very industrious with a tendency toward success.

	Never	Seldom	Sometimes	Usually	Mostly	Always	POINTS
	0	1	2	3	4	5	

Whatever givers touch seems to turn to gold. The endeavors they get involved in habitually succeed. True, givers are hard-working, but it's more than that. We believe that God prospers givers so that they can (and they usually do) give even more to the work of the Gospel.

When a giver, Patricia Stamets, moved to Seattle she was a single mother trying to get her kids through college. The economic cycle in Seattle was low but she was thrilled to get a job selling real estate, and was grateful when her mother loaned her enough money to buy a car, a necessity for the job.

One day during the first week Patricia was praising the Lord for His provision of the car when she heard Him ask, "Are you *really* thankful?"

"Oh, yes, Lord," she replied. "I am truly thankful."

"Then I want you to show it."

"But how, Lord?"

Then the Lord told her He wanted her to have "The Lord is my shepherd . . ." painted on the front doors and the tail gate of her station wagon in four-inch-high old English letters.

"Okay, Lord, I'll do it," she said.

It wasn't long before word got to the president of the real estate firm and Patricia was called into his office. He told her in no uncertain terms to get that "religious stuff" off her car or she'd lose her job.

The next day, Scriptures still in place, she went to a home to take a listing. And when the client was walking back to the car with Patricia she saw the words. "You know the Lord!" the woman exclaimed. She asked Patricia to come back into the house to pray with her for a desperate situation she was facing. At 10:30 that evening Patricia got a phone call from the woman saying that the crisis had been defused.

"While I never took the initiative to share my faith," Patricia told us, "day after day people responded to the Scripture, enabling me to pray and minister to their needs. My sales soared and within a couple of months I was a top performer in the industry. The Lord blessed me both financially and in opportunities to be a channel for His purposes. There are no economic down-cycles in God's economy."

She added that the president of the company, impressed with her success, never mentioned the Scripture on her automobile again. Patricia is now on her third car with "The Lord is my shepherd . . ." painted on it.

	Never	Seldom	Sometimes	Usually	Mostly	Always	
17. Has natural and effective business ability.	0	1	2	3	4	5	**POINTS**

Givers are good at making money. Even as children they are drawn into "business." They are the ones likely to open up a corner lemonade stand, or go door-to-door distributing homemade "business cards" offering baby-sitting or lawn-mowing or car washes.

Givers also learn to save money at an early age. My nephew Rex and his brother and two sisters lived with my family for a while. Whenever we gave the children spending money three of them would take off immediately for the grocery store. Not Rex. He would put his in his bank to save until he had enough to buy something he really wanted rather than spend it on candy.

When the kids were given nuts or candy Rex would only eat a little piece, then stash the rest away to eat later. Sometimes when I was cleaning house I would find his treasures hidden behind the cups in the china closet or under a sofa cushion. I kept his hiding places secret.

Today Rex continues to exhibit the characteristics of a giver: He works hard in his business, carefully invests his money, is building his own house, and takes his wife on an exciting two-week vacation each year.

18. Likes to get the best value for the money spent.

Never	Seldom	Sometimes	Usually	Mostly	Always	POINTS
0	1	2	3	4	5	

Givers don't like to waste money. When they give, they give the best. But when it comes to spending money on themselves they're frugal. They shop for bargains and sales. One giver said, "I never buy a garment for myself at full retail price. I check the sale racks or wait for post-season markdowns."

Mary Jane is a giver who has always clipped grocery coupons but was delighted to find a few years ago that her local supermarket would accept newspaper ad coupons from other stores.

"I save at least ten dollars a week this way," Mary Jane revealed. "What with the manufacturer's coupons that I pair up with another store's double-coupon offer, and the freebies and store coupons I clip from the newspaper, I sometimes get thirty-five dollar's worth of groceries for twenty dollars.

"I haven't paid for my weekly dozen eggs for two years since one store started making them their free incentive item. The other day I got a whole chicken and a sixty-four-ounce apple juice free as well. This kind of couponing only takes about thirty extra minutes of my time each week, and it releases about five hundred dollars a year for the Lord's work."

Never	Seldom	Sometimes	Usually	Mostly	Always	POINTS
0	1	2	3	4	5	

19. Is definitely not gullible.

We think God has supplied givers with this characteristic to protect them from those who would wrongly dissociate them from their money. They are not easily fooled. You can't pull the wool over their eyes.

This clear-eyed quality shows up in other areas besides financial ones. Lucy, a mature giver who owned a nursing home, demonstrated it every day in her relationships to the elderly people in her care.

A white-haired man wheeled up to her in his chair while I was there: "Please tell the nurse at the desk that it's okay for me to go to my daughter's this weekend."

"Now, Mr. Jones," Lucy would say, "you know your daughter only has you one weekend a month. You went last weekend."

Next a lady hobbled up complaining that her roommate was stealing her clothes. "No, Mrs. Smith," Lucy assured her, "she couldn't possibly do that. She can't even get out of her bed. You look again. Your clothes are all there, dear."

As we continued down the hall a half a dozen others reported crises, and Lucy quietly defused each one. Some were so convincing that we would have hurried to their rescue. But Lucy explained, "In this work you have to be able to discern the real from the imagined, the genuine from the attempted manipulation. Many live in the past or in a fantasy world. I'm grateful that God has gifted me with the ability not to be gullible."

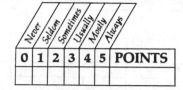

	Never	Seldom	Sometimes	Usually	Mostly	Always	
20. Possesses both natural and God-given wisdom.	0	1	2	3	4	5	**POINTS**

Givers are fair and objective. They are often wise beyond their years.

We cannot help but think of King Solomon, a biblical giver who prayed for wisdom and received much. In 1 Kings 3:16–28 we read that two women both claimed to be mother of a surviving baby. After hearing their claims Solomon asked for a sword and gave the order to "cut the living child in two and give half to one and half to the other."

What an awful-sounding command! But it was wisdom indeed, for the true mother cried out to spare the child, while the mother of the dead child agreed: "Neither I nor you shall have him. Cut him in two!"

Solomon's command had elicited from the women the responses that enabled him to determine the facts. Note the concluding verse: "When all Israel heard the verdict the king had given, they held the king in awe, because they saw that he had wisdom from God . . ." (NIV).

THE GIFT OF GIVING

Characteristics:

	Never	Seldom	Sometimes	Usually	Mostly	Always	POINTS
	0	1	2	3	4	5	
1.							
2.							
3.							
4.							
5.							
6.							
7.							
8.							
9.							
10.							
11.							
12.							
13.							
14.							
15.							
16.							
17.							
18.							
19.							
20.							
TOTAL							

1. Gives freely of money, possessions, time, energy, and love.
2. Loves to give without others knowing about it.
3. Wants to feel a part of the ministries to which he contributes.
4. Intercedes for needs and the salvation of souls.
5. Feels delighted when his gift is an answer to specific prayer.
6. Wants gifts to be of high quality or craftsmanship.
7. Gives only by the leading of the Holy Spirit.
8. Gives to support and bless others or to advance a ministry.
9. Views hospitality as an opportunity to give.
10. Handles finances with wisdom and frugality.
11. Quickly volunteers to help where a need is seen.
12. Seeks confirmation on the amount to give.
13. Has strong belief in tithing and in giving in addition to tithing.
14. Focuses on sharing the Gospel.
15. Believes God is the Source of his supply.
16. Is very industrious with a tendency toward success.
17. Has natural and effective business ability.
18. Likes to get the best value for the money spent.
19. Is definitely not gullible.
20. Possesses both natural and God-given wisdom.

PROBLEMS OF THE GIVER

20

Quite frankly, we find that givers do not have significant problem areas as frequently as the other motivational gifts, but we do list below the five that occur occasionally. It seems that givers wrestle mainly with the types of problems that all of us have, such as pride or lukewarmness.

Score yourself, asking the Holy Spirit to guide you.

	Never	Seldom	Sometimes	Usually	Mostly	Always	
	0	1	2	3	4	5	POINTS

1. May try to control how contributions are used.

While givers are generous, they can also give with strings attached. A classic example is the person who donates money for new church carpeting but wants to select the color himself. Or the person who gives to the organ fund but wants to head up the committee that selects it.

We ran into this type of problem in another country where one of the elders of a small church had donated a building for people to meet in and then insisted on having the final say on what happened there because "after all I paid for the building." The pastor had to confront him on the matter and ask him to decide whether he actually gave the building to the church, or was just letting the church use it, in which case they ought to be paying rent.

Just as parents need to cut the apron strings when their children are grown, so givers need to learn to cut any unseen strings that can remain attached to their gifts.

151

	Never	Seldom	Sometimes	Usually	Mostly	Always	POINTS
2. Tends to pressure others to give.	0	1	2	3	4	5	

As do recipients of each of the other gifts, givers see theirs as of primary importance. They don't understand why others don't give as much as they do. And so, consciously or unconsciously, they can be a source of pressure.

Janet had been a generous giver all her life. It was no problem until she got married. Up until then she had earned her own money and given to any cause she liked. Her husband was definitely not motivated in the same way. In fact, he was super-conservative about money. He agreed to tithe, but felt anything over and above that was overdoing it.

Janet found herself pressuring him to give each time a missionary came to the church, each time there was a special project to be funded, each time she heard of anyone in the church who had a genuine need.

"I didn't realize how much strain I was putting on our marriage," she admitted. "At first my husband didn't say much. Then he began to take a defensive stance about money in general. He started snapping at me over all kinds of things. He seemed to resent any suggestion from me, even about non-monetary matters."

It took a while for Janet to realize it had been her pushiness about giving that was at the root of the matter. "I asked the Lord to forgive me for pressuring my husband unwisely," Janet testified. "Then I asked my husband's forgiveness. I told him, 'Honey, you know how I love to give, but without you as a balance I might give away everything we have.'

"The most wonderful thing happened. He suggested that whenever either one of us was aware of a need we both pray about it—together—and find out what the Lord wanted. It's added a whole new dimension to our marriage."

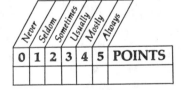

	Never	Seldom	Sometimes	Usually	Mostly	Always	POINTS
3. May upset family and friends with unpredictable patterns of giving.	0	1	2	3	4	5	

Since givers depend on the leading of the Holy Spirit, an observer may see no rhyme nor reason for their pattern of giving. In fact, the seemingly capriciousness can be a source of irritation to loved ones.

Blanche is a joyful giver who has her own source of income from a small home business. One day her daughter Trudy called from Hawaii. "Mom, I'm so depressed. Mark has broken off our engagement. I know it's for the best, but . . . could you come over for a week? I need some cheering up."

"Trudy, there's nothing I'd love more. But my work has piled up and I must meet the deadlines." Blanche felt bad as she hung up the phone.

Three hours later another call came, this time from a close family friend who'd moved to another state. "Blanche, I just had to talk with you. I'm feeling so blue."

"What's the matter, Alice?"

"Well, I know it sounds silly but I'm feeling so useless, so unneeded. I guess I've got the empty nest syndrome."

The Holy Spirit's timing was crystal clear to Blanche! "Alice," she said, "how would you like a week in Hawaii?"

"Who wouldn't," Alice replied, "but our finances are tight."

"No, I mean I'll pay your way." Blanche went on to outline Trudy's need and her own prior commitment.

"Trudy loves you so much and it would be such a blessing to me if you could take my place."

Blanche wired the money to Alice who left the next day for Hawaii, and did a wonderful job of being a substitute mom for Trudy. All three were blessed. Not so Blanche's husband who couldn't understand why, if there was money for a trip to Hawaii, he wasn't the one to go.

"At first I was upset with my husband's reaction," Blanche acknowledged. "Then I realized that he did not understand how a girl needs another woman's shoulder to cry on at such a time as this. I could see I needed to share my reasoning with him. And I asked him to forgive me for my unthinking independence."

	Never	Seldom	Sometimes	Usually	Mostly	Always	
4. Tends to spoil own children or other relatives.	0	1	2	3	4	5	**POINTS**

Givers love to give so much that they can spoil their children, nieces, or nephews.

Georgia admitted that she used to go overboard with gifts for her children on their birthdays and at Christmas. "I so overloaded my kids with presents that they didn't know what to play with first. Worse, they began to *expect* a heap of packages. I saw an attitude of the-world-owes-me-a-lot developing. So my husband and I came up with a plan.

"We sat down with the children and explained to them that Christmas was Jesus' birthday and that we could give gifts to Him by giving to those in need instead of each other. We were amazed how the children took to the idea. We "adopted" several needy families, got the names and ages of the children and took our kids shopping with us to help us pick out the presents. The joy on their faces told us we were doing the right thing.

"Christmas morning we sang 'happy birthday' to Jesus and then gathered up all the presents to deliver to the various families. What a delightful time we all had. We had invited two one-parent families from our church for Christmas dinner; afterward the kids from the three families played games while the adults talked.

"When we tucked our oldest daughter into bed she said, "This is the neatest Christmas we've ever had.' "

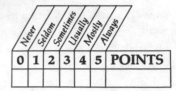

5. May use financial giving to get out of other responsibilities.

Never	Seldom	Sometimes	Usually	Mostly	Always	
0	1	2	3	4	5	**POINTS**

Sometimes givers figure that if they provide the money they've done their part.

Jim loved to give, but he also loved to make money. He enjoyed his job and often worked overtime. When his church—which had met for years in an old school—announced plans to build, he contributed a very generous amount to the building fund. But when it came time to put up the structure with mostly volunteer labor Jim was "too busy" to help.

He rationalized that he'd work overtime at his job on Saturdays during the project so he could make an additional contribution. But it wasn't long before the Holy Spirit brought him under conviction and he admitted to himself that it was simply that he preferred working at his office to physical labor. He repented.

When he showed up the next Saturday at the building site he found it was great fun working with the other men. He decided getting personally involved was an important part of giving, too.

POINTS	Never	Seldom	Sometimes	Usually	Mostly	Always	
	0	1	2	3	4	5	
1.							
2.							
3.							
4.							
5.							
							TOTAL

Typical problem areas of the gift of giving:

1. May try to control how contributions are used.
2. Tends to pressure others to give.
3. May upset family and friends with unpredictable patterns of giving.
4. Tends to spoil own children or other relatives.
5. May use financial giving to get out of other responsibilities.

Copyright © 1987, Don & Katie Fortune

155

BIBLICAL GIVERS
21

Givers are noted for their generosity, their ability to multiply assets, and their success in business. Abraham, the biblical example that we have selected for study in this chapter, is a prime example of all these qualities.

Givers also have a close walk with God and a great desire to share the Gospel with others. In Old Testament days the Gospel had not yet been given, but Abraham was the champion propagator of monotheism. The closeness of his walk with God enabled him to leave the security of his homeland and follow Him into the Promised Land.

Look for the giver's characteristics in the verses that follow:

Scripture: Genesis 13–14 (TAB)   *Your Comments:*

Genesis 13

2 Now Abram was extremely rich in livestock and in silver and in gold.

9 Is not the whole land before you? Separate yourself, I beg of you, from me. You take the left hand, then I will go to the right; or if you choose the right hand, then I will go to the left.

Genesis 14

14 When Abram heard that [his nephew] had been captured, he armed [led forth] his 318 trained servants, born in his own house, and pursued the enemy as far as Dan.

16 And he brought back all the goods, and also brought back his kinsman Lot and his possessions, the women also and the people.

19 And he (Melchizedek) blessed him and said, Blessed (favored with blessings, made blissful, joyful) be Abram by God Most High, possessor and maker of heaven and earth.

20 And blessed, praised and glorified be God Most High Who has given your foes into your hand! And [Abram] gave him a tenth of all [he had taken].

22 But Abram said to the king of Sodom, I have lifted up my hand and sworn to the Lord, God Most High, the possessor and maker of heaven and earth,

23 That I would not take a thread or a shoelace or anything that is yours, lest you should say, I have made Abram rich.

The giver's heart comes through in Abraham's life again and again. Here's what we saw in these passages:

Scripture: Genesis 13–14

Our Comments:

2 Now Abram was extremely rich in livestock and in silver and in gold.

#1 had possessions to share
#10 wise in finances
#16 successful in business

Our Comments:

9 Is not the whole land before you? Separate yourself, I beg of you, from me. You take the left hand, then I will go to the right; or if you choose the right hand, then I will go to the left.

#1 gave Lot choice of land
#8 blesses those around him
#15 faith in God's supply
#20 wisdom

Genesis 14

14 When the Abram heard that [his nephew] had been captured, he armed [led forth] his 318 trained servants, born in his own house, and pursued the enemy as far as Dan.

#1 gave energy and time
#11 helped Lot

16 And he brought back all the goods, and also brought back his kinsman Lot and his possessions, the women also and the people.

#1 gave back possessions
#11 helped Lot
#16 succeeds in undertaking

19 And he (Melchizedek) blessed him and said, Blessed (favored with blessings, made blissful, joyful) be Abram by God Most High, possessor and maker of heaven and earth.

#1 prosperous
#8 blessed for blessing others

20 And blessed, praised and glorified be God Most High Who has given your foes into your hand! And [Abram] gave him a tenth of all [he had taken].

#7 gives by God's leading
#13 first tither
#16 successful

22 But Abram said to the king of Sodom, I have lifted up my hand and sworn to the Lord, God Most High, the possessor and maker of heaven and earth.

#14 focus is on God

23 That I would not take a thread or a shoelace or anything that is yours, lest you should say, I have made Abram rich.

#15 God is his Source
#20 wise in decisions

God could trust Abraham with great riches because Abraham was generous and never let possessions become idolatrous. Here we see Abraham giving the choice of land to his nephew. Then he gives his time, energy, and personal resources to rescue Lot. After the battle was won he gave a tithe of all the spoils to Melchizedek, thus becoming the first recorded tither.

But the greatest giving of all is recorded in Genesis 22 in the story of how Abraham unquestioningly obeyed God when He asked him to give his only son, Isaac—the son through whom all the promises were to be fulfilled—as a burnt offering. God restrained Abraham from killing Isaac at the last moment saying, ". . . Now I know that you fear and revere God, since you have not held back from Me or begrudged giving Me your son, your only son" (Genesis 22:12, TAB).

Read for yourself the whole story of this remarkable giver in Genesis chapter 12 through 25:8. Also read about:

Dorcas—Acts 9:36–42

Cornelius—Acts 10:1–31

Epaphras—Colossians 1:7; 4:12, Philemon 23

Paul—Romans 1:1–20; Acts 9–28 (Note: Paul was also strongly gifted as a perceiver, teacher and exhorter. But his main role was to proclaim the Gospel to all the world.)

Lydia—Acts 16:14, 40

Zacchaeus—Luke 19:1–10

Solomon—1 Kings 1–11; 2 Chronicles 1–9

CHARACTERISTICS OF THE ADMINISTRATOR

22

The administrator is the born leader. He will emerge into leadership just as surely as Joseph, our biblical example, did.

We could have used other words for this gift: facilitator, organizer, ruler, leader, superintendent. According to *Strong's,* in the Greek the word is *proistemi,* from the verb "to stand before" or "to preside."

Score yourself as you go and transfer the total to your profile sheet.

1. Is highly motivated to organize that for which he's responsible.

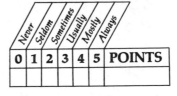

Never	Seldom	Sometimes	Usually	Mostly	Always	
0	1	2	3	4	5	POINTS

Administrators love a challenge. Don tells me that's why I love him so much, because he's a challenge. (There are times when I can say "amen" to that!)

They also love to "dig in" and develop or organize anything they're in charge of. The natural motivation is there—a creative desire to take "raw materials" and people, and produce something that has never been—like organizing an office, setting up a committee, or developing a project.

Although I've always been an organizer, from organizing neighborhood playmates to being responsible for 900 young people as Director of Christian Education in a large Methodist church, my favorite project was developing *Aglow* magazine.

The original challenge was to get the testimonies of Christian women out to those who could not come to our meetings. But as the women passed along the little magazine to friends and relatives and subscriptions started pouring in, we found that we had an unintended national publication on our hands.

The Lord kept adding competent personnel to our volunteer staff as we increased our vision and enlarged our operation. Every day was exciting. And we saw the magazine develop from twelve black-and-white pages into thirty-two pages in full color. By the end of seven years 100,000 copies were going out to sixty-five nations.

An organizer-leader is by job requirement a "jack of all trades but master of none." He must have a wide range of interests and abilities, but those who carry out specific tasks will be more capable and specialized. In order to supervise effectively he needs to know a little about a lot of things. I often praised the Lord for those with expertise in their fields. *Together* we made a team.

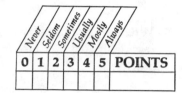

2. Expresses ideas and organization in ways that communicate clearly.

Administrators are excellent communicators. They look for ways to express what they want to say clearly and effectively. Believing that a picture is truly worth a thousand words, they like to use charts, diagrams, outlines, graphs, and other visual aids.

Guess why you have profile sheets and a scoring system in this book? Since this is my primary motivational gift, the first thing I thought of when I learned about the gifts was, "Why hasn't someone organized them into chart form so that people can test themselves?" What a joy it has been to see people all over the world use these testing sheets to discover their God-given gifts.

When I was editor of Aglow Publications, I also loved doing flow charts so we could see what happened to an order from the time it came in to the time the materials were shipped out. In addition I kept an up-to-date progress and sales chart on the back of my office door. At one glance I could see how we were doing financially.

Diagramming came so naturally to me that when Don and I were newlyweds and had our first disagreement I got out a piece of paper, drew a diagram of our differences, and outlined a solution. It was not exactly what he wanted to see. I thought it would clear up the whole matter but I had to learn there was a time and place for such things.

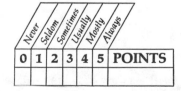

3. Prefers to be under authority in order to have authority.

Administrators understand, honor, and respect authority structures. They feel comfortable with them, whether they are at the top or somewhere within the system.

The centurion who came to Jesus to ask Him to heal his servant probably had the motivational gift of administration. When Jesus offered to go to the sick man's bedside the centurion replied, " 'Lord, I do not deserve to have you come under my roof. But just say the word, and my servant will be healed. For I myself am a man under authority, with soldiers under me. I tell this one, "Go," and he goes; and that one, "Come," and he comes. I say to my servant, "Do this," and he does it' " (Matthew 8:8–9, NIV).

Jesus commended the centurion's confidence in His authority, and the servant was healed.

Administrators want to know how much authority they have and what authority they do not have, for they respect those limits. They like to have exact parameters defined, so they will not inadvertently step outside of them, and they like the freedom, within those parameters, to "be their own boss." They are creative and productive given this situation, stifled and inhibited without it.

4. Will not take responsibility unless delegated by those in authority.

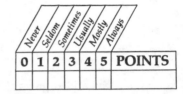

Never	Seldom	Sometimes	Usually	Mostly	Always	
0	1	2	3	4	5	POINTS

Because of his keen respect for authority the administrator will never deliberately usurp it. Therefore, in any situation where authority exists, the administrator will not try to move in to utilize his skills—no matter how needed—unless those in authority ask him to do so.

Some years ago I was the speaker at a women's retreat in Kansas City. On the last evening a women's quartet sang after my concluding message, then invited people to come up for individual ministry. About fifty women responded. I thought, "This is going to take hours. I'd love to go and help them." But I had not been told specifically by the leaders to assist in this prayer time. They had not said that I couldn't, either, but because I always submit my ministry to the leaders of the inviting group I felt I could not go beyond what had already been established.

"Glued" to my chair, I felt torn. I wanted to help but I "couldn't." Later I described my dilemma to the leaders.

"Oh, we simply assumed that you would help with the ministry time," they said in surprise. "We never thought to mention it."

But since they hadn't, I felt I couldn't participate.

There are lots of administrators who are not utilizing their abilities because of this characteristic. We encourage those in leadership positions to search out these facilitators and delegate areas of responsibility to them.

5. Will assume responsibilities if no specific leadership exists.

Never	Seldom	Sometimes	Usually	Mostly	Always	
0	1	2	3	4	5	POINTS

In situations where there is no existing leadership or authority structure it is the administrators who will most naturally step in and take charge. Divide a large group into subgroups and give each a task to do and it will be those with the motivational gift of administration who emerge as the spontaneous leaders of the individual units. True, they would prefer to be appointed ahead of time to take the lead, but where a group is floundering with no designated leadership, they will take the reins.

Dan, a young man with a degree in business administration, says, "I can't stand lack of leadership in an organization. If no one else will, I usually end up taking control to bring order out of the chaos."

In the early days of Aglow there was no one in leadership in the loosely knit fellowship. So I took the initiative in starting the magazine. But eight years later when the Lord showed me that I was to develop the Aglow television ministry, the organization had a well-established superstructure with a president and six vice-presidents (of which I was one). So I waited, without saying anything, until the time came that the whole board recognized it was time to start such a ministry and appointed me to do it.

6. Especially enjoys working on long-range goals and projects.

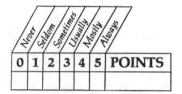

While the server enjoys short-term goals—two days or two weeks—the administrator thrives on two-year projects. "In fact," one administrator said confidently, "I really prefer a project that can take several years. I like something I can throw myself into, make long-range plans, and establish shorter-range goals along the way."

When you ask a person with the gift of compassion to set a goal he says, "Whatever for?" He lives one day at a time, or more precisely, one moment at a time. It's the administrators who attend time-management seminars. They want to increase their skills in handling projects of significant size.

Dorothy, a writer from the Pacific Northwest, told us she did not fully realize how much she enjoyed long-range challenges until she was nearly forty years old. "At that time," she explained, "I began to mix with other writers and found myself in charge of a writing group. My job was to encourage new or faltering writers and now it's almost become an obsession. I help them set personal long-range writing goals and keep after them to stick to a program that will enable them to reach these goals, even if it means neglecting my own writing."

7. Is a visionary person with a broad perspective.

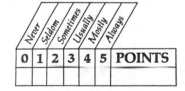

Proverbs 29:18 tells us, "Where there is no vision, the people perish...." Vision is needed to keep people in focus, whether in business or faith. A good leader is a person of vision, and in upholding that vision for others to see he can inspire great accomplishment.

That vision can be anything from a revelation of God as to His particular purposes for a particular group, to the simple ability to visualize how people can work together to accomplish a common goal.

Nehemiah had a vision for the rebuilding of the walls of Jerusalem. Joshua held onto the vision of the Promised Land. Joseph had a dream-vision showing how to spare the Middle East from seven years of devastating famine. David had a vision for his role as king but waited for the appointed time. Gideon had a vision of victory. The Bible is full of visionary leaders.

Along with vision comes a specific type of faith. Administrators believe that they can accomplish—with the help of others—that which they are able to visualize.

Administrators often have vision beyond the scope of the people they lead, but those who follow are spurred on and kept on course by the vision of the leader. Without this, the people would fail to achieve their potential.

8. Easily facilitates resources and people to accomplish tasks or goals.

Never	Seldom	Sometimes	Usually	Mostly	Always	POINTS
0	1	2	3	4	5	

Like one who loves to put pieces of a puzzle together, the administrator loves to fit people and resources together to facilitate a task.

Paul is a systems analyst for the Boeing Company. "I have to be an organizer, educator, and motivator of various people if I am to accomplish the goals I've been assigned," Paul explains. "I enjoy using organizational ability, logic, and persuasion as my basic tools for working with people to get the job done."

In contrast, Julia uses her administrator gift in her home. "First thing in the morning I always make out a list of things to be done during the day," she confides. "Then I think through the jobs, who will do them, and when. I schedule tasks for the kids. I get the resources ready—the broom and mop, the garden tools, the bathtub cleaner. I even 'organize' my husband. He's not always so happy about it but he knows if he does his part all the work will get done on schedule."

9. Enjoys delegating tasks and supervising people.

Never	Seldom	Sometimes	Usually	Mostly	Always	POINTS
0	1	2	3	4	5	

Administrators love to tell people what to do. We mean that in a positive sense. They easily see what jobs need to be done and they seem to know who can do them well. They enjoy distributing work in such a way that it will bring about maximum satisfaction and accomplishment.

Marvin was asked to take over the leadership of a large Christian organization that had bogged down with ineffective workers. Marvin's motivational gift of administration enabled him to trim the staff and place capable people in key positions. Then he delegated lots of responsibility, taught leadership principles to key staffers, and trained them to supervise effectively. The organization was turned around from financial failure to an effective ministry.

Our son Dave has this gift too. We used to chuckle when he'd come home from college on weekends and walk in the door with a string of delegations: "Dad, would you look at the car, it's running kinda funny. Mom, will you do this load of laundry for me, I didn't have time to do it myself this week. Dan, would you mow the lawn for me—I've got to study for a massive exam!" In a moment of time he had us all working on his delegated tasks while he pursued his most important goal.

10. Will endure criticism in order to accomplish the ultimate task.

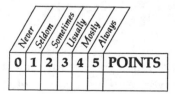

Leaders get criticized! It seems to be part of the "occupational hazard" of administration. There are always those who feel the leader should do things differently, or slower, or faster, or more carefully, or more daringly, or whatever.

A variation on Abraham Lincoln's famous statement might be, "You can please all of the people some of the time, and some of the people all of the time; but you can't please all of the people all of the time." However, this will not deter an administrator from his course.

One pastor said, "The problem working with a church is that you have people. When you have people you have problems."

Someone else once answered an outspoken critic of churches: "There are no perfect churches. And if you should find one and join it, it would not be perfect anymore!"

If you know any administrators, pray for them. The are being bombarded with more than their share of criticism.

11. Has great zeal and enthusiasm for whatever he is involved in.

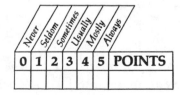

Enthusiasm emanates naturally from the administrator. The Amplified Bible says that administrators are to do their job with "zeal and singleness of mind." The Greek word is *spoude*, which in the King James is translated "diligence" and by Wuest "intense eagerness and effort." From *Strong's Concordance* we learn that the word also encompasses the ideas of speed, dispatch, earnestness, haste, intense effort, and determination.

It is as if God has given the administrator the ability to throw all of his efforts into a situation in order to see it to a conclusion.

Dennis, carrying several types of heavy administrative responsibilities, testifies, "I absolutely love what I am doing. I can hardly wait to get to work each day. I love the demands and challenges of my job. I enjoy seeing how quickly I can accomplish what I need to do and then move on to the next area with just as much zeal and enthusiasm."

Although the administrator's zeal is pure and altruistic it is so strong that others are often threatened or overwhelmed by it.

"I was responsible for a volunteer organization," Hazel says. "I was really sold on its purposes and threw myself wholeheartedly into the work. But some of the membership seemed suspicious of my enthusiasm and began to resist every idea I presented. I finally set up a teaching session on the motivational gifts so they could learn what to expect from the different ones. It helped. They began to accept my zeal and we worked together much better."

12. Finds greatest fulfillment and joy in working to accomplish goals.

	Never	Seldom	Sometimes	Usually	Mostly	Always	
	0	1	2	3	4	5	POINTS

Servers work toward immediate goals, experiencing joy as each one is accomplished. For administrators with their longer-range projects, the point of joy is often "'way down the road."

Each time I wrapped up an issue of the magazine—all the stories edited, pictures ready, captions and titles written, layout completed—and stuck the package in the mailbox to the printer, that was my point of joy. But it took three months to get there. (And I have to admit that there was a type of "anticipated joy" along the way.)

Wanda found her gift of administration invaluable in her job as Christian education coordinator of her church. "The first goal I worked on," she says, "was to organize a resource center that would supply the teachers with the materials they would need in order to do their job well. Then I spent months training them in teaching methods. What a sense of fulfillment there was at last, to see the whole staff working together to make our Sunday school the best it could be."

13. Is willing to let others get the credit in order to get a job done.

	Never	Seldom	Sometimes	Usually	Mostly	Always	
	0	1	2	3	4	5	POINTS

The mature administrator does not worry about getting credit for accomplishments. Like anyone else, he enjoys a pat on the back, but he would rather share that credit with the whole group. He sees success as a collective achievement. It is not false modesty when the administrator refuses accolades insisting, "None of this could have happened if it had not been for the excellent work of my associates." He really means it. He sees himself as a facilitator, the others as the real accomplishers.

Roy Burkhart, pastor of a large church in Ohio, addressing five hundred seminary students on the practical aspects of pastoring, asserted: "It's amazing what you can get accomplished in a church if you don't care who gets the credit."

In the business world Jeff has learned how well his staff operates with the liberal distribution of appreciation. "But I even go beyond that," he admits. "Whenever I drop a hint or an idea and one of my employees picks up on it and develops it, I give him credit for thinking of it. I love to see people feeling useful and valued. It makes me feel good, too."

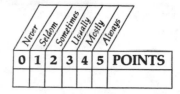

14. Prefers to move on to a new challenge once something is completed.

Never	Seldom	Sometimes	Usually	Mostly	Always	
0	1	2	3	4	5	POINTS

Once administrators complete a goal, they're ready to move on. Some assume that once an organizer gets a business or a church group functioning, he would enjoy staying at the helm and continuing to coordinate. No so. Once the system is running smoothly he'd rather turn it over to someone else and move on to new challenges.

After seven years *Aglow* magazine was running smoothly. We finally had paid staff, a good group of editors, and I no longer felt needed. With no pioneering work left to do I was bored and frustrated. I knew in advance what each day would hold. There was no adventure left.

Then, at the close of my eighth year, the whole television field opened up for us. It was unmapped, untried territory and I was delighted. I could glimpse the potential for women sharing the Gospel with other women in the privacy of their own homes.

I remember standing on the rooftop of a skyscraper in Chicago that housed a Christian television station and looking out in the darkness at vast numbers of high-rise apartment buildings, visualizing the thousands upon thousands of women in those apartments—some lonely, some abused, some afraid, many without hope. "Oh, God!" I cried. "This is how we can reach them! They probably wouldn't come out to a meeting, but they'll listen to another woman share her heart on their own TV sets."

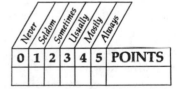

Never	Seldom	Sometimes	Usually	Mostly	Always	
0	1	2	3	4	5	POINTS

15. Constantly writes notes to self.

This characteristic applies to all with the gift of administration without exception. They daily write reminder notes to themselves and make lists of things to do, calls to make, goals to accomplish.

Administrators tend to have so many things on their mind that if they don't write something down when they think of it, they're apt to forget. At a writer's conference I was talking with the then-new editor of *Decision* magazine. He shared with me some of the things he liked about his new job and I could easily tell that he had the gift of administration. Just for fun I said, "You write notes to yourself, don't you?"

"How did you know?" he asked with astonishment.

"Because," I replied, "I can tell that you are an administrator by motivational gift and they *always* write notes to themselves!"

Adele admits, "I live my life by lists. Sometimes I spend more time making them than it would take to do the job. I have such a tendency to want to organize—but some things would be better left spontaneous."

Another administrator confided in us that whenever she did not have a piece of paper handy she'd jot notes on her hand, and then hope she didn't forget and wash her hands before she got the notes transferred!

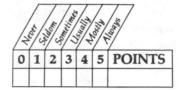

	Never	Seldom	Sometimes	Usually	Mostly	Always	
	0	1	2	3	4	5	POINTS

16. Is a natural and capable leader.

Is a bee drawn to honey? Does a cow come back to the barn? Just so an administrator is bound to lead—at least part of the time.

One of the things we have learned about administrators is that they do not do well in any kind of team leadership. They have strong convictions about the way they lead. Each one has his own style and two leaders will clash. They far prefer to be given specific areas in which they are in sole charge than to be placed in what they view as a no man's land of dual leadership. As one man put it, "I'd much rather follow than try to share leadership on an equal basis with another administrator."

One of the rare couples who share the motivational gift of administration is a young pastor and his wife, Duncan and Judy. Both were raised on farms and loved gardening. So in their first pastorate they decided to plant a vegetable garden in the backyard, and later related this scene to us:

"The rows should go north and south," Duncan declared.

"Oh, no," Judy insisted, "we always planted east to west."

"Well, the tall vegetables need to go over here on the south side to help shade the other crops," Duncan claimed.

"You've got to be kidding," Judy blurted out. "Anyone knows it's best to plant the corn and the beans on the north so the smaller plants get adequate sunshine." They spent the next hour arguing over where each vegetable should go.

"We were getting nowhere," Judy said. "We were both so sure we were right. I don't think we would ever have gotten our garden planted if God had not given Duncan some special wisdom. He got a stick and drew a line right down the middle of the plot and gave me the right side while he took the left. Our rows went in different directions and we each followed the methods we'd been used to. And you know what? We each had a beautiful, productive garden."

There can also be exceptions. My administrator friend Bette Ayers wrote, "Thought you would find it interesting that on occasion two leaders *can* work together. While I was the chairman of retreats for our church I had JoAnn McMoran as my right hand gal. I cannot tell you how wonderful it was working with her. I was so blessed to have her to pray with me and seek the Lord's will in every aspect. I found that when two administrators work that well together, it's because they have the Lord as the Administrator!"

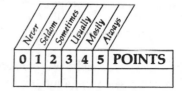

17. Knows when to keep old methods going and when to introduce new ones.

	Never	Seldom	Sometimes	Usually	Mostly	Always	
	0	1	2	3	4	5	POINTS

In any group or organization where a method of operation has been established, people feel at ease with it. But when an administrator is placed in leadership he or she may see that changes are necessary. Yet it is not easy to move people out of their "comfort zone." It calls for great wisdom, and administrators have it.

Jesus explained that a leader in the Kingdom of God "is like a householder who brings forth out of his storehouse treasure that is new and [treasure that is] old—the fresh [as well as] the familiar" (Matthew 13:52, TAB).

In Japan we visited Meiji-Mura, a restored village of the Meiji period. Our host, Pastor Tempei Wada, pointed out a house that had an old-fashioned storehouse out back. "That is like the storehouse Jesus mentioned," he said. "It was where the householder kept his treasure, his money, his silver dishes, anything of value.

"Notice there are no windows," he commented. "When the door was bolted there was no way for a thief to break in. The householder would store his valuables there—new purchases as well as family heirlooms, and bring them into the house to enjoy as he desired."

We thought the parallel was apt. The wise leader introduces new ideas or new ways of functioning one or two at a time, letting people hold onto much of the familiar while adjusting to the fresh. Then another new idea can be introduced, and then another, but not all at once.

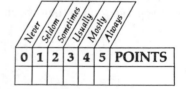

18. Enjoys working with and being around people.

	Never	Seldom	Sometimes	Usually	Mostly	Always	
	0	1	2	3	4	5	POINTS

Administrators are people people. They share this characteristic with the exhorters, except that the motivation in their case is not to encourage but to get to know, to learn from, to interact with. Administrators are great observers of human behavior and are constantly learning how to work with people more effectively.

We've watched our son Dave focus on people. In high school he loved being a part of a group, whether it was a football team, a Christian singing group, the church youth group, the student body leadership, or just his own gang of friends.

As a junior he noted that many of the students were unaware of the problems of people in third-world nations. He was especially interested in the plight of the people of Haiti, and came up with an idea to expose fellow students to their needs.

With the help of a teacher and a staff member of World Concern he arranged for eight students and two adults to go on a ten-day trip, first to Washington, D.C., to talk with a congressional aide, then on to Florida to visit a refugee camp, and finally to Haiti to visit Christian hospitals, schools, churches, and orphanages and to get acquainted with the people. "It was a real experience in interpersonal relationships," Dave said.

During his sophomore and junior years at Seattle Pacific University Dave became "peer advisor" of a dorm floor. It helped pay for his room and board but more importantly gave him the opportunity to interact with other students and to further develop his leadership skills.

When Dave told us he was considering running for student body president for his senior year we could encourage him to do so, for with his motivational gift of administration and his love for people we knew he'd do a great job. He was elected—and he did.

Dave's been accepted at Yale University Divinity School. He plans to become a pastor or a college professor so that, as he says, "I can have an impact on as many people's lives as possible."

19. Wants to see things completed as quickly as possible.

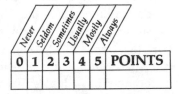

Administrators want to get the job done—fast! They do not like delays, red tape, or people dragging their feet.

One administrator mother said, "I get very upset and frustrated when I can't finish a simple project quickly. The greatest obstacle is not knowing where things are. With a family as large as mine [she has six children] it's amazing what disappears or doesn't get back to its rightful place."

Jenni, who has taken on the directorship of a girls' drill team, shared how frustrating it is when the youngsters do not pay attention or apply themselves. "They have the potential to be champions but that takes work. Often they simply play at learning the formations. It's delayed our progress; I wish they wouldn't waste time."

20. Does not enjoy doing routine tasks.

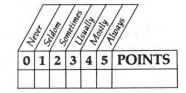

"Boring!" That sums up the administrator's opinion of repetitive work. No challenge. No interest.

We estimate that an administrator would last no more than one day on an assembly line job. Servers on the other hand might enjoy the security of a work routine where they knew exactly what was expected of them. No wonder administrators love having servers on their team, so they can delegate this kind of work to them.

Susan, an administrator from Kamloups, Canada, wrote us that while she is doing routine tasks around the house she beats the boredom by organizing her current projects in her head. "Not only does the housework become more tolerable," she reported, "but when I'm free to work on the project, most of the planning is already completed and so I save time."

Gladys says she copes with routine housework by listening to teaching tapes. Wilma has a similar system, only with her it's good music. Mark wears his Walkman and headphones when he mows the lawn. Georgia prays as she vacuums and scrubs floors. And Pete memorizes Scripture on his half-hour drive to and from work. All good ideas for administrators!

THE GIFT OF ADMINISTRATION

	Never 0	Seldom 1	Sometimes 2	Usually 3	Mostly 4	Always 5	POINTS
1.							
2.							
3.							
4.							
5.							
6.							
7.							
8.							
9.							
10.							
11.							
12.							
13.							
14.							
15.							
16.							
17.							
18.							
19.							
20.							
						TOTAL	

Characteristics:

1. Is highly motivated to organize that for which he's responsible
2. Expresses ideas and organization in ways that communicate clearly.
3. Prefers to be under authority in order to have authority.
4. Will not take responsibility unless delegated by those in authority.
5. Will assume responsibilities if no specific leadership exists.
6. Especially enjoys working on long-range goals and projects.
7. Is a visionary person with a broad perspective.
8. Easily facilitates resources and people to accomplish tasks or goals.
9. Enjoys delegating tasks and supervising people.
10. Will endure criticism in order to accomplish the ultimate task.
11. Has great zeal and enthusiasm for whatever he is involved in.
12. Finds greatest fulfillment and joy in working to accomplish goals.
13. Is willing to let others get the credit in order to get a job done.
14. Prefers to move on to a new challenge once something is completed.
15. Constantly writes notes to self.
16. Is a natural and capable leader.
17. Knows when to keep old methods going and when to introduce new ones.
18. Enjoys working with and being around people.
19. Wants to see things completed as quickly as possible.
20. Does not enjoy doing routine tasks.

Copyright © 1987, Don & Katie Fortune

171

PROBLEMS OF THE ADMINISTRATOR

23

There's a major pitfall lying in wait for people with the gift of administration: When they carry their positive characteristics to an extreme they *become* problem areas. God has equipped them with enablings and giftedness to accomplish tasks and achieve goals. Yet, if they don't slow down enough to "smell the roses," their gift scrunches life's priorities into configurations that were never meant to be.

One dear saint from Australia told us that if Satan cannot get a Christian to sin deliberately his next tactic is to push him to operate in good works to an extreme until everything is out-of-balance and his witness no longer effective. As you score yourself be aware of the need for moderation in all things.

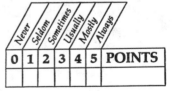

Never	Seldom	Sometimes	Usually	Mostly	Always	
0	1	2	3	4	5	POINTS

1. Becomes upset when others do not share the same vision or goals.

As mentioned, the administrator finds it difficult to work in team leadership to begin with, but when his co-workers have stunted vision that hampers the accomplishment of goals, it is to him as a millstone around the neck.

One administrator, Ed, worked for an organization that was structured so that all seven men who headed up departments also served as the governing board. Their policy was not to move ahead on any project unless *all* were in agreement. It seemed an ideal way to govern, but in practice there were frustrations when the negative vote of one person became the determining factor.

"There were several on the board who were quite conservative and automatically suspicious of any new idea," Ed reported. "Each time I'd present a proposal to increase the organization's effectiveness one of them was sure to dig in his heels and we'd hear, 'Well, we've never tried it before,' or, 'We'd better put that on the shelf for now.'

"I would get so upset," Ed admitted. "Their lack of vision was absolutely frustrating. I finally blew up. I'm not proud of it but I told them we'd never make any progress if they continued to let the person of least vision determine the level of our work.

"The Lord dealt with me about my attitude, but He also showed me that that particular authority structure was not for me. I was able to move on to another job where I didn't feel so many restraints."

Perhaps the most important thing for the administrator to learn is that prayer changes things. Persuasion and the presentation of facts only go so far in changing another's limited perspective. But God can move mountains—and people—and enlarge the vision of others if we just ask.

2. Develops outer callousness due to being a target for criticism.

	Never	Seldom	Sometimes	Usually	Mostly	Always	
	0	1	2	3	4	5	**POINTS**

If it is true, as psychologists tell us, that for every negative word spoken against us we need four positive words to neutralize the negative effects, then it's clear why many administrators build up a callousness to protect themselves from the barrage of criticism their position invites.

Malcolm, an administrator with an executive position, is married to a woman who used to pick at him constantly. She majored on his weak points, and bombarded him with unkind comments.

"I could take criticism at work," he insisted, "but it was the critical attitude of my wife that defeated me. I built walls of silence and sarcasm and determined I was not going to let her hurt me anymore. We were living in the same house but that was all. Our marriage was falling apart and I kept telling myself I didn't care.

"Fortunately our pastor did. He called us in for counseling and helped me to begin to let down the walls as he also taught my wife how to communicate without criticizing. It took time, but what we both learned was worth it, and now we are helping to counsel others with similar problems."

3. Can regress into "using" people to accomplish own goals.

	Never	Seldom	Sometimes	Usually	Mostly	Always	
	0	1	2	3	4	5	**POINTS**

Administrators are so goal-oriented that they can forget that people are not pawns to be moved about as in a game of chess. It's not that they mean to do this, it just happens that they push a good quality to an extreme until they become inconsiderate of—even hurtful to—others.

I remember how, in the early days of Aglow when our editorial and publishing "office" was in the room over our unusually large garage, I would lapse into this from time to time. Most of our volunteer staff worked just until four o'clock so they'd be home before their husbands were.

One day I could see that we could finish mailing out the magazine if everyone would work only half-an-hour longer. I asked if they would.

"My husband gets very upset if I'm late," one woman apologized. "He doesn't mind my doing volunteer work, as long as it doesn't interfere with our home life."

"I'd like to stay and help," said another, equally apologetic, "but my baby sitter can't stay past 4:15."

"I can stay an extra ten minutes," one person ventured, "but I've got to shop and get dinner on the table or my son will miss basketball practice."

I suddenly realized what I was doing. I'd started looking at them as so many hands to get a job done, rather than seeing them as real people with real families with real needs to be met. *I* was the one who needed to apologize!

	Never	Seldom	Sometimes	Usually	Mostly	Always	POINTS
4. Tends to drive self and neglect personal and family needs.	0	1	2	3	4	5	

Priorities! That's what administrators need to keep in mind. As one told us, "I give myself one hundred percent to whatever I do." But this potentially admirable quality can also wreak havoc in other areas of life.

Administrators can get overextended, be too committed to a task, or take on too much for either their own good or their family's well-being. Their zeal for their work or ministry can leave those they love the most feeling neglected.

Some excellent advice is given in the beautiful description in Proverbs 31, "She considers a new field before she buys or accepts it—expanding prudently [and not courting neglect of her present duties by assuming others]" (verse 16a, TAB). Whenever administrators are considering new fields of endeavor they need to take stock of their present obligations and take on new responsibilities only if they can do so without neglecting spouse, children, job, church commitments—and time for devotions, exercise, and recreation.

	Never	Seldom	Sometimes	Usually	Mostly	Always	POINTS
5. Neglects routine home responsibilities due to intense interest in "job."	0	1	2	3	4	5	

I was tremendously relieved to learn that administrator women do not have to love housework! I used to feel so guilty about it. I do get it done—eventually. But I'll have to admit that our house looks lived in.

I procrastinate. I don't love dusting. I do it and the next day the dust just resettles on everything. I make the bed and then, of all things, we sleep in it, and I have to make it again the next day. I wash clothes and soon they need to be washed again. There's no end to routine. (I'm so grateful for the reports that there is no dirt or dust in heaven.)

Housework must be done. But I've got a long phone cord so I can be loading the dishwasher while I talk on the phone. I listen to tapes while I do floors. I watch my favorite TV program while I fold laundry and iron. I've learned to make housework endurable.

And for you administrator men, it's okay to hate yardwork, and cleaning out the gutters, and repainting the house, but just remember that those things still need to be done. You are the men, along with you career women, most likely to become "workaholics" or "married to your job." So watch it!

For *all* of us administrators, we need to remember that our love for our job, our volunteer projects, our church work, or whatever we're involved in must not put us in a position of neglecting life's necessary responsibilities.

Typical problem areas of the gift of administration:

1. Becomes upset when others do not share the same vision or goals.
2. Develops outer callousness due to being a target for criticism.
3. Can regress into "using" people to accomplish own goals.
4. Tends to drive self and neglect personal and family needs.
5. Neglects routine home responsibilities due to intense interest in "job."

	Never	Seldom	Sometimes	Usually	Mostly	Always	POINTS
	0	1	2	3	4	5	
1.							
2.							
3.							
4.							
5.							TOTAL

176

BIBLICAL ADMINISTRATORS

24

In the Bible administrators are often kings, priests, or bishops. Such people may assume leadership not only because of their giftedness but also because of the advantages of birth, position, or power. The example of the motivational gift of administration that we have chosen to examine, however, is a person who rose to leadership without special status or influence.

Joseph was born into an important Jewish family and he was indeed favored by his father, Jacob. But this was not enough to help him out of trouble. Joseph's mistake was announcing his governing abilities before anyone else was prepared to accept them. Then, after his brothers sold Joseph into slavery, there was nothing in his family ties or credentials that helped him rise to leadership.

See how many characteristics of the gift of administration you can find in the following references:

Scripture: Genesis 37–50 (TAB)   *Your Comments:*

Genesis 37

9 But Joseph dreamed yet another dream and told it to his brothers [also]. He said, See here, I have dreamed again, and behold, [this time not only] eleven stars, but

also the sun and the moon bowed
down and did reverence to me!

10 And he told it to his father
[as well as] his brethren. But his
father rebuked him and said to him,
What is the meaning of this dream that
you have dreamed? Shall I and your
mother and your brothers actually come
to bow down ourselves to the earth
and do homage to you?

Genesis 39

4 So Joseph pleased [Potiphar] and
found favor in his sight, and he
served him. And [his master] made
him supervisor over his house, and he
put all that he had in his charge.

Genesis 41

29 Take note! Seven years of
great plenty throughout all the
land of Egypt are coming.

30 Then there will come seven years
of hunger and famine; and [there will
be so much want that] all the great
abundance of the previous years will
be forgotten in the land of Egypt;
and hunger (destitution, starvation)
will exhaust (consume, finish) the land.

40 You shall have charge over my
house, and all my people shall be
governed according to your word
[with reverence, submission and
obedience]. Only in matters of the
throne will I be greater than you are.

God had a plan for Joseph's leadership ability. He operated in his gift first in prison, then over the whole of Egypt and surrounding lands. Here are the characteristics we see suggested:

Scripture: Genesis 37–40, (TAB)   *Our Comments:*

Genesis 37

9   But Joseph dreamed yet another
dream and told it to his brothers
[also]. He said, See here, I have
dreamed again, and behold, [this
time not only] eleven stars, but
also the sun and the moon bowed
down and did reverence to me!

#7   a visionary person
#11   zeal for dream
#16   leadership capabilities revealed by dream
#19   wants quick fulfillment of dream

10   And he told it to his father
[as well as] his brethren. But his
father rebuked him and said to him,
What is the meaning of this dream that
you have dreamed? Shall I and your
mother and your brothers actually come
to bow down ourselves to the earth and
do homage to you?

#10   draws criticism

Genesis 39

4   So Joseph pleased [Potiphar] and
found favor in his sight, and he
served him. And [his master] made
him supervisor over his house and he
put all that he had in his charge.

#3   worked under authority
#5   assumed responsibilities
#8   facilitating abilities recognized
#9   enjoys supervising
#16   a leader even in jail

Genesis 41

29   Take note! Seven years of
great plenty throughout all the
land of Egypt are coming.

#7   a visionary

30   Then there will come seven years
of hunger and famine; and [there will
be so much want that] all the great
abundance of the previous years will
be forgotten in the land of Egypt;
and hunger (destitution, starvation)
will exhaust (consume, finish) the land.

#6   sets long range goals
#7   a visionary
#14   enjoys a challenge

Our Comments:

40 You shall have charge over my house, and all my people shall be governed according to your word [with reverence, submission and obedience]. Only in matters of the throne will I be greater than you are.

#1 motivated to organize
#3 accepts authority
#6 given long-range goals
#7 broad perspective
#8 a facilitator
#16 a capable leader

Have you ever wondered what would have happened to all of those Middle Eastern countries if a person with such an outstanding gift of administration had *not* been available? Joseph's farsighted leadership saved millions of people.

Now take time to look up more about Joseph, and some of the other biblical examples of the gift of administration:

Joseph—Genesis 30–40
Nehemiah—Nehemiah 1–7
Deborah—Judges 4–5
David—1 Samuel 16–31; 2 Samuel; 1 Kings 1–2; 1 Chronicles 10:13–29:30
Annas—Luke 3:2; John 18:13–24; Acts 4:5–6
James, brother of Jesus—Matthew 13:55; Mark 6:3; Acts 12:17; 15:13; 21:18; 1 Corinthians 15:7; Galatians 1:19; 2:9
Jairus—Matthew 9:18; Mark 5:22–43; Luke 8:41–45

Characteristics of the Compassion Person

25

Of all the gifts, that of compassion is by far the most frequently bestowed. How wonderful that this is so! "What this world needs now is love, sweet love," as the song tells us. Maybe it's because so many people are hurting that God has created such a vast number of compassionate people. On our survey they made up thirty percent of the primary gifts. That's almost one-third of the population.

"To have mercy" in Greek is *eleeo*. *Strong's* defines it: "to *compassionate* (by word or deed, specifically by divine grace): have compassion, (pity on), have (obtain, receive, shew) mercy (on)." (We have elected to use the word "compassion," rather than "mercy," because the latter can carry negative connotation of weakness.)

The compassion person is to show his compassion with cheerfulness, *hilarotes* in the Greek, according to Vine, signifying "that readiness of mind, that joyousness, which is prompt to do anything; hence, cheerful." Wuest notes that our word *hilarity* comes from this Greek word. Vincent defines it "the joyfulness, the amiable grace, the affability going the length of gaiety, which make the visitor a sunbeam penetrating into the sick-chamber, and to the heart of the afflicted." The Amplified Bible states that our acts of mercy or compassion are to be done "with genuine cheerfulness and joyful eagerness."

Remember there is no eighth gift type. This is the final gift in the list. So, complete this adventure in discovering your giftedness. When you've transferred your compassion total to your profile sheet, you'll see the whole picture of your giftedness. In the chapter that closes this section we'll take a look at what your profile sheet indicates and how to evaluate it.

	Never	Seldom	Sometimes	Usually	Mostly	Always	
	0	1	2	3	4	5	**POINTS**

1. Has tremendous capacity to show love.

Of all the motivational gifts, this is the one with the greatest capacity and ability to show love to others. Reflecting the nature of their heavenly Father, compassion people seem to be an unending source of *agape* love. The more opportunity they have to give love, the more joyful and fulfilled they are.

I was teaching the motivational gift seminar at a women's retreat in western Pennsylvania some years ago when I noticed a woman on the first row with tears rolling down her cheeks. I wondered if I had said something to upset her. At the next break she came up to me.

"I just wanted you to know those were tears of joy you saw," she told me. "I've been sitting through all the sessions saying, 'This doesn't fit me, nor does this,' and getting pretty discouraged. I said, 'Lord, am I going to fit into any of these gifts?'

"Then as you started to share about the gift of compassion the Lord spoke to me and said, 'This is the gift I've given you and now I'm going to enlarge your heart so that you can give more of my love to others.'

"Katie, I felt a sensation in my physical heart, just as if it were being stretched, and then I felt the love of God pour into my heart and I could see how He truly loves and cares for everyone in the world. I was overwhelmed with the greatness of His love and with the fact that He had gifted me in such a way that I could be a channel for His love. I couldn't help crying for joy."

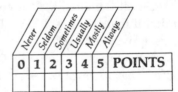

	Never	Seldom	Sometimes	Usually	Mostly	Always	
	0	1	2	3	4	5	**POINTS**

2. Always looks for good in people.

Compassion people are non-critical. It's almost as if they have built-in blinders that keep them from seeing bad things in others. Their focus remains on the good, both real and potential. Neither do they want to hear others talk about the negatives in people.

Barbara Ann Chase who served as an international officer of Aglow for several years was an excellent example of this characteristic. Whenever she would hear any of us talking about someone's negative traits she would interject with, "But that person has so many *good* qualities. Why just the other day I saw her . . ." and she would go on to list all the positive things she knew about the person.

Her beautiful focus on the good qualities of others was an important check on the rest of us, for we can always find bad points in anyone if we look hard enough.

Dixie Choyce, a lovely senior citizen in our church with a spontaneously flowing gift of compassion, shared this memory with us: "I decided at about age eighteen that there had to be something good about everyone no matter how unpleasant the person was to get along with. So I tried to find that positive quality and value it." She's spent a lifetime looking for, and finding, the good in people.

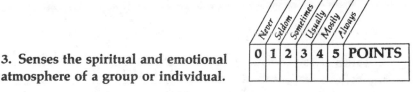

3. Senses the spiritual and emotional atmosphere of a group or individual.

	Never	Seldom	Sometimes	Usually	Mostly	Always	
	0	1	2	3	4	5	POINTS

One can almost visualize invisible feelers or antennae on the heads of those with the motivational gift of compassion. They are incredibly sensitive to the emotional status of others. They know if people are up or down, elated or blue, confident or fearful.

Jeanette told us she's always been sensitive to the spiritual needs of people. "God has gifted me with the ability to see when people are intimidated or hurt by other people in conversation. I'm automatically drawn to help them."

Compassion people are also good at reading body language. Some experts in communication have proposed that seventy-five to eighty-five percent of human communication is nonverbal. The way we stand, sit, or even hold our arms, can say, "I'm open to you" or, "I won't receive a thing you say" or, "I'm hanging loose today." On top of this our facial expressions are often a dead giveaway of feelings even when we don't say a thing. Or if we do, the tone of our voice can reveal far more than the words we use.

All of us can "read" this type of communication to some degree, but the compassion person is the expert. And since he functions in this area constantly he is more or less always in tune with the deepest feelings of others.

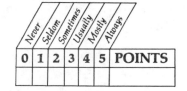

4. Is attracted to people who are hurting or in distress.

	Never	Seldom	Sometimes	Usually	Mostly	Always	
	0	1	2	3	4	5	POINTS

This is an always-present, ready-to-function characteristic of compassion people. It starts in early childhood and continues all through their lives.

They are the ones as children who brought home the lost dogs and the stray cats. They also brought home the lonely kids no one else cared for.

Our daughter Linda was that way. We remember how in her older grade school days she started to bring home some unusual new girlfriends. One was such a social misfit that we asked, "Linda, why do you want to play with *her?*"

She replied, "This girl doesn't have a single friend at school. So I'm going to be her friend!"

Not everyone understands the compassion person's attraction to the hurting, nor can everyone handle it.

Arlene tells how—when she was ten years old—she found out that a little Mexican girl in her small town had never had or even seen a Christmas tree. So she invited her over for Christmas dinner. "When Maria arrived in her ragged clothes my mother was horrified," Arlene recalled. "Mother had been raised with a lot of racial and class prejudice, and she just couldn't understand why I'd invite such a person to our home. When Mother said she'd have to leave I cried my heart out. Marie got to stay for dinner, and see our tree, but Mother was far from comfortable about it."

	Never	Seldom	Sometimes	Usually	Mostly	Always	
	0	1	2	3	4	5	**POINTS**

5. Takes action to remove hurts and relieve distress in others.

Compassion people are not only drawn to the hurting, they also do something about it.

A woman with this gift gave us a capsule definition of the difference between sympathy, empathy, and compassion:

Sympathy says: "I'm sorry you hurt!"

Empathy says: "I'm sorry you hurt, and I hurt with you!"

Compassion says: "I'm sorry you hurt, and I hurt with you, and I'm going to stay right here with you until the hurt is gone."

Mollie, a nurse who loves ministering to others, told us, "Working with the American Indians in the field of public health and midwifery has given me the opportunity to share my gift and help others in a very practical way."

Bonnie, who today works with Parents in Crisis, a support organization for those dealing with child abuse and drug addiction, tells how she wanted to help the hurting from the time she was a child.

"When I was six years old," she relates, "I used to rush home from school and go over to a neighbor's to share what I had learned that day with their little girl who was five years old and still confined to a baby buggy. She had an enormous head, the body of a baby, and a large growth on her back. I felt so bad for her, and wanted to help, and this was the only way I knew how."

	Never	Seldom	Sometimes	Usually	Mostly	Always	
	0	1	2	3	4	5	**POINTS**

6. Is more concerned for mental and emotional distress than physical distress.

Suppose you have to go to the hospital. Guess who's going to be the first to come and visit you? The compassion person will inquire about your comfort and the medical prognosis. But he will then move on to find out how you are *feeling* about being in the hospital. Are you worried about things getting taken care of at home? Are you battling fear? Do you sense the Lord's presence in this time of need? Do you need prayer?

He may just sit by your bed and hold your hand. He will literally weep with those who weep.

Sharon was so concerned about people in distress that she started a group in her church called Caring & Sharing, where people can come together and talk about their hurts and find others in similar situations.

Jacquie, who heads up the prayer chain at her church, has found herself drawn to informal counseling. "I always seem to have someone in my life who needs my emotional support. As soon as I'm able to help one work through her problems, the Lord sends me another."

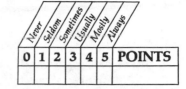

7. Is motivated to help people have right relationships with one another.

Compassion people grieve over broken relationships. They are builders of bridges and menders of breaches. They are the peacemakers. They want to see the Body of Christ united and functioning in love. They love Jesus' prayer in John 17, and work to that end.

Robin Adams, now a missionary in Japan, exemplifies this characteristic constantly in her life. While she was still living in the United States we watched her arrange gatherings in her home, bringing together people from different churches and different backgrounds so that they could get to know and love one another.

When we visited her in Japan we saw that she was continuing to do the same thing. She would invite Japanese people she had met in different settings to come to her residence for dinner. "It gives them a chance to get to know Christians outside their own church," she said. "The Japanese tend to limit their Christian fellowship to their own small group. They need to know there are many more who love the Lord, too. I love to see friendships spark and develop from these encounters. I'm delighted if I can expand anyone's vision of the Body of Christ."

We've seen Barbara Ann Chase try to bring whole Christian organizations together to work for common causes.

And David DuPlessis with his outstanding compassion gift used to visit the heads of every denomination to foster understanding, love, and fellowship among churches.

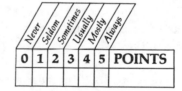

8. Loves opportunities to give preference or place to others.

These are the people who will open the door for you, let you step in line in front of them, give you the best chair.

Lynn Koontz had a 9:30 A.M. doctor's appointment for back pain. The doctor was running late when about 10:30 an elderly woman came into the waiting room, obviously very ill. The receptionist said that they were already overbooked but that they would try to work her in as soon as possible.

Lynn couldn't stand it. She got up and went over to the receptionist. "Please, let that woman have my appointment. I'll wait to be worked in."

Lynn had to wait until noon to see the doctor, but sat there with a hurting back and a rejoicing heart.

9. Takes care with words and actions to avoid hurting others.

	Never	Seldom	Sometimes	Usually	Mostly	Always	POINTS
	0	1	2	3	4	5	

The last thing a compassion person wants is to be the cause of hurt to another person. Therefore they are careful of their own actions and speech. We've seen them stop in the middle of a sentence in order to choose just the right word, lest they say something that might offend.

Dixie shared with us, "When I was just five years old I refused to choose between my parents when my father would ask, 'Which of us do you love the most?' Though I loved Mother more, I'd always answer, 'I love you both the same.'

"Then at age nine, when I had to be sent into isolation with a contagious disease, my father asked, 'Who do you want to go with you, Mother or me?' I knew I was again being asked which I loved more. So I said, 'I can go by myself. I don't want either of you to catch it.'"

Henry tells how this characteristic affected his job. "I was working in the complaint department of a department store and when customers would come in 'hoppin' mad,' instead of arguing I immediately empathized with them, and spoke to them with such genuine concern that they sometimes forgot what they were mad about. Often they would drop their complaint altogether. My boss was so pleased I got a nice raise in pay!"

10. Easily detects insincerity or wrong motives.

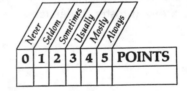

	Never	Seldom	Sometimes	Usually	Mostly	Always	POINTS
	0	1	2	3	4	5	

The compassion person's "built-in radar system" helps him to detect ulterior motives or insincerity of any kind. He will back off from a person or a group when he senses this.

Virginia had gone to a prayer group upon the recommendation of a friend. At first she was impressed. The leader seemed to be committed to praying for the world and the nation as well as individual needs. "But something bothered me about her," Virginia said. "At first I couldn't put my finger on it—it was just a little 'warning signal' going off inside me."

Virginia returned to the group the next week. "About halfway through the morning I suddenly realized what had been bothering me," she declared. "The leader had mixed motives. I think she really believed in the power of prayer, but she was also controlling the women in the group. It was not just firm leadership, she was dominating the direction of the meeting and relishing her power. I never went back again."

Jill, a woman with a compassion gift who as a child spent most of her time with animals "because they loved me so much," explained to us: "Insincerity in people bothered me as a little girl. It still does."

Shelly said, "I sense insincerity quickly and have learned to trust my impressions. Even when people come for prayer I can tell if their motives are right. I've learned to minister as the Lord directs, not necessarily as people request."

11. Is drawn to others with the gift of compassion.

Never	Seldom	Sometimes	Usually	Mostly	Always	POINTS
0	1	2	3	4	5	

Those with the motivational gift of compassion are naturally drawn to each other. They enjoy sharing with each other, praying together, just being together. It isn't that they think alike, but that they *feel* alike. They have the same emotional reactions to people and situations. They share the same concerns.

It's amazing how many compassion people have confided in us that their best friend is another compassion person. This is especially true while growing up. They often cannot relate well to those with the speaking gifts—the perceiver, the teacher, the exhorter, and the administrator—feeling rather overwhelmed by them. But they can relate well to the server, the giver, and especially to fellow compassion people.

While fewer than one percent of people marry someone with the same gift, about half of those who do are compassion people. Our daughter is married to a compassion person. Her Don (Simms) is gentle, loving, and caring. "That's why I was drawn to him," Linda tells us. "He's so good to me!"

When a person marries someone with the same gift, and the couple is immature, the negative characteristics tend to be amplified in the relationship. But we've run across several mature "compassion couples" who have what they describe as a marriage made in heaven. They are so loving and caring for each other that it's a beautiful thing to behold. Even some of these admit, though, that it was not always so, and that they had to work through a variety of problems in the early years of their marriage.

12. Loves to do thoughtful things for others.

Never	Seldom	Sometimes	Usually	Mostly	Always	POINTS
0	1	2	3	4	5	

These are the people who remember birthdays, anniversaries, Mother's and Father's Day, Valentine's Day, and find a host of other occasions on which to send cards or notes just to say they care.

If you're married to one of these, you're fortunate. A compassion husband will whisk his wife off to a dinner rendezvous more often than a man with any other type of gift. A compassion wife will serve an intimate candlelight meal more often than those with other gift types would ever think to do.

The thoughtfulness extends to every relationship. Compassion daughters and sons will be more affectionate to their parents, and vice versa. Compassion friends tend to put a lot more of themselves into friendships.

Gail was a single woman in our home group for many years. Her compassion gift prompted her to bless many of us with her kindnesses. Sometimes she would single out people just to tell them how special they were to her. How often the rest of us forget to do things like that!

We would get beautiful cards from her on Father's Day and Mother's Day, saying that she loved us just like another dad and mom. Sometimes we'd get unbirthday cards, or just a note for "no reason at all except to tell you how much you mean to me."

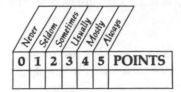

	Never	Seldom	Sometimes	Usually	Mostly	Always	POINTS
13. Is trusting and trustworthy.	0	1	2	3	4	5	

It's because they are trustworthy that compassion people expect others to be so too. They assume that everyone is honest and reliable, until absolutely proven otherwise. They can be so trusting, in fact, that they become gullible.

They are greatly disappointed when someone proves not to be reliable. But you know what? They will continue to expect the best from that person anyway. They believe in people's capacity to change for the better. Often this very expectation brings out the best in those around them. But it can also work to the compassion person's harm.

From compassion people who have taken our seminar we've heard these comments:

Doug: "I am trusting sometimes to the point of being stupid. I always expect people to treat me in the same way I would treat them. And even if I'm burnt, I will continue to trust."

Donna: "My attitude has always been that every person I meet is a good person. I still experience a feeling of shock when occasionally I find out that's not true. I'm crushed when someone is dishonest."

Cathy: "When someone I have trusted has taken advantage of me I get angry—mostly at myself for being so easily fooled."

	Never	Seldom	Sometimes	Usually	Mostly	Always	POINTS
14. Avoids conflicts and confrontations.	0	1	2	3	4	5	

Even small children with the compassion gift find it very difficult to cope with conflict. They long for peace and harmony in the home and when parents quarrel or split up, the compassionate youngster assumes it is his fault: "If I had just been a better child my mom and dad would still be together." Here's how two of them expressed it:

Ben: "When my parents fought, I found myself crying and begging them to make up. I kept telling them how much I loved them and asking them to love each other."

Ruth: "I always disliked conflict, but I seemed to be the 'middle man' in strained relationships, including my parents'. I was always trying to repair relationships and at the same time keep people from being hurt."

Compassion people are not confronters. They may hint that they are unhappy about something, but will seldom—unlike the perceiver or exhorter—address a problem straight on.

The effect of this characteristic on young boys can be a problem since they usually avoid fighting, and may be labeled sissies by their classmates.

Michael recalls, "I never fought back when bullies picked on me because I never believed fighting was worthwhile. Most of my friends were the quiet type, like me. We were the ones who played on the fringes of the playground to stay clear of the more aggressive kids."

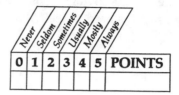

15. Doesn't like to be rushed in a job or activity.

	Never	Seldom	Sometimes	Usually	Mostly	Always	POINTS
	0	1	2	3	4	5	

Compassion people have one speed, and it's *slow* forward. As children, these were the kids who had to be pushed out the door so they'd get to school on time. They just didn't pay much attention to clocks.

How often we used to say to Linda, "Hurry up or you'll miss the school bus!" I wish I had the proverbial nickel for every time I had to drive her to school.

Punctuality remains a problem as they grow older. Given a job to do, they will finish it, but not necessarily on schedule. Somehow time just isn't that important to them. They are *now* people. They live for the moment. They figure the future will take care of itself, as long as they are about their Father's business in the present.

One compassion woman we worked with was always late to meetings. She'd show up fifteen minutes after we'd started, always with a "good excuse." She'd say something like, "I ran into a friend who needed prayer." Or, "I was so caught up in my devotions that the time slipped by before I realized how late it was."

We really needed her to be with us from the beginning of the meeting but we couldn't afford to waste everyone else's time. So, we decided to schedule the actual starting time fifteen minutes later, without informing her. Unsuspectingly, she made the start of every meeting!

16. Is typically cheerful and joyful.

	Never	Seldom	Sometimes	Usually	Mostly	Always	POINTS
	0	1	2	3	4	5	

Compassion people are positive people. The Amplified Bible says they are to show mercy and compassion "with . . . genuine cheerfulness and joyful eagerness" (Romans 12:8). They love showing love. It gives them joy to do so.

One person said, "I love being around compassion people. Their cheerfulness buoys me up."

Since they yearn to relieve hurts and encourage relationships, they are constantly working to bring the level of happiness in others up to their own and beyond. How often we all need that kind of help!

One compassionate man had the responsibility of caring for his elderly parents. Both were somewhat senile and their care demanded much of Bart's time. As a result there were many events he and his wife were unable to participate in. Yet each time we did see him he would assure us that things were going "just great" for him. No complaints. He considered it a joy to help his parents.

Robert has the reputation of being especially loving to his wife, both in public and at home. Other women say they wish their husbands treated them as well. But we notice that Robert treats everyone lovingly. His voice and manner are so gentle, and his face glows with an inner joy. It's hard to feel "down" around Robert.

Never	Seldom	Sometimes	Usually	Mostly	Always	POINTS
0	1	2	3	4	5	

17. Is ruled by the heart rather than head.

The heart plays the major role in the compassion person's life. His heart is the channel through which he shares God's wonderful love with others.

Compassion people are not what are normally tagged thinkers, intellectuals, or analyzers. Rather, they are the *feelers*. They rely on emotions rather than mental processes to guide their lives. They're the ones who could say, "Don't confuse me with the facts, my feelings are already made up." This is not to say that they do not use their minds. They do, but always in relationship to what they feel.

We'd shared our testimony at an Anglican church in Timaru, on the South Island of New Zealand, when a man came to talk with us. "What you said touched me deeply," he said, "but I wish I didn't cry so easily when I feel that way. It seems unmanly. I try to hold back the tears but they come anyway."

We asked him several questions about himself and determined quickly that he had a compassion gift. "Don't hold back the tears," we advised. "God has given you a sensitive and caring heart and He expects you to respond with deep feelings. The world needs more men who are free to care and to cry."

"You mean it's okay to be this way?" he asked.

"Of course," we replied, briefly describing the gift of compassion.

"What a relief," he said, looking as though a weight had been taken off his shoulders. "All my life I've condemned myself for being this way."

It is obviously more difficult for a man to have this gift than for a woman. Society allows a woman to be led by her heart and easily moved to tears. Not so a man. The social expectations of most cultures tend to pressure a man into a macho mold, but the compassion gift is just not going to fit. Our hope is that wider understanding of the motivational gifts will allow compassion people of both sexes to be the beautiful, tenderhearted people they were created to be.

Never	Seldom	Sometimes	Usually	Mostly	Always	POINTS
0	1	2	3	4	5	

18. Rejoices to see others blessed and grieves to see others hurt.

The person with the compassion gift has an immense capacity to identify with what others are going through. He will literally rejoice with those who rejoice, and weep with those who weep. There are times in all of our lives when we need someone to do just that with us.

Have you ever shared some great happiness with someone only to have him reply indifferently, "Oh, that's happened to me many times, it's no big deal." You wish you'd never brought it up.

But share the good news with a compassion person and he's apt to jump for joy, saying, "I'm so happy for you," or, "Praise God. I'm so glad you told me." And you are too.

Earl admits his gift just spills out. "I can just put my arms around a hurting person and feel his pain. And if someone's joyous, I share that joy as if it were my own."

There are times in our lives when we need someone to empathize with our sorrow or hurt. We don't need advice, or exhortation, or evaluation, but just someone who can sit and feel for and with us. We need someone who cares.

When Jane was in the hospital after a serious automobile accident and knew that if she did survive she would never look the same, the visitor who meant the most to her was a compassionate friend who would just sit by her bedside, hold her hand, and weep. "Very few words were said," Jane told us, "but my friend's tears spoke volumes."

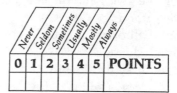

	Never	Seldom	Sometimes	Usually	Mostly	Always	
	0	1	2	3	4	5	POINTS
19. Is a crusader for good causes.							

In the eyes of the compassion person, right needs to prevail. If there is evil at work in society he strives to overcome it, usually in "silent witness" fashion, like sit-ins, picketing, peace marches, or mail-outs. Those who have more extroverted personalities or a strong secondary "speaking gift" may also address political rallies or appear on TV. But all work to bring about change.

They tend to be altruistic, not wanting any special benefit for themselves, but for others.

Shannon shared how her gift went into action when her first husband's mother died leaving his brother, eighteen, and sister, thirteen, orphaned. "My husband, who has a secondary gift of compassion, and I went to court to fight an uncle who wanted the kids separated. We brought them to live with us. The boy finished high school and eventually got a good job and went out on his own. The girl stayed with me, even after my husband died, until she married. I still like to champion a good cause."

Stan tells how he lost his job one time (in 1974) because he went on strike, not for more wages for himself, but for equal benefits for the women in his office.

We suspect that a high percentage of the "flower children" of the sixties were compassion people who could not cope with an "unjust war." The subculture they formed enabled them to venture out to champion causes in society as a whole, while withdrawing from time to time into the security of their group.

	Never	Seldom	Sometimes	Usually	Mostly	Always	
	0	1	2	3	4	5	POINTS

20. Intercedes for the hurts and problems of others.

This is the third of the seven motivational gifts that is called to and anointed for intercessory prayer. They intercede primarily for the hurts and problems they have become aware of in other people's lives.

Theirs are deep, heartfelt prayers. If you've heard a compassion gift in action at a prayer meeting you may have thought, "Oh, how beautiful. I wish I could pray like that."

They are so expressive because they feel what they are praying so deeply. It is not unusual for them to be moved to tears as they intercede. They pray with abandonment, almost forgetting there are others present, unashamed of their tears or other expressions of emotion.

Those who are drawn to become regular members of an intercessory prayer group are the perceiver, the giver, and the compassion person. Each will bring his own special approach to the gathering.

The *perceiver* will pray for the will of God to be done in nations, in churches and other groups, and in individual lives.

The *giver* will pray for the salvation of lost souls, specifically and generally.

The *compassion person* will pray for the problems and hurts of people and for unity in the Body of Christ.

It is a beautiful thing to behold such a group in action. We believe it is the actualization of Jesus' declaration:

"Again I tell you, if two of you on earth agree (harmonize together, together make a symphony) about—anything and everything—whatever they shall ask, it will come to pass and be done for them by My Father in heaven. For wherever two or three are gathered (drawn together as My followers) in (into) My name, there I AM in the midst of them" (Matthew 18:19–20, TAB).

Notice that "agree" (the Greek word is *sumphoneo*) means to "harmonize together, or make a symphony," a beautiful picture of what happens when these three gifts pray together. Just as a chord is richer and lovelier than a single note, so when each gifted person prays wholeheartedly from his unique perspective, the resulting harmony is exquisite. It touches the heart of God and produces results.

We encourage churches not to pressure *everyone* to come to intercessory prayer meetings, but to let the Holy Spirit draw those who are called. Three or four people from the three gift groups mentioned above will accomplish more in intercession than dozens of people from the other four.

This does not mean that we are not all to pray. We are *all* called to pray. But not all are called to intercession.

THE GIFT OF COMPASSION

Characteristics:

1. Has tremendous capacity to show love.
2. Always looks for good in people.
3. Senses the spiritual and emotional atmosphere of a group or individual.
4. Is attracted to people who are hurting or in distress.
5. Takes action to remove hurts and relieve distress in others.
6. Is more concerned for mental and emotional distress than physical distress.
7. Is motivated to help people have right relationships with one another.
8. Loves opportunities to give preference or place to others.
9. Takes care with words and actions to avoid hurting others.
10. Easily detects insincerity or wrong motives.
11. Is drawn to others with the gift of compassion.
12. Loves to do thoughtful things for others.
13. Is trusting and trustworthy.
14. Avoids conflicts and confrontations.
15. Doesn't like to be rushed in a job or activity.
16. Is typically cheerful and joyful.
17. Is ruled by the heart rather than head.
18. Rejoices to see others blessed and grieves to see others hurt.
19. Is a crusader for good causes.
20. Intercedes for the hurts and problems of others.

	Never	Seldom	Sometimes	Usually	Mostly	Always	POINTS
	0	1	2	3	4	5	
1.							
2.							
3.							
4.							
5.							
6.							
7.							
8.							
9.							
10.							
11.							
12.							
13.							
14.							
15.							
16.							
17.							
18.							
19.							
20.							
TOTAL							

PROBLEMS OF THE COMPASSION PERSON

26

The motivational gift of compassion is potentially both the most beautiful gift of all and the most emotionally destructive. It all depends upon the degree to which the compassion person has overcome his own emotional wounds.

Compassionate people are the most vulnerable to hurts because their hearts are most open to others. When they are betrayed there is virtually no protection, no shell, no tough hide or callousness to deflect the attack.

Of all the recipients of gifts, the compassion child needs the most love, tenderness, and adult protection. Those who receive this nurturing emerge into adulthood reasonably whole emotionally and able to cope with life's challenges. Those who don't, often require much encouragement, counseling, deliverance, and healing in order to come into their rightful inheritance of a life free of encumbrances.

We've found that the compassion person is more apt to become an alcoholic, drug abuser, or in need of psychiatric care than any other. Compassion people are also idealists who are prone to live in a fantasy world if the real world becomes intolerable.

Unfortunately many compassionate people grow up in homes where strife and unkind-nesses—even abuse and molestation—prevail. But the good news is that Jesus can heal all those hurts. Our experience with ministering to the emotionally hurt has verified this.

So, if you find you are hurting, let Jesus heal you and set you free. Often that happens even as you ask. Or, let someone else assist you, your pastor, or a mature Christian who ministers inner healing. Then you will be able to function in all the beauty and fullness of your gift.

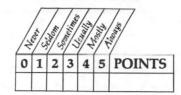

1. Tends to be indecisive.

	Never	Seldom	Sometimes	Usually	Mostly	Always	
	0	1	2	3	4	5	**POINTS**

It is difficult for the compassion person to make decisions. He will ponder the possible consequences, delay as long as he can, or transfer the responsibility to others if possible.

One young man with the gift of compassion fell in love with a young woman from our church with the same gift. The first year of their marriage was a real challenge.

"Let's go out to dinner tonight," he would say.

"Okay," she'd reply.

"Where would you like to go?"

"Oh, I don't care, you decide."

"No, you pick the place."

"I'd feel better if you did."

"I had to make the choice last time. It's your turn."

"Well, any place is okay with me."

"Just pick one, then."

"I don't want to!"

"Well, I don't either."

By this time they'd be too angry to go out together. The problem was they went at every decision this way, until finally they went to their pastor for counseling in decision-making.

This characteristic is especially detrimental in child-rearing. Often compassion parents are not willing to confront their children with their improper behavior. They hope the other parent will take care of it. Actually, they *are* training their children—to be disobedient and disrespectful.

2. Is often prone to take up another person's offense.

	Never	Seldom	Sometimes	Usually	Mostly	Always	
	0	1	2	3	4	5	**POINTS**

Because a compassion person cannot stand to see another person hurt or offended, he is quick to take up the offended person's cause.

Here's how it goes. Person A says something hurtful to person B. The compassion person observes this and joins person B in being upset with person A. Meanwhile A and B make up and restore their relationship. But the compassion person is still holding a grudge against person A.

They need to learn, first, that these matters are none of their business, except as they pray for those involved. We are not accountable for the actions of others unless we are in a position of authority with them, like a parent, pastor, teacher, or group leader.

And second, they need to learn that prayer *will* move mountains. Just as prayer can defuse the perceiver's critical attitude, so prayer can defuse the compassion person's tendency to take up offenses. He needs to give the offense to the Lord, let Him deal with the situation, and then let go of it.

Sometimes the taking up of an offense gets in the way of God's dealing with another person. The compassion person also has a tendency to be easily offended himself. He reads meaning into other people's words or actions that are not there at all.

A good prayer for the compassion person is, "Lord, help me to be slow to be offended, on my own behalf or another's."

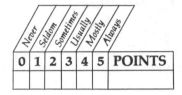

Never	Seldom	Sometimes	Usually	Mostly	Always	POINTS
0	1	2	3	4	5	

3. Is easily hurt by others.

This is the big one! No one gets hurt as easily as the compassion person. They are the most vulnerable.

It usually starts in childhood, even in infancy. One woman we counseled was an unwanted child. She was an inconvenience and her parents never let her forget it. As an adult she continued to feel she was in people's way. She would often break down and sob, "Please, somebody love me." Jesus did—in a very personal encounter—and she was healed.

Brian shared that he had a difficult home life. "My mom and dad would get in fierce yelling arguments. My heart would bleed, but I was afraid, so I'd pretend I didn't hear anything. To this day it hurts to hear people fight."

Unfortunately compassion children often assume the blame for strife between parents. They tend to take everything so personally.

Gary was only seven when his parents divorced. "I was sure it was my fault," he recalls. "Along the way I kept thinking, if only I could be a better child, maybe all this would not happen. The guilt was almost unbearable at times. It's taken years of counseling to enable me to see that I was not the cause of my parents' problems."

It's ironical, but the very people who are the best at relieving the hurts of others are the ones who are most easily hurt themselves. Or . . . is it that God doesn't waste anything that we go through—if we let Him use it?

Never	Seldom	Sometimes	Usually	Mostly	Always	POINTS
0	1	2	3	4	5	

4. Empathizes too much with the suffering of others.

This is another danger area for those with the gift of compassion. If they empathize too completely with the suffering of others, it can weigh them down and render them ineffective in ministry.

Dinah wrote to us about this problem in her life. "I always want to help someone who is hurting because I hurt for them. But I have a tendency to take their worries on myself and go through it all with them. Then I'm not objective enough to really be of help."

Dinah's answer was to remember that Jesus has already borne our sorrows and griefs. He's the only One with a heart large enough to carry them. We need to commit the suffering of the world to Him, rather than trying to take it upon ourselves.

In some cases we've even seen compassion people take on the illnesses of others. We're not to do that either. Jesus bore our sicknesses on the cross at the same time that He bore our sins.

One woman in California (we'll call her Amanda) was hurting for a friend who had cancer. Amanda had begun to exhibit similar cancer symptoms in her own body, although her doctor could find no physical base for them.

We cautioned Amanda that she must not try to take a sickness into her own body, no matter how deeply she cared about her friend. She kept insisting that she wanted to suffer with her friend. Even Amanda's husband could not get her to stop. She became almost completely debilitated.

5. Affectionate nature is often misinterpreted by opposite sex.

Never	Seldom	Sometimes	Usually	Mostly	Always	POINTS
0	1	2	3	4	5	

Because the compassion person has such ability to show love, and because so many people need to feel loved, it is easy for their affection to be misconstrued by a member of the opposite sex.

One time when we were responsible for a tour group to the Holy Land there were two single women with the compassion gift along. They wanted so much to share the love of Jesus with the tour guide and the bus driver that they took every opportunity to make conversation. Soon Don and I could see that the men were taking the women's *agape* love as personal interest. When we found out that they'd been invited to the guide's apartment Don had to put the brakes on the situation.

At first the women resented his interference, for they saw the invitation as an opportunity to talk to the two men about Jesus. He convinced them at last that he was acting for their own protection; if the men were really ready to hear the Gospel, they could do so within the safety of the group.

Sheila, a college student with a score of ninety-eight on compassion, shared this: "I have to be very careful ministering to the opposite sex even within our church's young adult group. More than once a 'brother' has fallen in love with me just because I showed some loving concern for him, and boy—what a problem. It's so difficult to be able to straighten out their perspective and not hurt their feelings in the process."

We recommend that a compassion person *never*, and we mean *never* counsel someone of the opposite sex *alone*. (In fact, this is a good rule for everyone.)

If you know some compassion people, take time to let them know you love them, and minister positive input into their lives.

	Never	Seldom	Sometimes	Usually	Mostly	Always	POINTS
	0	1	2	3	4	5	
1.							
2.							
3.							
4.							
5.							
						TOTAL	

Typical problem areas of the gift of compassion:

1. Tends to be indecisive.
2. Is often prone to take up another person's offense.
3. Is easily hurt by others.
4. Empathizes too much with the suffering of others.
5. Affectionate nature is often misinterpreted by opposite sex.

BIBLICAL COMPASSION PEOPLE

27

Those with the gift of compassion are the easiest of all to spot in action: These are feeling people and their deeds of caring and mercy give identifiable evidence.

Jesus' story of the Good Samaritan is a classic portrait of a compassion person. The setting underscores the tremendous importance of this gift. Jesus has just pinpointed to a devious lawyer that life in the Kingdom of God has to do with loving God and loving one's neighbor.

Scripture: Luke 10:30–35 (TAB)

Your Comments:

Luke 10

30 A certain man was going from Jerusalem down to Jericho and he fell among robbers, who stripped him of his clothes and belongings, and beat him, and went their way [unconcernedly] leaving him half dead, as it happened.

31 Now by coincidence a certain priest was going down along that road; and when he saw him he passed by on the other side.

32 A Levite likewise came down to the place and saw him, and passed by on the other side [of the road].

33 But a certain Samaritan, as he traveled along came down to where he was, and when he saw him was moved with pity and sympathy [for him].

34 And went to him and dressed his wounds, pouring on [them] oil and wine. Then he set him on his own beast, and brought him to an inn, and took care of him.

35 And the next day he took out two denarii [two days' wages], and gave [them] to the innkeeper, saying, Take care of him; and whatever more you spend, I [myself] will repay you when I return.

Neither the priest nor the Levite, the religious leaders of their time, showed any compassion for the man who had been robbed and beaten. Religiosity without the Spirit can insulate us from "feeling with" the people around us.

The Samaritan, on the other hand, was so full of the gift of compassion that his caring broke through the social barriers that separated Samaritans and Jews. Though ostracized by Jews, the compassionate traveler reached out to a fellow human being in need. Here are our observations:

Scripture: Luke 10:30–35

Our Comments:

Luke 10

30 A certain man was going from Jerusalem down to Jericho and he fell among robbers, who stripped him of his clothes and belongings, and beat him, and went their way [unconcernedly] leaving him half dead, as it happened.

31 Now by coincidence a certain priest was going down along that

Note: the priest had no compassion

Scripture: Luke 10:30–35 (TAB)   *Our Comments:*

road; and when he saw him he passed
by on the other side.

32   A Levite likewise came down to   Note: the Levite had no compassion
the place and saw him, and passed by
on the other side [of the road].

33   But a certain Samaritan, as he   #1   great capacity for love
traveled along came down to where he   #4   drawn to the hurting
was, and when he saw him was moved   #17   response of the heart
with pity and sympathy [for him].   #18   empathized

34   And went to him and dressed his   #5   took action to remove hurt
wounds, pouring on [them] oil and   #6   removed physical distress
wine. Then he set him on his own   #17   ruled by heart
beast, and brought him to an inn,
and took care of him.

35   And the next day he took out   #6   removed potential emotional
two denarii [two days' wages], and   distress
gave [them] to the innkeeper,   #12   thoughtful actions
                                             #13   trusted innkeeper

saying, Take care of him; and
whatever more you spend, I [myself]
will repay you when I return.

We see the Good Samaritan not only taking care of the victim's physical hurt, but also anticipating his emotional distress: coming out of his coma in an inn and realizing that he had no money to pay for his care. Truly the Samaritan covered all the bases of compassion as only those with this gift can do.

Another obvious example of the motivational gift of compassion is John, "the disciple whom Jesus loved." Certainly compassionate people are exceptionally lovable. In addition, we see John's loving, sensitive nature coming through in his writing. See how much the gift is evidenced in his Gospel!

Other compassion people to look at are:

Ruth—Ruth
Joseph, the legal father of Jesus—Matthew 1:16–24; 2:13; Luke 1:27; 2:4–51; 3:23; 4:22; John 1:45; 6:42
Jeremiah (but with the *call* of a prophet; note that he's often called the "weeping prophet")
Rachel—Genesis 29–31, 35, 46, 48:7; Ruth 4:11; 1 Samuel 10:2; Jeremiah 31:15
Rebekah—Genesis 22:23; 24:29; 35:8; 49:31

EVALUATING YOUR PROFILE SHEET

28

Now you have your profile sheet completed. Your scores have all been tallied and transferred and you see something like the following sample profile sheet. What does this all mean? How can you evaluate it? What if you have a tie for first and second place? What if there's not much difference between any of your seven scores? What if your scores seem too high? Or too low? We'll try to answer these questions.

We'll use our own profile sheets as examples:

Name: Katie Fortune	0	10	20	30	40	50	60	70	80	90	100
Perceiver								(3)			
Server					(7)						
Teacher									(2)		
Exhorter							(4)				
Giver						(5)					
Administrator											(1)
Compassion person					(6)						

Evaluating Your Profile Sheet

Here's what we see from my profile sheet:

1) My primary gift is administration. It is a high score (94) indicating that I function in it nearly all the time. It means that I am capable of and comfortable in leadership and that I organize easily.

2) My secondary gift of teaching (82) is high too. This indicates that I am also operating in that gift a lot of the time. It shows that my teaching gift is constantly modifying my primary gift of administration. It also indicates that I can operate specifically in my secondary gift, although the way in which it functions will still be colored by my primary gift. For instance, when I prepare to teach, I will do lots of research, but always with the overall picture in mind and a view to systematically organizing the material.

3) My third gift of perceiving (74) is medium high. Therefore this third gift will have some influence in my life, but not nearly so much as the first two. It is not high enough to make me a regular intercessor, especially since my first two gifts are not intercessory gifts. However, it is strong enough to provide me with a keen sense of right and wrong and a desire to see God's will done through the use of my primary gifts.

4) Close to my third gift is exhorter (72), which is—like the first three—a *speaking* gift. Therefore my communication skills are fluent.

5) My three lowest gifts are the *serving* gifts—giving (63), compassion (56), and serving (42)—which means that I am not adapted well to serving in general.

6) My lowest score is server, indicating that I am least capable in that area. My viewpoint, of course, is that I "serve" when I give myself to leadership and teaching for the benefit of others.

7) The fact that Don and I both scored low on server indicates that our home and yard will sometimes get neglected in favor of involvement with people in areas where we can both use our speaking gifts.

Name: Don Fortune	0	10	20	30	40	50	60	70	80	90	100
Perceiver								(3)			
Server							(5)				
Teacher							(7)				
Exhorter									(1)		
Giver							(2)				
Administrator						(6					
Compassion person						(4)					

Now about Don's profile sheet.

1) Don's primary gift is exhortation. The high score of 89 reveals that he functions in it most of the time. Don just naturally encourages people in every situation in which he finds himself. This is also a speaking and leadership gift, and he does a lot of both.

2) His secondary gift of giving (73) is strong, too. This has given him a keen interest in missions and evangelism and it's why he especially likes ministering on the mission field. This gift also motivates him to support missionaries and outreach projects financially.

3) Perceiver (69), his third gift, is close to his giver gift; from this combination comes his call to a ministry of prayer and intercession. He finds his participation in the early morning prayer meeting from 6:00 to 7:00 A.M. each day at church both essential and fruitful.

4) Compassion (62) and serving (61) are almost a tie for fourth and fifth place, while Don's two lowest scores, administration (55) and teaching (54) are also only a point apart. Don's teaching ability stems from his exhortation gift, not his teaching gift.

5) Notice that his last two gifts are my first two. This means we are complementary to each other in our approach to things. This makes for some interesting challenges from time to time in our marriage, but one thing for sure, we are never bored.

Don exercises his primary gifts as a home fellowship leader and church elder, in teaching seminars in many countries, in heading up missions outreach at our church, in overseeing the caring ministries like the food bank, and in counseling.

This is the kind of evaluation you can make from your profile sheet. Remember, there's only one of you in all the world, and God has designed you to be a vital part of the body of Christ.

REASONS FOR CLOSE SCORES

In some cases a person will have such close scores that he has difficulty determining his primary gift. There can be a number of reasons for this:

1. First of all, it may be that your motivational gifts have been squelched in childhood or are being hindered by some present circumstance. Therefore, another gift may at this point be taking precedence over the primary one.

2. A second reason could be a self-image so poor that you are unable to get in touch with your underlying personality and your actual giftedness.

3. A third reason may be that you are currently involved in activities or employment that make use of some secondary gift; your scoring may be influenced more by your present involvement than by your innate giftedness.

4. A fourth reason could be that you're trying to be something you're not (or trying not to be something you are).

5. Finally, you may indeed have two motivational gifts that are equally strong because God gifted you in just that way. It has been our experience that when this happens the two gifts modify each other in order to bring the balance that is needed for the type of ministry that person is to have. See the end of the chapter for more information on this.

TIE BREAKERS

If you find that you have nearly identical scores on your first two gifts, how do you determine whether they are in fact equally strong, or whether one belongs ahead of the other? Here's a test to show which gift is stronger. The questions are based on a matter of preference—yours. It is a subjective way of determining which gift is primarily motivating you.

Answer every question, even if you feel, "I really like to do both." *Make yourself make a choice,* even if the margin of preference is very small.

If two or three of your answers are (a), yours is probably the first of the two gifts named. If the majority of your answers are (b), then yours is the second gift.

This procedure can also be used as a tie-breaker in determining the relative strength of your second and third gifts, or your third and fourth gifts, and so on.

PERCEIVER/SERVER

1. *Would you rather spend time*
   - _____ a. interceding for others (or)
   - _____ b. entertaining house guests?
2. *Would you consider it more loving and caring to*
   - _____ a. help a person to change for the better (or)
   - _____ b. do something to meet a special need he has?
3. *Would you rather help a person to get rid of*
   - _____ a. sin in his life (or)
   - _____ b. clutter in his house?

PERCEIVER/TEACHER

1. *When you share Scriptures with people would you most likely*
   - _____ a. tell them if their interpretation is right or wrong (or)
   - _____ b. instruct them to study and find the truth themselves?
2. *Would you rather*
   - _____ a. spend time in intercessory prayer (or)
   - _____ b. teach a Bible study class for believers?
3. *To form an opinion about something would you probably*
   - _____ a. go by what you feel and/or believe already (or)
   - _____ b. research it until you are confident enough?

PERCEIVER/EXHORTER

1. *To be of genuine help to people would you rather*
   - _____ a. tell them to repent and change their ways (or)
   - _____ b. encourage them to get their relationships right?
2. *In counseling people do you*
   - _____ a. tell them where they are wrong and what to do (or)
   - _____ b. accept them where they are, then suggest change?
3. *In giving advice do you*
   - _____ a. quote Scripture as an absolute basis for action (or)
   - _____ b. give practical steps of action to follow?

PERCEIVER/GIVER

1. *To be helpful to others would you tend to*
   - _____ a. give scriptural advice (or)
   - _____ b. do something for them?

2. *Would you rather*

_____ a. pray for someone (or)

_____ b. provide for him?

3. *When dealing with unbelievers would you more likely*

_____ a. tell them they are sinners and need to repent (or)

_____ b. simply show them the way of salvation?

PERCEIVER/ADMINISTRATOR

1. *When helping someone spiritually would you more likely*

_____ a. tell him, "This is what Scripture says" (or)

_____ b. help him to see the overall view of Scripture?

2. *In giving advice to people would you*

_____ a. tell them where they're right or wrong (or)

_____ b. try first to find out all you can about their problems?

3. *Would you rather spend time*

_____ a. in prayer and fasting (or)

_____ b. organizing a Christian project?

PERCEIVER/COMPASSION PERSON

1. *In helping people do you tend to meet*

_____ a. their spiritual needs first (or)

_____ b. their emotional needs first?

2. *When someone is hurting do you*

_____ a. show from Scripture how to overcome the hurt (or)

_____ b. identify with the hurt, staying with him until it's gone?

3. *Would you rather participate in*

_____ a. an intercessory prayer group (or)

_____ b. a program to help the poor?

SERVER/TEACHER

1. *Do you teach primarily by*

_____ a. demonstrating the caring nature of God (or)

_____ b. expounding on the Word of God?

2. *If someone needs something would you rather*

_____ a. provide it for him (or)

_____ b. show him how to provide for himself?

3. *Would you rather*

_____ a. help set up for or serve a church dinner (or)

_____ b. speak to the group after dinner?

SERVER/EXHORTER

1. *Would you rather*

_____ a. work with your hands (or)

_____ b. speak with your mouth?

2. *If a person didn't follow your instructions properly would you*
　　_____ a. just go ahead and do it yourself (or)
　　_____ b. explain more thoroughly so he could do it?

3. *After a meeting do you feel it is more important to*
　　_____ a. make sure the room is left in order (or)
　　_____ b. spend time socializing?

SERVER/GIVER

1. *Do you view hospitality mainly as an opportunity to*
　　_____ a. serve (or)
　　_____ b give?

2. *Would you rather*
　　_____ a. help people with their practical needs (or)
　　_____ b. spend time witnessing?

3. *Would you rather help someone in need by*
　　_____ a. doing something for him (or)
　　_____ b. anonymously giving money?

SERVER/ADMINISTRATOR

1. *Would you rather*
　　_____ a. help someone accomplish something (or)
　　_____ b. tell him how to accomplish it on his own?

2. *If a room needed to be cleaned, would you*
　　_____ a. get a broom and sweep it (or)
　　_____ b. figure out who could do the job best?

3. *Do you*
　　_____ a. take things as they come (or)
　　_____ b. plan ahead?

SERVER/COMPASSION PERSON

1. *Do you care more about*
　　_____ a. people's practical needs (or)
　　_____ b. how people feel?

2. *Would you rather*
　　_____ a. help with a church work party (or)
　　_____ b. visit the shut-ins?

3. *Do you*
　　_____ a. work at a project until it's completed (or)
　　_____ b. get sidetracked by the emotional needs of others?

TEACHER/EXHORTER

1. *Would you rather help people by*
　　_____ a. teaching a Bible study class (or)
　　_____ b. counseling them with their problems?

2. *Would you prefer to*
　　_____ a. read a good book (or)
　　_____ b. be with people?

3. *Do you like to have*

_____ a. a few select friends with similar interests (or)

_____ b. lots of friends, the more the better?

TEACHER/GIVER

1. *Would you like to see God increase your ability*

_____ a. to teach effectively (or)

_____ b. to give generously?

2. *Would you rather*

_____ a. research and study (or)

_____ b. witness and evangelize?

3. *Are you most likely to be successful in a*

_____ a. teaching career (or)

_____ b. business venture?

TEACHER/ADMINISTRATOR

1. *Would you rather*

_____ a. train others to do a job (or)

_____ b. delegate work to others?

2. *Do you find that more often you are*

_____ a. reading a good book (or)

_____ b. making lists of things to do?

3. *Would you rather*

_____ a. do thorough research on a subject (or)

_____ b. organize and lead a group project?

TEACHER/COMPASSION PERSON

1. *Is your decision-making*

_____ a. based on research (or)

_____ b. difficult for you?

2. *Do you*

_____ a. keep your emotions in control (or)

_____ b. cry easily?

3. *Do you find that you*

_____ a. are drawn to intellectual pursuits (or)

_____ b. daydream or fantasize a lot?

EXHORTER/GIVER

1. *Do you encourage people*

_____ a. by sharing your own experiences (or)

_____ b. by giving them practical help?

2. *Would you rather*

_____ a. let your life be an example to an unbeliever (or)

_____ b. lead someone to the Lord through verbal witnessing?

3. *Would you prefer to*

_____ a. speak in front of a group (or)

_____ b. function supportively in the background?

EXHORTER/ADMINISTRATOR

1. *Would you prefer to*

_____ a. do individual counseling (or)

_____ b. take on group leadership?

2. *When working on a project do you tend to*

_____ a. stay with it until it is finished (or)

_____ b. delegate as much as you can to others?

3. *Do you find that you*

_____ a. adapt easily in almost any situation (or)

_____ b. get frustrated with delays and red tape?

EXHORTER/COMPASSION PERSON

1. *Would you rather*

_____ a. do personal counseling (or)

_____ b. help with caring-type ministries?

2. *Are you*

_____ a. likely to see a problem as a challenge (or)

_____ b. sometimes overwhelmed by a problem?

3. *Are decisions*

_____ a. easy for you (or)

_____ b. hard to make?

GIVER/ADMINISTRATOR

1. *Would you rather*

_____ a. assist a going project (or)

_____ b. organize a project?

2. *Would you rather be*

_____ a. a supporter (or)

_____ b. a leader?

3. *Would you prefer to spend your time*

_____ a. doing door-to-door witnessing (or)

_____ b. pioneering a new project?

GIVER/COMPASSION PERSON

1. *Is your prime interest in*

_____ a. people's needs (or)

_____ b. people's feelings?

2. *If you're working on a project when someone expresses a need, would you*

_____ a. finish the project and then meet the need (or)

_____ b. meet the need and then finish the project?

3. *Would you rather encourage people to*

_____ a. give generously to further the Gospel (or)

_____ b. minister to those who are hurting?

ADMINISTRATOR/COMPASSION PERSON

1. *When you look at situations do you focus on*

_____ a. the long-range view (or)

_____ b. what's happening now?

2. *Would you prefer to spend your time*

     _____ a. organizing people and projects (or)

     _____ b. ministering to someone in distress?

3. *Would you rather work with*

     _____ a. a group (or)

     _____ b. one person at a time?

CLARIFYING CLOSE SCORES

Here are some other suggestions that can help you make sure of your primary motivational gift:

1. Set your test aside for a few days, a few weeks, even a few months. Become more observant of your behavior, your interests, and what seems to be motivating you. Now that you're familiar with the seven gifts, you'll be more aware of them operating in your life. Then take the test again; this time it may be more decisive.

2. If you tended to avoid giving yourself fives and zeros, do the test again with a willingness to record the extremes where appropriate. Remember, it is not prideful to score a five. If you always do something, this is just a fact.

3. Look for patterns. Go over the scoring sheets for consistency within a major gift. For instance, you may have had a similar score on two gifts but on one the scores range from twos to fives, while on the other, most of the scores are fours. The latter is most likely your primary gift.

4. Look at the problem characteristics. Some people have told us, "The problem area shouted the loudest, 'That's you!'" This will be especially true if you are a fairly new Christian or one who still has a lot of problems to resolve.

5. Examine the children's characteristics in chapter thirty-three beginning on page 247. Many have said that as they thought back into their growing up years they saw their giftedness clearly. (This will not help, however, if your personality was squelched or controlled in your growing-up years.)

Some have found it helpful to personalize that chapter by circling all the traits that were characteristic of them as children. Then look to see which gift predominates.

Another device is to score yourself on the youth scoring sheets, or even the children's scoring sheets (also found in chapter thirty-three). Be sure to score *as you were at that age.*

6. Ask your spouse or a close friend or relative to help you score or even to score the test for you. He may be able to see things about you that you don't see. However, use this only as confirmation, for the person who knows you best is you!

7. Ask the Lord. This may well be the most important thing you can do. After all, He created you and He knows you best of all. If He knows (and He does) how many hairs are on your head at this moment (and you certainly don't), He surely knows the gifts that He has built into you. Remember, He wants you to be a well-functioning member of His Body. He wants you to use your gifts to help others. He wants you to have the joy that comes from using your motivational gift(s) to the fullest.

COMBINATION GIFTS

Suppose that you've done all of the above and two (or more) gifts are still tied for first place in your makeup. Accept this: *Some people have combination gifts.* This means that God has created them with two motivational gifts of equal strength because they need both for the work of their ministry.

What happens is that the two gifts *modify* each other. It is this modification that enables them to better do what they do.

Each combination produces an interesting modification. For instance, a person gifted in both perceiving and compassion will find that his perceiver gift is softened by the compassion gift. Sensitive to the hurts of others, he will not be so blunt and judgmental.

His compassion gift is also modified in such a way that he is able to be reasonably decisive and to counsel with a reliable amount of objectivity. His tendency to compromise is balanced by his perceiver's refusal to compromise—which means he will compromise only when there is valid reason.

The teacher/exhorter combination produces an individual especially suited to teaching, with the ability not only to present well-researched facts but to get them across with colorful, interesting, and life-related anecdotes.

The giver/perceiver combination equips a person to become a powerful evangelist or missionary, with outstanding success at calling people to repentance and salvation.

The server/giver combination creates a well-rounded Christian who both serves in person and provides financial support for others' ministries.

The list goes on and on. If you have a combination gift, praise God for your unique blend of equipping.

BIBLICAL EXHORTATIONS

No matter what gift or combination of gifts you have been given, the most important thing to remember is that it should be operated in love—always!

Following the list of motivational gifts in Romans 12, the remainder of the chapter is devoted to various exhortations setting forth the way in which we are to put love into action as we use our gifts. While some verses may seem to relate specifically to certain motivational gifts, we think they relate to *all* the gifts, and that we are *all* to practice the principles laid out here. Such things as hospitality, harmony, forgiveness, and kindness are both the privilege and the responsibility of every believer. It seems as if Paul has pin-pointed the most important exhortations from his own writings and other biblical sources and condensed them into a precise presentation of positive Christian conduct.

One could say that if a person—no matter what his motivational gift—were to live by these exhortations, life would be good and relationships would be healthy. The converse is also true: to the degree that we do not abide by them we fall short of fulfilling the law of love. Here is a capsulized prescription for following Paul's exhortations.

1. Love others (Romans 12:9a).
2. Hate evil (Romans 12:9b).
3. Focus on good (Romans 12:9c).
4. Practice brotherly love (Romans 12:10a).
5. Honor others (Romans 12:10b).
6. Be zealous in Spirit (Romans 12:11a).
7. Serve the Lord (Romans 12:11b).

8. Be joyful in hope (Romans 12:12a).
9. Endure affliction (Romans 12:12b).
10. Pray faithfully (Romans 12:12c).
11. Share with others (Romans 12:13a).
12. Practice hospitality (Romans 12:13b).
13. Bless when persecuted (Romans 12:14a).
14. Don't curse (Romans 12:14b).
15. Rejoice with rejoicers (Romans 12:15a).
16. Mourn with mourners (Romans 12:15b).
17. Live in harmony (Romans 12:16a).
18. Avoid pride (Romans 12:16b).
19. Don't be conceited (Romans 12:16c).
20. Don't return evil (Romans 12:17a).
21. Do what is right (Romans 12:17b).
22. Live at peace (Romans 12:18).
23. Don't take revenge (Romans 12:19a).
24. Let God settle accounts (Romans 12:19b).
25. Show kindness to enemies (Romans 12:20).
26. Overcome evil with good (Romans 12:21).

JESUS' CHARACTERISTICS

29

Only Jesus has demonstrated the complete and perfect operation of all seven of the motivational gifts in His life.

AS A PERCEIVER:

1. He spoke only what He heard the Father speak.

"For I did not speak of my own accord, but the Father who sent me commanded me what to say and how to say it" (John 12:49, NIV).

2. He was the Truth.

Jesus answered, "I am the way and the truth and the life" (John 14:6, NIV).

3. He saw into people's hearts.

"The fact is, you have had five husbands, and the man you now have is not your husband . . ." (John 4:18, NIV).

"You brood of vipers, how can you who are evil say anything good? For out of the overflow of the heart the mouth speaks" (Matthew 12:34, NIV).

4. He prayed and interceded.

Very early in the morning, while it was still dark, Jesus got up, left the house and went off to a solitary place, where he prayed (Mark 1:35, NIV).

5. He hated evil.

"It is written," he said to them, " 'My house will be called a house of prayer,' but you are making it a 'den of robbers' " (Matthew 21:13, NIV).

6. He was frank and outspoken.

"Woe to you, teachers of the law and Pharisees, you hypocrites! You are like white-washed tombs, which look beautiful on the outside but on the inside are full of dead men's bones and everything unclean" (Matthew 23:27, NIV).

AS A SERVER:

1. He worked with his hands, a carpenter with His father Joseph.

Then he went down to Nazareth with them and was obedient to them (Luke 2:51, NIV).

2. He demonstrated service.

After that, he poured water into a basin and began to wash his disciples' feet . . . (John 13:5, NIV).

3. He exalted serving.

". . . Whoever wants to become great among you must be your servant . . ." (Mark 10:43, NIV).

4. He had a high energy level and kept pace with the demands of His ministry.

Again crowds of people came to him, and as was his custom, he taught them (Mark 10:1, NIV).

AS A TEACHER:

1. He taught God's truth.

He told them another parable: "The kingdom of heaven is like a mustard seed, which a man took and planted in his field" (Matthew 13:31, NIV).

2. He fulfilled the Law.

"Do not think that I have come to abolish the Law or the Prophets; I have not come to abolish them but to fulfill them" (Matthew 5:17, NIV).

3. He quoted Scriptures.

Jesus answered, "It is written: 'Man does not live on bread alone, but on every word that comes from the mouth of God' " (Matthew 4:4, NIV, quoting Deuteronomy 8:3).

4. He built on scriptural truth.

"You have heard that it was said to the people long ago, 'Do not murder, and anyone who murders will be subject to judgment.' But I tell you that anyone who is angry with his brother will be subject to judgment . . ." (Matthew 5:21–22, NIV).

5. He was intelligent and curious.

After three days they found him in the temple courts, sitting among the teachers, listening to them and asking them questions (Luke 2:46, NIV).

6. He was self-controlled.

He plied him with many questions, but Jesus gave him no answer. . . . Then Herod and his soldiers ridiculed and mocked him . . . (Luke 23:9–11, NIV).

AS AN EXHORTER:

1. He taught people to live victoriously.
   The Sermon on the Mount, Matthew 5–7.

2. He gave positive exhortations.
   ". . . Love your enemies . . . bless . . . give . . . lend . . . be kind . . . be merciful . . . judge not . . . forgive . . ." (Luke 6:27–35, NIV).

3. He prescribed precise steps of action.
   "Go now and leave your life of sin" (John 8:11, NIV).
   Jesus answered, "If you want to be perfect, go, sell your possessions and give to the poor. . . . Then come, follow me" (Matthew 19:21, NIV).

4. He accepted people as they were.
   The woman at the well (John 4:4–30), the tax collector (Mark 2:13–16).

5. His own life was a witness to the truth.
   Jesus answered . . . "In fact, for this reason I was born, and for this I came into the world, to testify to the truth . . ." (John 18:37, NIV).

AS A GIVER:

1. He fed the five thousand.
   Taking the five loaves and the two fish . . . he gave them to his disciples to set before the people . . . (Mark 6:41, NIV).

2. He gave His time, energy, abilities, and love to others.
   He trained His disciples, taught the multitudes, healed the sick, cast out evil spirits, raised the dead.

3. He taught on giving.
   But a poor widow came and put in two very small copper coins, worth only a fraction of a penny. Calling his disciples to him, Jesus said, "I tell you the truth, this poor widow has put more into the treasury than all the others" (Mark 12:42–43, NIV).

4. He had a strong focus on the Gospel.
   But he said, "I must preach the good news of the kingdom of God to the other towns also, because that is why I was sent" (Luke 4:43, NIV).

5. He gave His life for us.
   "Greater love has no one than this, that he lay down his life for his friends" (John 15:13, NIV).

AS AN ADMINISTRATOR:

1. He organized His followers.
   (He had an inner circle of three.) After six days Jesus took Peter, James and John with him and led them up a high mountain, where they were all alone . . . (Mark 9:2, NIV).

(He trained twelve disciples.) Jesus went up on a mountainside and called to him those he wanted, and they came to him. He appointed twelve—designating them apostles . . . (Mark 3:13–14, NIV).

(He sent out the seventy two by two.) After this the Lord appointed seventy others and sent them two by two ahead of him to every town and place where he was about to go (Luke 10:1, NIV).

2. He was highly motivated to fulfill His mission.

. . . Jesus . . . who for the joy set before him endured the cross, scorning its shame, and sat down at the right hand of the throne of God (Herbrews 12:2, NIV).

3. He was a man under authority and taught about authority.

Then Jesus . . . said, "All authority in heaven and on earth has been given to me" (Matthew 28:18, NIV).

4. He was an effective leader.

These twelve Jesus sent out with the following instructions: ". . . Heal the sick, raise the dead . . . freely give . . ." (Matthew 10:5–8, NIV).

5. He endured criticism for the long-range goal of the cross.

". . . the Son of Man . . . came . . . to give his life as a ransom for many" (Matthew 20:28, NIV).

AS A COMPASSION PERSON:

1. He had a tremendous capacity to show love.

When Jesus . . . saw a large crowd, he had compassion on them and healed their sick (Matthew 14:14, NIV).

2. He was aware of people's physical needs.

Jesus said, "I have compassion for these people; they have already been with me three days and have nothing to eat. I do not want to send them away hungry, or they may collapse on the way" (Matthew 15:32, NIV).

3. He was alert to emotional and psychological needs.

When he saw the crowds, he had compassion on them, because they were harassed and helpless, like sheep without a shepherd (Matthew 9:36, NIV).

4. He cared for children.

Jesus said, "Let the little children come to me, and do not hinder them . . ." (Matthew 19:14, NIV).

5. He had empathy for others.

When the Lord saw [the widow whose son had died], his heart went out to her and he said, "Don't cry" (Luke 7:13, NIV).

6. He expressed emotion.

Jesus wept (John 11:35, NIV).

7. He mourned over Jerusalem.

"O Jerusalem, Jerusalem . . . how often I have longed to gather your children together, as a hen gathers her chicks under her wings, but you were not willing" (Matthew 23:37, NIV).

Each of us, as part of the corporate Body of Christ on this earth, has received one or more of the motivational gifts to enable us to continue the work He began here. Working together, we can (in a sense) accomplish as much and even more than Jesus did in His three years' earthly ministry.

"I tell you the truth, anyone who has faith in me will do what I have been doing. He will do even greater things than these, because I am going to the Father" (John 14:12, NIV).

Even the Communion service has taken on greater meaning for Don and me since we've come to understand how the motivational gifts tie in with it. We can almost see Jesus at that Last Supper as He broke the bread, representing the body through which He had ministered to people, saying something like:

"Here, Peter. You are obviously part of My gift of exhortation. I want you to increase in your capacity to speak boldly for this group.

"Here, Thomas. I want you to continue as the part of My gift of teaching that I have made you. Always check out purported truth by what I have taught you.

"And here, John. I want you to continue to grow as part of My gift of compassion. Let My Father's love increasingly flow through your life to others."

Jesus exhibited perfectly *all* of the motivational gifts. As His Body today we can work with Him to minister to and bless others. When Don and I take Communion now we look around at the people with whom we are joined and say with deep appreciation, "Thank You, Jesus, for Pastor Mike who gives so endlessly of himself to this flock. His gifts of teaching, administration, and serving are such a marvelous combination. And thank You, Lord, for Pati and the candid but loving honesty that comes through her perceiver gift. How we praise You for Claudia's gift of serving. What would we do without her faithfulness to handle all the detailed tasks behind the scenes? And Lord, we so appreciate John's ability to exhort and encourage people as he teaches. Thanks for Phil's giving gift: It's so good to see him bringing people to You. We are grateful for Bonnie's blossoming gift of administration and Ted's meticulous research into Your Word. And thank You, Lord, for Lynn's beautiful, gentle, and abundant gift of compassion."

Each time we take Communion we celebrate with joy the fact that each person in the Body of Christ is gifted generously by God!

PART
3

PRACTICAL
APPLICATIONS

LIVING YOUR GIFT

30

Now that you know your giftedness you can follow the commands found in 1 Peter 4:10 and Romans 12:6 to use it. You will discover what a joy it is to function in your gifts. Even if you've realized that you have been doing so naturally and spontaneously in the past, you will be more delighted as you consciously observe your gift in action in the future.

You will be able to make wise choices and decisions. You will be able to live life to the fullest, to deliberately be a blessing to others, and to accept and appreciate others as they operate in their giftedness. Truly, you will be able to know experientially the fulfillment of Jesus' prayer in the seventeenth chapter of John.

In any given situation you will be able to recognize the motivational gifts in action—in conversations, in groups, in preachers, in leaders, and in those who work quietly behind the scenes. You'll spot a person's gift as he speaks or teaches, even as he appears on television or radio. Biographies will make more sense. Even newspaper reports, if enough details are given, will reveal a person's giftedness.

We'd like to share the following example that shows how naturally the motivational gifts go into action.

Suppose that you have seven people over for dinner and each just happens to have a different motivational gift. You are bringing three salad plates to the table when one slips from your grip and crashes to the floor, scattering bits of glass and salad in one big mess. How will each person react?

Perceiver: "That's what happens when you try to carry too many plates."

Server: "I'll clean it up."

Teacher: "The reason you dropped that plate was that it was not balanced properly."

Exhorter: "Next time, let someone help you carry the plates."

Giver: "I'll be glad to help you make another salad."

Compassion person: "Don't feel embarrassed, it could have happened to anyone."

Administrator: "John, get the broom and dustpan. Sally, bring the mop. Marie, help me fix another salad."

MARRIAGE CHALLENGES

We have found that opposites usually attract in marriage. Usually one will have a speaking-type gift and the other will have a serving type gift. A perceiver may be attracted to a compassion person, or a teacher to an exhorter, or a server to an administrator—seemingly contrary gifts.

We could write a whole book on this subject (and we may!) but we'd like to say here that many marriage conflicts and stresses can be eliminated simply by coming to know and accept the motivational gifts of the mate.

Take Tim and Darlene, for instance. Tim is the quiet type who likes to work with his hands, a boat builder by trade. He is easily moved to tears, easily swayed in the stands he takes. Darlene is more outgoing, highly opinionated, unmovable in her standards, and drawn to a ministry of prayer.

There were many conflicts at first for them. Darlene would get irritated at Tim's "wishy-washiness" and changeability. He was upset with her dogmatic and unbending ways and easily hurt by her outspokenness.

Then the motivational gift test revealed that she was a perceiver and he was a compassion person. Almost immediately their relationship improved. Darlene realized that she needed to pray more and comment less. She began to appreciate her husband's sensitivity and gentleness as a beautiful gift from the Lord, and understood that he could hear from God, too.

Tim realized that Darlene's giftedness was from the Lord and that he could value, rather than be threatened by, her strong standards. He saw that it was okay for her to be the more verbal of the two.

They began to encourage each other's giftedness instead of resisting it. Differences were seen as an asset, and they have since become one of the most loving and spiritually mature couples we know. Darlene said, "I realized if both of us were just alike, one of us wouldn't be needed."

Then there's Gill and Gloria. He's a dynamic speaker type who for years tried to push his quiet, reserved wife into public ministry with him, accusing her of stubbornness and rebellion for not complying. Her attempts to talk in front of groups left her drained, embarrassed, and devastated. She, on the other hand, accused Gill of being dominating, controlling, and prideful for wanting such a visible public ministry.

After taking the motivational gift test they both repented for their judgments of each other. They discovered he was an administrator/perceiver combination and she was a server with a secondary gift of compassion. Gill released Gloria to be a behind-the-scenes support person and she accepted the fact that Gill's giftedness, not pride, was the reason he enjoyed a high-profile ministry. They are getting along just fine now.

We recommend that every married couple, and every couple considering marriage, get to know their motivational gifts.

All types of relationships, not just husband/wife, can benefit from a heightened awareness of giftedness. Use the following chart to gain insight into the people with whom you tend to have problems or conflicts. Write the names and the relationship to you in the first column. Then in the second column briefly define the problems in that relationship. In the third column list what you think their gifts might be (you may even want to give them the test if they'd be open to that) and how these relate to the frictions between you. The fourth column is for possible solutions. Indicate what you can do to help reduce the stresses. It may be that just seeing how different your gifts are (or in some cases, how similar) will relieve much of the pressure.

THE PERSON & THE RELATIONSHIP	CONFLICTS & PROBLEMS	MOTIVATIONAL GIFT	POSSIBLE SOLUTIONS
husband/wife:			
mother/father:			
brother/sister:			
other:			

Others you might list include your employer, fellow worker, pastor, leader, teacher, in-law, child, friend, roommate or neighbor.

Ask the Lord to guide you as you seek solutions. Remember, *you cannot change anyone else, but you can change yourself, both your attitudes and your actions.*

COUNSELING CLUES

We find that knowing a person's motivational gift is invaluable in the counseling we do. A polluted gift may well be responsible for the difficulty he is having. Or he may simply be in conflict with someone who has an opposite gift or in competition with someone who has the same gift. The counsel we give to one type of gift is different from that which we give another type of gift. Sometimes the very nature of the problem is an indicator of the gift. A wife who feels constantly crushed by her husband may be a compassion person. A father who expects too high a level of academic performance from his son may be a teacher parent with a server child.

Often we can discern a person's gift by interviewing him or asking a few pointed questions. We asked a man who expected unquestioning obedience from his wife if he believed he was always right about everything. His "yes" answer was a clue to his perceiver gift.

Other times we give the motivational gift test to the counselee to score at home and bring back to the next counseling session.

Here are some problems we encounter repeatedly:

Perceiver: Judgmental, intolerant, critical, prideful, domineering, controlling, unforgiving, poor self-image.

Server: Perfectionist, critical, interfering, over dependent on appreciation, won't cut apron strings.

Teacher: Prideful, intolerant, legalistic, dogmatic, opinionated, aloof, unromantic, know-it-all attitude.

Exhorter: Opinionated, interruptive, compromising, over talkative, pushy, stretches the truth.

Giver: Stingy, manipulative, too focused on money, workaholic, too frugal, spoils children, steals.

Administrator: Bossy, domineering, insensitive, callous, over-zealous, procrastinates, neglects routine work.

Compassion person: Easily wounded, over-emotional, compromising, indecisive, undependable, tardy, illogical, overly empathetic.

We can't imagine being able to counsel constructively without such clues and an understanding of the counselees motivational gifts.

WITNESSING STYLES

Most classes and seminars on witnessing assume there is a basic formula that works for everyone. We have not found this to be so. Rather, the most effective witnessing approach will be different wih each of the seven motivational gifts. Therefore we see great value in knowing something about the person's giftedness before sharing our faith. The buckshot method may win some to Christ, but how much better it is to target our witnessing.

I can remember at age fifteen being accosted by a group of well-meaning but over zealous Christian young people who confronted me in a public place with, "Are you saved?" They succeeded only in making me mad.

First of all, they were brash and abrupt. They made no effort to strike up a conversation first or give any opportunity for me to relate to them.

Secondly, the statement was threatening and judgmental. It implied that if I didn't answer yes I was by implication "lost." They were using "Christianese," which does not communicate with unbelievers—or even believers from more traditional backgrounds.

Thirdly, they knew nothing of my individual approach to new ideas, and so I automatically rejected what they said. I answered, "Of course I am!" even though I had no real idea of what they were asking. I only knew it got them off my back and I walked away thinking, "I'm glad I'm not like them!"

That encounter, far from being an effective witness, prompted me to ignore future witnessing attempts for the next eleven years. It had done more harm than good.

Here are some observations on witnessing within the framework of a person's gift that will at least earn you the right to be heard. In all cases strive to build a bridge first. Let the person know you are genuinely interested in him, his needs, and his opinions.

Perceivers will respond best to questions about right and wrong, good versus evil, God's justice, or other ultimate things: "Why do you think there is so much evil in the world?" or "How can God be both loving and just?" or "Do you know what happens to people when they die?" Depending on their answers you can lead into what you believe about these things and why.

Servers will respond to a Gospel that is practical and useful. Questions like "What is a man's greatest need?" or "Do you think 'good works' will help a person get into heaven?" or "Have you ever considered how much Jesus focused on the importance of having a servant's heart?" will arouse interest and response.

Teachers will want to know facts and the reliable basis or proof for what you share. Ask something like "Why do you think God sent Jesus to live on this earth?" or "Look at this verse. Isn't that compelling proof that Jesus really was the unique Son of God?" or "Have you ever considered the claims of Christ? Do you think they are valid?"

Exhorters are concerned with people and their problems and what they can do to help. Questions like "What's the best way to help people overcome their problems?" or "What do you consider to be of greatest importance for having a fulfilled life?" or "Would you like to hear how I dealt with the same problem you are facing now?" will bring responses.

Givers have an inborn eager responsiveness to the Gospel. Your approach can be more direct: "Do you know what it means to be born again?" or "What do you think the word *salvation* means in the Bible?" or "What is the greatest gift you can give to God?"

Administrators are interested in the overall view of life and the universe. Catch their interest with "Why do you think God created people?" or "What is the most important thing that the Bible teaches?" or "What do you think will happen to the human race?"

Compassion people will relate best on a feeling level; logic leaves them cold. Try "How do you feel God wants us to treat each other?" or "If Jesus were here today, what do you feel He'd want to spend His time doing?" or "Do you feel there is any hope for the suffering people in the world?"

You'll develop your own questions, of course. Just remember that the focal point for each gift is different. After you've attracted the interest of a person, you will find that each comes to Jesus with a different emphasis:

The *perceiver* will likely feel the need to repent and make salvation a deliberate choice of the will.

The *server* will be attracted by the good works of Jesus and receive Him because he wants to do good works, too.

The *teacher* may want to read through the New Testament to gain the facts needed to make an intellectual decision.

The *exhorter* will be glad to learn about Jesus' methods of helping people and want to be joined together with Him.

The *giver* will be excited when the Gospel suddenly makes sense and will want to witness to others right away.

The *administrator* will examine the whole story from creation to the Millennium before deciding Jesus is the Son of God.

The *compassion person* will be moved to tears of joy over the greatness of God's love for him personally.

Every Christian a "Minister"

31

Growing up in a traditional church I thought that the only person who was a minister was the pastor. I never had a clue that every Christian was a minister.

In Ephesians 4:12 Paul tells us that all of us are to be equipped for the work of the ministry, which will help build up and mature the Body of Christ. But we will minister in various ways, depending upon our motivational gift(s), our possible ministry gift (verse 11), and how we flow in the manifestation gifts.

Not everyone is called, as those with ministry gifts are, to the full-time Christian service of equipping the "saints," but *all of us are called to minister in the name of the Lord Jesus Christ.* Most of us will have a full-time job outside the organizational church or a full-time responsibility in the home. We will find, however, that there are plenty of opportunities to minister our gifts to others: the neighbor with a problem, our son's best friend, the elderly shut-in down the street, the wrong number who turned out to be in crisis, the guy at work, the discouraged woman in the prayer group.

Here are some specific instances:

MINISTRY TO NEIGHBORS

An illness keeps a woman bedridden for a month. If each of her seven immediate neighbors has a different motivational gift, how will each one express love to her?

The *perceiver* will pray both privately and at her bedside for healing, strength, and endurance.

The *server* will take over meals, offer to do housework, run errands, mow the lawn.

The *teacher* will find it hard to relate to her, but will finally take her some good books and tapes.

The *exhorter* will go right over to encourage her, and share uplifting Scripture.

The *giver* will bring food and other gifts, spend time talking and listening.

The *administrator* will find out what she needs and organize the neighborhood to meet those needs.

The *compassion person* will ask how she feels, empathize, hug, weep, and stay by her bedside.

MINISTRY IN SUNDAY SCHOOL

There's a place for everyone to minister in a Sunday school program. Not everyone will want to teach, but there are plenty of other jobs.

The *perceiver* will want to teach, especially the older youth or the adult classes.

The *server* will prefer to assist a teacher, or help in the nursery, handle the custodial work, or be the Sunday school secretary.

The *teacher* will aim at teaching the adult or college-age classes, or preparing and providing enrichment material.

The *exhorter* will be happy to teach any age and will be especially good with children and teenagers.

The *giver* will do well teaching any age, and may also want to handle finances, or promote missionary support and offerings.

The *administrator* will be delighted to be in charge, or be a department superintendent, or teach an adult class.

The *compassion person* will migrate to teaching or helping in the primary age, pre-school, or nursery departments.

MINISTRY IN BIBLE STUDIES

Everyone can minister by teaching a Bible study group. But the subject and approach will differ with each gift:

The *perceiver* will:
1. Spend much time in prayerful preparation.
2. Use the Bible as the basic text.
3. Focus on subjects like prayer, prophecy, and God's will.

The *server* will:
1. Prefer to use prepared materials.
2. Do a detailed preparation of the lesson.
3. Focus on practical subjects that demonstrate faith.

The *teacher* will:
1. Want to prepare his own lesson plans.
2. Spend much time in biblical research.
3. Prefer teaching an entire book of the Bible or a thematic topic.

The *exhorter* will:
1. Use prepared materials.

    2. Draw from life experience for illustrations.

    3. Choose subjects that help people live victoriously.

The *giver* will:

    1. Enjoy doing his own preparation.

    2. Tend to gear each lesson to win someone to Christ.

    3. Focus on subjects like evangelism and missions.

The *administrator* will:

    1. Organize materials into his own special lesson plan.

    2. Bring in resource people for added interest.

    3. Cover broad subjects from a variety of aspects.

The *compassion person* will:

    1. Use prepared materials.

    2. Be spontaneous in teaching methods.

    3. Focus on God's love and right relationships.

MINISTRY TO THE BODY OF CHRIST & OTHERS

Paul tells us in Ephesians 4:16 that the Body of Christ actually grows and builds itself up in love and maturity as *each part* does its work properly. Every person is needed. Every person ministers to others, knowingly or unknowingly.

Perhaps you've never thought of some of the spontaneous things you do to help others as being ministry, but they are. We are naturally drawn to those types of ministries that enable us to use our motivational gifts. If you don't function in your giftedness in ministry to others, there is a lack in the Body of Christ. You are needed!

To demonstrate the wide variety of service areas available we've compiled the following list, grouped under general headings, although many overlap. We have indicated which motivational gift usually ministers in these areas, but that does not mean that other gifts do not minister in those areas, too. Two other possibilities are listed in parentheses. Also, your secondary gift may lead you into areas of ministry that your primary gift might not otherwise be drawn to.

As you study this list ask the Holy Spirit to trigger ideas for ways in which you could minister.

Possible areas of ministry

PRAYER AND HEALING MINISTRIES: Perceivers (givers and compassion people)

__ intercessory prayer	__ prayer groups	__ prayer chain
__ anointing with oil	__ hospital calls	__ fasting
__ prayer breakfasts	__ praying by phone	__ prayer counseling

PRACTICAL MINISTRIES: Servers (givers and compassion people)

__ office help	__ church kitchen help	__ custodial work
__ church secretary	__ nursery work	__ repairing
__ doing mail-outs	__ organizing files	__ bake sales

Every Christian a "Minister"

- writing letters
- preparing Communion
- childcare
- financial support
- rolling bandages
- bazaar crafts
- tape ministry
- baby showers
- phone-calling
- handling registration
- advertising
- making gifts
- missionary barrels
- sports programs
- ushering
- wedding showers
- wedding hostess
- making choir robes
- hospitality
- church treasurer
- work parties
- recreation programs
- helping people move
- news releases

EDUCATIONAL MINISTRIES: Teachers (administrators and perceivers)

- Bible teacher
- workshop leader
- youth ministry
- retreat speaker
- researching
- church library
- seminar leader
- adult classes
- children's ministry
- discipling
- word studies
- book reviewing
- Sunday school teacher
- women's Bible study
- editing
- Bible school instructor
- tutoring
- teaching new believers

COUNSELING MINISTRIES: Exhorters (perceivers and compassion people)

- prayer counseling
- marriage counseling
- teen counseling
- pregnancy counseling
- encouraging others
- home visitation
- hospital visitation
- problem solving
- follow-up calls
- crisis center
- inner healing
- hotline help

OUTREACH MINISTRIES: Givers (perceivers and exhorters)

- child evangelism
- mime teams
- bus ministry
- drama
- in high schools
- political causes
- missions
- crusades
- TV/radio programs
- to college students
- street witnessing
- outreach center
- coffeehouse outreach
- men's breakfasts
- women's luncheons
- door-to-door witness
- Vacation Bible School
- placing Bibles

LEADERSHIP MINISTRIES: Administrators (exhorters and teachers)

- organizer
- emcee
- Sunday school supt.
- department head
- planner
- troubleshooter
- home group leader
- missions coordinator
- leader
- committee chairman
- Christian educ. dir.
- church administrator

CARING MINISTRIES: Compassion person (servers and givers)

- hospitality
- food bank
- hospital visitation
- food for shut-ins
- overnight guests
- clothing bank
- nursing homes
- deliver Communion
- entertaining
- prison visitation
- helping elderly
- food for new moms

— driving service
— baby sitting
— AA/Al-Anon
— dial-a-prayer
— missions
— street ministry

— crisis center
— hospice care
— assisting retarded
— prayer help line
— abuse aid
— women's shelter

— helping handicapped
— helping needy
— rides to church
— feeding hungry
— halfway house
— help unwed mothers

CREATIVE MINISTRIES: All the gifts (depends on talents and interests)

— music
— choirs
— playing piano
— dramatic readings
— trio/quartet
— translation work
— designing posters

— drama
— leading worship
— playing organ
— mime presentations
— puppetry
— interpreting
— bulletin boards

— writing
— songwriting
— church orchestra
— church band
— decorate church
— making banners
— arts and crafts

In addition to all of these personal and church-related ministries there are hundreds of civic, environmental, and para-church organizations in which you may be led to be involved. Just remember to keep your priorities straight: God, family, job, and then outside ministry.

CAREERS AND JOBS

32

One of the questions most frequently asked us is, "How do I relate my motivational gift scores to my career or job?" In this chapter we have related the gifts to 180 of the most common careers and jobs. If you do not find yours in the list, you can probably find similar ones and draw appropriate conclusions from the comparison.

But first, we want you to consider a specific way of relating your motivational gift(s) to any job you might consider, including the job you have now. Here are some general guidelines for determining how likely you are to be successful and fulfilled in a job or career.

YOUR BUILT-IN TRAITS

As part of your motivational gift you have received certain built-in traits or modes of operating. Making use of these traits is what gives you satisfaction and a feeling of accomplishment. Whenever you are considering particular employment, you should ask yourself the following question: To what degree will this enable me to do what I am motivated to do?

To assist you in answering that question we have prepared the following lists that are indicative of what each motivational gift enjoys doing. Go over the items listed under your primary gift—and your secondary gift if it's a strong one—and check off all the things that you would be able to do in a given job. If many of the items are checked, it is likely that you will be happy and successful in that work. If very few items are checked, it is probable that you are not suited to it. How much better to be able to recognize ahead of time whether or not a job is one you will enjoy, rather than to become committed to it and struggle with ongoing frustration.

Practical Applications

Statistics indicate that two out of every three people are dissatisfied with their present jobs. How sad! Many people spend all their working years doing something that fails to use their motivational gifts.

We do not believe that is God's intention. He wants us to feel fulfilled in what we do. Adam may have been placed under the "curse" of work, but Jesus has set us free to *enjoy* our work. Our motivational gifts are to be a blessing to us and a blessing to others.

Motivational gift of perception

___ admonish
___ advocate
___ advise
___ analyze
___ assess
___ caution
___ challenge
___ change
___ combat
___ convict
___ convince
___ correct
___ decide

___ defend
___ discipline
___ dramatize
___ enforce
___ evaluate
___ evoke
___ expose
___ forewarn
___ identify
___ impact
___ inspire
___ intercede
___ moralize

___ judge
___ negotiate
___ overcome
___ persevere
___ persuade
___ preach
___ prevail
___ proclaim
___ reveal
___ solve
___ strengthen
___ urge
___ warn

Motivational gift of serving

___ assemble
___ assist
___ be useful
___ carry through
___ carry out plans
___ build
___ complete
___ construct
___ detail
___ develop
___ do
___ entertain guests
___ finish

___ fix
___ follow
___ follow up
___ fulfill expectations
___ handle
___ help
___ host
___ implement
___ maintain
___ make
___ make effective
___ make work
___ master

___ meet needs
___ minister
___ obey
___ operate
___ perfect
___ persist
___ produce
___ repair
___ run effectively
___ serve
___ tend
___ wait on
___ work for

Motivational gift of teaching

___ analyze
___ communicate
___ comprehend

___ figure out
___ formulate
___ improve

___ recommend
___ research
___ search

— discipline
— discover
— edit
— educate
— enlighten
— establish truth
— evaluate
— examine
— experiment
— expound

— inspire
— instruct
— interpret
— interview
— investigate
— learn
— lecture
— observe
— present truth
— publish

— solve
— study
— systematize
— teach
— theorize
— train
— tutor
— use logic
— validate
— write

Motivational gift of exhortation

— achieve potential
— admonish
— advise
— advocate
— assure
— build up
— coach
— communicate
— convince
— counsel
— cultivate
— demonstrate
— develop

— direct
— edify
— endure
— encourage
— entreat
— exhort
— expound
— explain
— foster
  gain response
— give opinions
— guide
— improve

— influence
— inspire
— instruct
— modify
— motivate
— persuade
— prescribe
— relate
— stimulate
— strengthen
— talk
— teach (practical)
— urge

Motivational gift of giving

— accommodate
— acquire
— advocate
— aid
— assist
— back up
— bargain
— benefit
— bless
— bolster
— budget
— contribute
— corroborate
— develop
— donate
— encourage

— endow
— entertain
— espouse
— evangelize
— expedite
— furnish
— gain
— give
— grant
— host
— help
— improve
— invent
— invest
— improvise
— make better

— modify
— multiply assets
— patronize
— perform
— proclaim
— procure
— prompt
— rescue
— share
— shore up
— succeed
— supply
— support
— sustain
— testify
— witness

Motivational gift of administration

__ achieve	__ develop	__ oversee
__ accomplish	__ design	__ motivate
__ administrate	__ envision	__ pioneer
__ attain	__ establish	__ plan
__ authorize	__ excel	__ preside
__ be challenged	__ explore	__ proceduralize
__ be in charge	__ facilitate	__ promote
__ be responsible	__ govern	__ put together
__ build	__ guide	__ rule
__ command	__ handle projects	__ schedule
__ communicate	__ influence	__ set goals
__ conduct	__ initiate	__ shape
__ control	__ instigate	__ shoulder
__ coordinate	__ lead	__ strategize
__ create	__ operate	__ supervise
__ delegate	__ organize	__ visualize

Motivational gift of compassion

__ accept	__ comfort	__ nurse
__ accommodate	__ compassionate	__ promote unity
__ affirm	__ console	__ relieve distress
__ assist	__ crusade	__ relieve hurts
__ assure	__ defer to	__ renew
__ avoid hurting	__ empathize	__ repair hearts
__ be gentle	__ feel	__ rescue
__ be thoughtful	__ forgive	__ respond
__ befriend	__ give preference	__ restore
__ bring together	__ heal	__ serve
__ build relationships	__ harmonize	__ show kindness
__ build up	__ help	__ show mercy
__ care for	__ intercede	__ support
__ cheer up	__ look after	__ sustain
__ cherish	__ love	__ sympathize
__ condole	__ nurture	__ trust

These lists can also be applied when you are asked to help with a project, program, or task in your church, as well as the selection of an appropriate ministry or do volunteer work.

OCCUPATIONAL SUCCESS PROBABILITIES

We list 180 career and job possibilities, indicating to what degree we feel each of the motivational gifts will cause a person to be fulfilled and successful in these fields. We offer the chart simply as our *opinion*, based on twelve years of research and working with people in the area of the motivational gifts. We hope it will be helpful as you seek God's will for your life's work.

Remember that many other factors besides giftedness contribute to success in any field: talents, special abilities, training, education, background, emotional stability, dependability, commitment, adaptability, and so forth. A person with little gifting in an area can succeed because of his eagerness to learn and apply himself, whereas a person with great gifting in the same area can fail because of poor attitude, laziness, indifference, or unwillingness to make a nine-to-five commitment.

Some fields are so broad that everyone can find a place where his motivational gifts are well-utilized—a writing career, for example. Anyone can enter this field. However, the gifts can determine what types of writing jobs each person will be drawn to and excel in. Let's look at this field more closely to show you what I mean.

When I taught at a Billy Graham Writers' Conference my goal was not only to help writers discover their motivational gifts but also to identify the various kinds of writing in which they might be successful.

For instance, *perceivers* will do well in high-pressure jobs such as news reporting and editorial positions. Their field of interest will be strictly nonfiction. They will be good at writing articles and books that deal with good and evil, spiritual principles, politics, prophecy, prayer, character development, and spiritual growth. They make good drama critics, probing interviewers, and challenging editorialists. Their writing is persuasive, highly opinionated, and often blunt.

Servers will not be happy in high-stress jobs or in leadership positions. They do well as editorial assistants, copy editors, or rewriters. They are good at proofreading, detailed writing, and being supportive staff persons. Servers like fiction, poetry, and writing for the children's market. They write excellent articles dealing with the practical application of Christian principles, how-to subjects, and self-help ideas.

Teachers will excel in almost every area of writing and will make the finest editors and nonfiction book authors. They work well under stress and within schedules. They are top-notch curriculum and Bible study writers and do well on any biblical subject. They love research and often include generous amounts of information. They are good at writing about education, religion, science, medicine, history, and law. They write probing editorials and excellent descriptive pieces. They make good reporters and also do well with textbooks or research books. They could also be good playwrights and poets.

Exhorters will excel in writing anything with a self-help or how-to approach. Their writing is practical and encouraging and often drawn from their own experiences. They are good at biographies and nonfiction and they make dialogue come alive. Their focus will be people, not facts or places. They are among the most prolific writers and their material is exceptionally readable. They write true-life stories, inspirational pieces, how-to articles and books, testimonies, advice columns, articles on psychology, ministry, interpersonal relationships, also humor, poetry—anything life-related.

Givers are so well-rounded that they are able to write on a wide range of subjects and handle a variety of jobs. They make especially good editors and publishers. Ghostwriting is acceptable. They write both fiction and nonfiction with a focus on business and success, evangelism, and missionary endeavors.

The *administrator* will also make an excellent editor or publisher, and will do well in other management positions. Bored with copy editing or routine writing assignments, they'd rather pioneer. Their area is definitely nonfiction with comprehensive coverage of broad subjects. They will organize their material well. Freelancers will find it a challenge to discipline themselves to "office hours" at the typewriter because of their desire to interact with people. They will delegate routine writing tasks to others, if possible.

Compassion people are the most creative of all writers—with a focus on fiction, from true confessions to science fiction. They are exceptionally good with children's stories, devotionals, and poetry. Their articles and books deal with feelings, human interest episodes, interpersonal relationships, animals, inspiration, and overcoming handicaps. They are not into research, and are not suited to newspaper or magazine reporting unless it is strictly human interest writing.

Thus, there is a place for each gift in the field of writing, and this applies to many other careers as well. To identify these something-for-everyone occupations in our list we have placed a plus sign (+) immediately following them.

HOW TO SCORE

Here's how we've coded the following 180 occupations.

If success in a job is *highly unlikely* for a person with a particular motivational gift (because it would not use the person's natural motivations or because the demands of the job go beyond the capabilities of that motivational gift) then we've given the job a *minus sign* (−) in the column under the gift.

If success is *not likely*, but there could be other factors enabling an individual to enjoy this work (like a strong secondary gift) then we have coded the job by leaving the *space blank*.

If success is *possible*, especially with other positive factors entering in, then we have coded it with an *asterisk* (*).

If success is *very possible*—if that person's motivational gift would be an asset in the job—then we have coded it with *two asterisks* (**).

If success is *highly probable*—if that person's motivational gift is especially suited to the job and he would excel and be fulfilled—then we have coded it with three *asterisks* (***).

To score your probability for success circle all the three-star (***) and two-star (**) codes under your primary motivational gift. If you have a strong secondary gift, do the same in that column. Then put a check mark in front of all the occupations thus identified. Now look to see which jobs have the highest number of stars. Write those occupations (except for ones that you already know you would not be interested in) in the spaces provided at the end of the chapter. It will be from among these that you could confidently choose a career, knowing that you are well-gifted for top performance in any of them. For nstance, if you circle three-star codes for a certain occupation beneath both your primary and your secondary gift, such a career would be one of the very best that you could follow.

> **Here's the scoring at a glance. Success is:**
>
> | | |
> |---|---|
> | — | highly unlikely |
> | (blank) | not likely |
> | * | possible |
> | ** | very possible |
> | *** | highly probable |

Now proceed to circle the two-star and three-star codes under your motivational gift(s):

	Perceiver	Server	Teacher	Exhorter	Giver	Administrator	Compassion person
accountant	**	***	*		**	—	
actor	**	*	—	*	***		*
advertising executive	*	—	**	***	**	***	—
agricultural worker	*	***			**	—	*
air traffic controller	***	**	**	*	*	***	—
airplane pilot	***	*	**	**	*	***	
ambassador	***	*	**	***	*	***	*
anthropologist	*	*	***	**	*	**	**
archaeologist	*	*	***	*	*	**	**
architect	**	***	**	*	*	**	
artist +	*	**	*	*	*	*	***
assembly line worker		***	—		**	—	*
astronomer	**	*	***	*	*	**	*
auctioneer	*	*		***	**	*	—
auditor	**	***	**	*	***	*	
automobile dealer		*		**	**	**	
bank teller	*	***	*	*	***	*	*
banker	**	*	*	*	***	**	
barber/beautician		***		*	**		**
biologist	*	*	***	*	*	**	*
bookkeeper	*	***	*		***		
botanist	*	**	***	*	**	*	**
builder	*	***	*	*	**	**	*
bus driver		***		*	**		*
business consultant	**	*	*	*	***	**	—
business owner +	**	*	**	**	***	***	
buyer	**	*	**	*	***	**	
cashier/checker		***		*	**		**

	Perceiver	Server	Teacher	Exhorter	Giver	Administrator	Compassion person
carpenter	*	***		*	***		*
chemist	**	*	***	*	*	**	
childcare provider	*	***		**	**		***
chiropractor	**	*	***	**	*	**	*
city planner	**	—	**	**	*	***	—
civil servant +	*	***	*	**	**	*	**
clerk	*	***	—	*	***	—	**
college professor	**		***	**	*	***	
conductor (music)	*		**	*		***	**
composer +	*	*	***	**	*	**	***
commercial artist	*	**	*	*	*	**	***
computer operator		***	*	*	**		**
computer programmer	*	***	***	*	**	**	
cook	*	***		*	**	*	**
conservationist	**	**	**	**	*	**	***
contractor	**	*	*	**	***	***	
criminologist	***	*	**	**	*	**	—
curator	*	*	***		*	**	
dental hygienist		***		*	**		*
dentist	**	*	**	**	*	*	
department store manager	**		**	**	**	***	
dietitian	**	**	*	**	*	*	**
dock worker		***	—	*	***	—	
doctor +	**	*	***	**	**	**	**
economist	*	*	**	*	***	**	
electrician	*	***		*	***	—	*
engineer	**	*	***	**	*	**	
evangelist	**	*		**	***	*	*
farmer	*	***			***	*	**

	Perceiver	Server	Teacher	Exhorter	Giver	Administrator	Compassion person
fashion designer		**		*	**	*	***
firefighter	*	***		*	**		*
fisherman		***	—	*	**	—	*
flight attendant	*	***		*	**	*	**
florist		**		*	**		***
forest ranger	*	***		*	**		**
funeral director	*	**		*	**		*
geographer	*	***	**	*	*	*	*
geologist	**	**	***		**	*	
guidance counselor	***	*	**	***	*	***	**
heavy equipment operator		***		*	**		
home economist	*	**	*	**	**	*	***
hospital administrator	**		**	**	*	***	
hotel manager	**		**	**	*	***	
industrial designer	*	***	**	*	**	*	
inspector	***	*	**	*	*	**	
interior decorator	*	***	*	*	**	*	***
investment fund manager	**		**	**	***	**	
janitor		***	—	*	***	—	**
journalist +	**	*	***	**	*	**	*
judge	***		**	*	*	***	—
landscaper		***		**	***		*
lawyer	***		**	*	*	***	—
librarian	*	***	***	*	**		**
licensed practical nurse	*	***		**	**		***
life insurance agent	***	*	*	**	*	**	*
manufacturer	**	*	*	*	***	**	
market researcher/analyst	***	*	***	**	*	***	*
marketing executive	**		*	**	**	***	

	Perceiver	Server	Teacher	Exhorter	Giver	Administrator	Compassion person
mason		***		*	***		*
mathematician	**	***	***	*	**	**	*
mechanic	*	***		*	***		*
mechanical drawing	*	***	*	*	**		**
medical technologist	**	**	***	**	**	*	*
metalworker		***		*	***		*
meteorologist	*	**	***	*	**	**	*
military officer	***		**	**	*	***	
miner	*	***			***		*
minister +	***	**	***	***	**	***	**
missionary +	***	**	**	**	***	**	**
model		**		**	*		***
musician +	*	**	**	*	**	*	***
nurse (RN) +	*	**	*	*	**	*	***
nutritionist	**	**	***	*	**	*	***
occupational therapist	*	**	*	***	**	*	***
oceanographer	*	**	***	*	**	*	*
office worker	*	***		*	***		***
optometrist	**	*	***	**	*	**	*
paramedic	***	**	**	**	***	*	*
personnel manager	*		*	***		***	*
pet groomer		***		*	**		***
performing artist +	**	*	*	**	**	*	***
pharmacist	*	**	***	*	**	*	***
philosopher	***		***	*	*	**	***
photographer	*	**	*	*	**	*	***
physical therapist	*	**	*	*	**		***
physician +	**	*	***	**	**	**	**
physicist	**		***	*		**	

	Perceiver	Server	Teacher	Exhorter	Giver	Administrator	Compassion person
plumber		***		*	**		*
politician	**	*	*	**	*	***	
postman		***		**	**		*
printer	*	**	*	*	**	**	*
professional housecleaner		***		*	**		**
proofreader	*	*	***	*	*	**	*
psychiatrist	**	*	***	**	*	**	*
psychologist	**		***	***		**	*
public administrator	**		**	**	*	***	
public relations director	*		*	***	*	***	*
purchasing agent	*	**	*	*	**	**	
radio/TV announcer	*		*	***	*	**	
radio/TV producer	**		**	**	*	***	
railroad engineer	*	**		*	**		
realtor	*	*	*	***	**	**	*
receptionist		***		***	**		**
recreation director	*	*		***	**	***	*
religious education director	**		**	***	*	***	*
reporter	***	*	***	**	*	***	*
research scientist	**	*	***		*	**	
researcher	**	*	***		*	**	
restaurant manager	**	*	*	**	**	***	
retailer +	**	*	*	**	***	**	
salesman	**	*	*	**	***	***	
school administrator	**		***	**	*	***	
scientist +	***	*	***	*	*	**	*
seamstress/tailor	*	***			**		**
secretary	*	***		*	**		**
shipbuilder	*	***		*	**		*

	Perceiver	Server	Teacher	Exhorter	Giver	Administrator	Compassion person
social worker	*	*		***	**	*	***
sociologist +	**	*	**	***	**	**	**
speech therapist		**	**	***	*	*	***
statistician	*	***	**	*	**	*	*
surgeon	*	***	***	*	*	**	
surveyor	*	***		*	**	*	*
systems analyst	***	**	**	*	**	**	
taxidermist		***			*		*
teacher (art)	*	**	**	*	*	*	***
teacher (business ed.)	*	***	*	**	***	*	**
teacher (drama)	***		**	**	*	*	***
teacher (elementary) +	*	*	*	**	**	*	***
teacher (English)	*	*	***	*	*	*	**
teacher (foreign language)	*	*	***	*	**	*	*
teacher (home economics)	*	**	*	**	*	*	***
teacher (history)	**	*	***	**	*	**	*
teacher (mathematics)	*	**	***	*	**	*	*
teacher (music) +	*	*	**	*	*	*	***
teacher (physical ed.)	*	*		***	**	***	
teacher (science)	***	*	***	*	**	**	*
teacher (social studies)	**	*	**	***	**	**	***
teacher (special ed.)	*	*	***	***	**	**	***
technician	*	***	**	*	***	*	*
telephone operator		***		*	**	*	***
theologian	***		***	*	*	***	
toolmaker		***			***		*
travel agent	*	*	*	***	***	***	*
truck driver	*	***		*	***		**
waiter/waitress		***		**	***		***

	Perceiver	Server	Teacher	Exhorter	Giver	Administrator	Compassion person
welder	*	***			***		**
wholesaler	*			*	***	***	
writer +	**	*	***	**	*	***	**
veterinarian		**			**	*	***
zookeeper		***			**		***
zoologist	*	***	**	*	**	**	***
X-ray technician	*	***		*	**		**

Now, record the occupations in which you have the highest number of stars. You could be successful in any of these. Remember, these "success probabilities" are just *guidelines and suggestions.* Individual circumstances, opportunities, and anointing will also help determine your actual choice. The most important thing is to pray about it and seek the Lord's guidance.

Commit the choice (or change) of your vocation to the Lord. He is the one who has gifted you, and He has a specific plan for your life. Ask Him to lead you in this decision.

MY LIST OF OCCUPATIONAL POSSIBILITIES

1. _____
2. _____
3. _____
4. _____
5. _____
6. _____

YOUR CHILDREN'S GIFTS

33

Over the past twelve years we have distributed a two-page questionnaire to seminar participants in order to learn more about their motivational gifts as they were growing up. Today with over one thousand responses we've assembled a composite portrait that enables parents not only to discover the motivational gifts of their children, but also to know better how to train their children up in their giftedness as Proverbs 22:6 indicates we should do.

The feedback questionnaires were collected from a broad cross-section of people from both the United States and Canada, representing all walks of life, ages, and most denominations. Allowing for the variables discussed earlier, we've found normative characteristics that consistently show up in the lives of even young children, depending on their motivational gifts.

The subject deserves a book to itself. Here we can present only a general picture, stressing that the recognition of the motivational gifts in children makes us aware of the need to treat children differently. There is no such thing as a model child any more than there is any one type of model adult. Rather, we could say there are seven.

CHILDREN'S LEARNING STYLES

Just as the different learning styles of children have been recognized in secular education circles, so it is evident from the study of motivational gifts that children learn in various ways.

While we cannot cover the subject in detail here, we've observed that children with the "serving" gifts (serving, giving, and compassion) perform better when separated from the more aggressive "speaking" gift children (perceiver, teacher, exhorter, and administrator). The former are not competitive and are easily overwhelmed by those who thrive on competition.

When the teachers that we work with divide these two groups of children for some activities, they've seen the "server" children function much better academically and socially.

PARENTING STYLES AND CHILDREN'S GIFTS

Children with different motivational gifts require different types of care, discipline, and training in the family setting. We found that our perceiver son required about four times the amount of discipline as our administrator son or our compassion daughter. Compassion children are the most easily wounded and the most in need of protection. Yet they also need to be taught how to express appropriately the negative feelings that they often hold in; otherwise they could suffer deep emotional damage.

Teacher children will exasperate you with their questions and challenges while exhorter children will talk your ear off. Server children will delight you with their helpfulness but be hurt if you don't show appreciation. Giver children will amaze you with their frugality yet often prove to be stingy. And administrator children may try to take over the organizing of family activities, yet thrill you with their accomplishments at school.

We hope the following brief overview will give you at least some clues to enhance your parenting skills.

AN OVERVIEW OF THE TALLIED DATA

We have tallied more than a thousand responses to this questionnaire.

Please answer all the following questions about your childhood experiences and feelings as descriptively as possible.

1. Emotions: Describe your emotional makeup as a child.
2. Expression: How easy was it for you to communicate verbally?
3. Self-image: How did you feel about yourself as a person?
4. Approach to life: Describe how you generally approached life (i.e., realistically, idealistically, systematically).
5. Reality/imagination: To what degree were you imaginative or realistic?
6. Behavior: Describe your usual behavior patterns.
7. Personal habits: What were your good and bad habits?
8. Friends: How many friends did you usually have? How did you feel about it?
9. Relationships: How did you relate to peers, older children, parents, and teachers?
10. Intellect: Describe your mental capacity as a child.
11. Leadership: To what degree were you a leader or follower?
12. School: How well did you do in school?
13. Best subjects: What were your best subjects in school?
14. Reading: What did you like to read for enjoyment?
15. Sports: In what sports did you participate regularly?
16. Games/toys: What were your favorite games and toys?
17. Pets: Did you have pets? How did you feel about them?

18. Qualities: List three positive qualities that were evident in you as a child.
19. Interests: What were your general interests?
20. Joy: What brought you the most joy as a child?
21. Other comments on your childhood:

We have summarized the various responses in the chart beginning on page 247 based on the gifts evident in the adults who filled out the questionnaire. The age span covers earliest memories to high school age. While the data is typical for each gift, please remember that the child's secondary gift, the variables in life, and the freedom from polluting factors can all affect the degree to which the child may match the data.

To use this tool we suggest that you select a different colored pencil for each child. Then read the description across from each of the twenty-one categories, and circle the qualities that match one child. The heading with the most circles will most likely be his primary gift. Then do the same for the next child, and so on.

Record the information below.

NAME OF CHILD	COLOR CODE	PRIMARY MOTIVATIONAL GIFT
1.		
2.		
3.		
4.		
5.		
6.		
7.		
8.		
9.		
10.		

CATEGORY	PERCEIVER	SERVER	TEACHER	EXHORTER	GIVER	ADMINISTRATOR	COMPASSION
1. Emotions	Sensitive Intense Extremes of secure & insecure	Shy Sensitive Emotional Easily embarrassed	Stable disposition Unemotional Reserved	Happy Sensitive Balanced	Happy Expressive of feelings Sometimes shy	Stable Confident Sensitive Happy Enthusiastic	Sensitive Shy Hard to express negative feelings
2. Expression	Verbalizes easily	Verbalizes with difficulty Quiet Shy in class	Verbalizes easily Articulate Dislikes small talk	Very verbal! Likes public speaking	Some verbalize easily Some verbalize with difficulty	Very verbal Expresses self easily	Verbalization hard to easy depending on feelings Softspoken
3. Self-image	Self-image problems Negative Introspective	Low self-image Needs to be appreciated Security in doing	Good self-image Objective	Most have good self-image Positive personality	Average self-image	Average to very good self-image Basically secure	Poor to good self-image Insecure Takes guilt for conflict
4. Approach to life	Idealistic Practical Creative Can get depressed	Practical Idealistic & realistic Oriented toward doing	Realistic Idealistic Practical Searcher for truth	Idealistic Creative Realistic Practical Adaptable	Balanced between realistic & idealistic Wholehearted	Practical Systematic Creative Wide areas of interest	Idealistic Creative Subjective Loving Peacemaker
5. Reality/ imagination	Can be both but mostly imaginative	Excellent imagination Good at pretending Realistic	Very realistic Poor imagination	Imaginative and also practical	Very imaginative	Both realistic & imaginative	Very imaginative Daydreamer

CATEGORY	PERCEIVER	SERVER	TEACHER	EXHORTER	GIVER	ADMINISTRATOR	COMPASSION
6. Behavior	Obedient Extremes of good/bad Very strong-willed	Obedient Quiet Likes to do things on own terms	Obedient Independent Entertains self easily	Obedient Outgoing Adaptable	Obedient Industrious	Obedient Gregarious Competitive Pleasing	Obedient Loving Indecisive Crusader for good causes
7. Personal habits	Dependable Wants to be right! Tattletale	Neat, tidy Helpful Completes projects	Neat Good study habits Punctual Intolerant	Neat, clean Helpful Accepting Not saver Interrupts	Neat Helpful Friendly Makes money Saves money	Studious Plans ahead Saves things Procrastinates	Neat, clean Helpful Unorganized Not punctual
8. Friends	Few or no friends Loner	Only a few friends	Just a few friends Often a loner	Many friends Gregarious Joiner Well-liked	Just a few friends Supportive	Average to many friends Likes large groups Joiner	A few close friends Drawn to friendless
9. Relationships	Relates best to adults & teachers Relates poorly to peers	Relates best to parents & teachers Good to teachers Shy toward peers	Relates best to parents & teachers Some difficulty with peers	Relates well to everyone	Relates well to everyone	Relates very well to all Tends toward broad relationships	Relates best to adults & teachers Average to peers
10. Intellect	Above average	Average to good Good at details	Very intelligent Highest IQ's Investigative	Above average to excellent	Average to good	Good to excellent Investigative	Average to above average Concern for feelings

CATEGORY	PERCEIVER	SERVER	TEACHER	EXHORTER	GIVER	ADMINISTRATOR	COMPASSION
11. Leadership	Can be either leader or follower	Follower Prefers smaller groups	Some are leaders	Mostly leaders	Primarily follower Sometimes will lead	Excellent leader Organizer Delegates	Follower Occasionally will lead
12. School	Above average Focuses on facts and truths	Average to good Meticulous	Excellent student! Self-motivated Over-prepares	Above average	Average to good	Excellent student Excels Enjoys a challenge	Average to above average
13. Best subjects	1. English 2. Math 3. History 4. Art 5. Drama	1. Math 2. English 3. History 4. Science 5. Home Ec/shop	1. History 2. English 3. Good in all subjects	1. English 2. Math 3. History 4. Likes most subjects	1. English 2. Math 3. Business 4. History	1. English 2. Math 3. History 4. Good in all subjects	1. English 2. Math 3. Art/music 4. History
14. Reading	1. Biography 2. Romance 3. Adventure 4. Mystery	1. Adventure 2. Mystery 3. Romance 4. Historical novel	1. Prolific reader 2. Historical novel 3. Mystery	1. Biography 2. Fiction 3. Nonfiction	1. Loves to read 2. Fiction 3. Adventure 4. Animal	1. Wide range of interests 2. Mystery 3. Biography	1. Romance 2. Mystery 3. Fairy tale & fantasy 4. Animal
15. Sports	Prefers individual sports—swim, ski, bicycle	Group sports Non-competitive sports—swim, skate Some: none	Not much interest Prefers watching or books	Loves active sports Group sports Swimming	Most like group sports Some don't like any sports	Group sports Competitive sports	No sports or non-competitive sports

CATEGORY	PERCEIVER	SERVER	TEACHER	EXHORTER	GIVER	ADMINISTRATOR	COMPASSION
16. Games & toys	Makes up own games Plays alone Toys—real things	Card games Table games Manual skill & crafts Puzzles	Table games Active games Prefers books	Active games Group games Toys with a purpose—ball, skates	Outdoor games Construction toys Creative play	Table games Group games Creative play	Table games Card games Quiet imaginative play
17. Pets	Loves pets	Loves pets Feels they are special friends	Indifferent about pets Would rather read a book	Likes them but prefers people	Enjoys pets but people even more	Loves pets but not the routine care	Adores pets They are their friends Brings home strays
18. Qualities	1. Sensitive 2. Honest 3. Loyal 4. Responsible	1. Helpful 2. Reliable 3. Sensitive 4. Obedient	1. Diligent 2. Dependable 3. Considerate 4. Perfectionist	1. Friendly 2. Loving 3. Obedient 4. Happy	1. Helpful 2. Kind 3. Honest 4. Thrifty	1. Capable 2. Responsible 3. Honest 4. Gregarious	1. Loving 2. Caring 3. Helpful 4. Obedient
19. Interests	1. Reading 2. Sports 3. Music	1. Handwork 2. Animals 3. Homemaking skills/build/fix	1. Reading 2. Studying 3. The arts	1. People 2. Outdoor activities 3. Reading	1. Reading 2. Friends 3. Domestic 4. Make money	1. Wide areas of interest 2. Doing with others 3. Reading	1. Music/Art 2. Reading 3. People
20. Joy	1. Family activities 2. Nature 3. "Being"	1. Family activities 2. Appreciation 3. Serving	1. Family activities 2. Learning 3. Being accepted	1. Family activities 2. Making others happy 3. People	1. Family activities 2. Helping others 3. Travel	1. Family activities 2. Accomplishments 3. People	1. Family activities 2. Friendships 3. Being appreciated
21. Other	Strong conscience Opinionated Blunt	Good dexterity Not college-oriented	Bookworm Teacher's pet	Encourager Gives lots of advice	All-around personality Gives generously	Makes lists Writes notes Plans	Easily hurt Easily moved to tears

TESTING SHEETS DESIGNED FOR CHILDREN

Through teaching about motivational gifts in Christian schools, from primary grades through high school, we have gained much insight in actually testing students at various levels. This, along with the information gleaned over the years from the survey feedback sheets, is the basis for the children's questionnaire on pages 252–259.

It is designed for young people from nine to twelve years old, or grades four through six. The testing should be done with the help of a parent or teacher. Some concepts are just too difficult to put into simple language and will need some explanation on the part of the assisting adult.

Notice that the scoring is somewhat simplified. Only five options are given: never (0), seldom (1), sometimes (2), usually (3), and always (4). Explain that the child is to score according to how true the statement is about himself. Total the scores and shade them in from left to right on the profile sheet. Parents may want to retest their children every year or so. The older the child the more reliable the test scores usually are.

TESTING SHEETS DESIGNED FOR YOUTH

We have especially enjoyed working with teenagers, in school settings and church groups as well as individually. We find they are very eager to know about themselves. And, since they are at an age where they are making life long career decisions, it is especially helpful for them to discover their motivational gifts.

It also helps them to build an acceptable self-image and to understand some of the teenage problems and stresses they are going through. It helps them with their interpersonal relationships with peers and parents, and to be able to make more responsible decisions in the future, including the choice of a mate. So often adults say, "Oh, how I wish I had known about the gifts when I was a teenager." We would personally love to see every teenager discover his motivational gift.

(College students can use this test, found on pages 260–267, or the adult one.)

The scoring procedure is the same as the adult one described in chapter six. Remember that the negative characteristics do *not* go on the profile sheet. They're to be scored just for the young person's own information and to provide an indicator of areas that need prayer and maturing.

Additional copies of the children's and youth questionnaires are available. See page 275.

Children's Questionnaire

CHILDREN'S MOTIVATIONAL GIFT PROFILE SHEET

Gift	0	10	20	30	40	50	60	70	80	90	100
Perceiver											
Server											
Teacher											
Exhorter											
Giver											
Administrator											
Compassion Person											

NAME _____   #1 GIFT _____

AGE _____ GRADE _____ DATE _____   #2 GIFT _____

PARENT/TEACHER _____   #3 GIFT _____

© Copyright 1987, Don & Katie Fortune

252

	Never	Seldom	Sometimes	Usually	Mostly	Always	POINTS
	0	1	2	3	4	5	
1.							
2.							
3.							
4.							
5.							
6.							
7.							
8.							
9.							
10.							
11.							
12.							
13.							
14.							
15.							
16.							
17.							
18.							
19.							
20.							
21.							
22.							
23.							
24.							
25.							
						TOTAL	

GIFT OF PERCEPTION

Children's Questionnaire

1. My greatest joy is seeing God's will being done.
2. I want to help people do what is right.
3. I'm so idealistic that I can get depressed easily.
4. I'm always trying to analyze myself.
5. My emotions seem to go from one extreme to the other.
6. It's easy for me to talk because what I say is the truth.
7. I am strong-willed.
8. I always know what God wants me to do.
9. I am basically a loner with few or no friends.
10. I'd rather be around adults than others my own age.
11. I would usually rather be a leader than a follower.
12. I do above-average work in school.
13. I prefer to read biographies.
14. I am very dependable.
15. I like active individual sports best.
16. I prefer real things to toys.
17. I have a strong conscience.
18. I see things as black or white, good or evil, right or wrong.
19. I can easily sense the character of others.
20. I see problems as opportunities for growth.
21. I am frank and outspoken.
22. I view the Bible as the basis for truth.
23. My opinions are strong and right.
24. I get very sad over the sins of others.
25. I feel God wants me to spend much time praying for others.

253

	Never	Seldom	Sometimes	Usually	Mostly	Always	POINTS
	0	1	2	3	4	5	
1.							
2.							
3.							
4.							
5.							
6.							
7.							
8.							
9.							
10.							
11.							
12.							
13.							
14.							
15.							
16.							
17.							
18.							
19.							
20.							
21.							
22.							
23.							
24.							
25.							
TOTAL							

Children's Questionnaire

THE GIFT OF SERVING

1. My greatest joy is doing things for others.
2. I like to do things with my hands.
3. I am very realistic and practical.
4. I need appreciation in order to feel good about myself.
5. I am shy and easily embarrassed.
6. I don't like to speak in front of a class.
7. I like to do things the way I like to do them.
8. I'm good at imitating and pretending.
9. I have just a few close friends.
10. I feel more comfortable around my parents than other kids.
11. I would rather be a follower than a leader.
12. I am an average student and good at details.
13. I prefer to read adventure stories.
14. I am very helpful.
15. I prefer noncompetitive sports.
16. I love to work on things like crafts, collections, and puzzles.
17. I am especially good with my hands.
18. I am very neat.
19. I always want to finish what I start.
20. I have a hard time saying no when asked to help.
21. I usually do more than I'm asked to do.
22. I'd rather work on a short project than a long one.
23. I want everything I do to be perfect.
24. I show love for others by what I do for them.
25. I always have lots of energy.

	Never	Seldom	Sometimes	Usually	Mostly	Always	POINTS
	0	1	2	3	4	5	
1.							
2.							
3.							
4.							
5.							
6.							
7.							
8.							
9.							
10.							
11.							
12.							
13.							
14.							
15.							
16.							
17.							
18.							
19.							
20.							
							TOTAL

Children's Questionnaire

THE GIFT OF TEACHING

1. My greatest joy is learning.
2. I'd rather read a book than anything else.
3. I love to search for truth.
4. I am very objective about myself.
5. My emotions are very stable.
6. I can speak easily and well.
7. I am very independent.
8. It's hard for me to pretend or to use my imagination.
9. I have a few friends but also enjoy being alone.
10. I'd rather be with my parents or teacher than with other kids.
11. I enjoy being a leader.
12. I am an excellent student.
13. I love to read books on almost any subject.
14. I am always on time.
15. I'm really not interested in sports.
16. I prefer word games.
17. I am a bookworm.
18. I like things like operas, art, music, and ballet.
19. I love to study and do research.
20. I like things to be logical, systematic, and organized.
21. I like to develop and use a large vocabulary.
22. I believe Scriptures should always be used in the right context.
23. I believe truth has the power to change people.
24. I have strong convictions and opinions.
25. I am self-disciplined.

	Never	Seldom	Sometimes	Usually	Mostly	Always	POINTS
	0	1	2	3	4	5	
1.							
2.							
3.							
4.							
5.							
6.							
7.							
8.							
9.							
10.							
11.							
12.							
13.							
14.							
15.							
16.							
17.							
18.							
19.							
20.							
21.							
22.							
23.							
24.							
25.							
TOTAL							

Children's Questionnaire

THE GIFT OF EXHORTATION

1. My greatest joy is encouraging others.
2. I'd rather be with people than anything else.
3. I am very adaptable.
4. I have a positive personality.
5. I am a happy person.
6. I absolutely love to talk.
7. I always look for ways to make tasks easier.
8. I am very practical about everything.
9. I have lots of friends.
10. I get along well with my parents, teachers, and all my friends.
11. I enjoy being either a leader or a follower.
12. I am an above-average student.
13. I prefer to read biographies.
14. I'm very accepting of others.
15. I like active and group sports.
16. I like toys with a purpose.
17. I am not good with my hands.
18. I love to show others how to be happy.
19. I prefer to learn about things I can apply in my daily life.
20. I believe that truth is best learned in everyday experience.
21. I love to help others solve their problems.
22. I think problems help me grow and develop character.
23. I clear up problems with others as quickly as possible.
24. I find that others like me because I'm so positive.
25. I prefer to share the Lord by how I live rather than by what I say.

© *Copyright 1987, Don & Katie Fortune*

	Never	Seldom	Sometimes	Usually	Mostly	Always	POINTS
	0	1	2	3	4	5	
1.							
2.							
3.							
4.							
5.							
6.							
7.							
8.							
9.							
10.							
11.							
12.							
13.							
14.							
15.							
16.							
17.							
18.							
19.							
20.							
21.							
22.							
23.							
24.							
25.							
						TOTAL	

Children's Questionnaire

THE GIFT OF GIVING

1. My greatest joy is giving to help others.
2. I do everything I can to witness to others.
3. I try to live my life wholeheartedly.
4. I think I am about average in how I feel about myself.
5. I am a happy person.
6. I am about average in my ability to express myself.
7. I am industrious.
8. I have a good imagination.
9. I have a few friends and I'm very supportive of them.
10. I enjoy everyone.
11. I usually prefer to be a follower rather than a leader.
12. I am usually a good student.
13. I love to read, especially fictional stories.
14. I am good at making and saving money.
15. I have about an average interest in sports.
16. I like toys and games that are constructive.
17. I believe in giving a tithe and even more if possible.
18. I like to give quietly, without others knowing about it.
19. I am delighted when my gift is an answer to prayer.
20. I want my gifts to be the best I can make or buy.
21. I pray often for those who are sharing the Gospel a lot.
22. I love to help entertain visitors in our home.
23. I am quick to help whenever I see a need for help.
24. I'm not gullible.
25. I think I have an all-around personality.

POINTS	Never	Seldom	Sometimes	Usually	Mostly	Always	POINTS												
	0	1	2	3	4	5													
1.																			
2.																			
3.																			
4.																			
5.																			
6.																			
7.																			
8.																			
9.																			
10.																			
11.																			
12.																			
13.																			
14.																			
15.																			
16.																			
17.																			
18.																			
19.																			
20.																			
21.																			
22.																			
23.																			
24.																			
25.																			
TOTAL																			

Children's Questionnaire

THE GIFT OF ADMINISTRATION

1. My greatest joy comes in accomplishing something.
2. I have a wide area of interests.
3. I love to plan and to work on projects.
4. I am basically self-accepting.
5. I am confident and enthusiastic about whatever I do.
6. It's easy for me to express myself.
7. I always want to be first or best.
8. I can be either realistic or imaginative, depending on the situation.
9. I have many friends and enjoy large groups.
10. I feel I get along well with parents, teachers, and friends.
11. I love to be a leader and to organize.
12. I am an excellent student who enjoys a challenge.
13. I love to read on a wide range of subjects.
14. I have to admit that my room is usually untidy.
15. I love competitive sports.
16. I like group games.
17. I'm always making lists and writing notes to myself.
18. I've always felt it's important to obey authority.
19. I'm quick to take a leadership role if no one else will.
20. It's easy to see the overall picture and set long-range goals.
21. I do not enjoy doing routine tasks.
22. I like to be in charge and tell others what to do.
23. I'm willing to take criticism in order to get something done.
24. I'll work hard to get something done even if another gets the credit.
25. I really enjoy working with people.

© Copyright 1987, Don & Katie Fortune.

POINTS	Never 0	Seldom 1	Sometimes 2	Usually 3	Mostly 4	Always 5
1.						
2.						
3.						
4.						
5.						
6.						
7.						
8.						
9.						
10.						
11.						
12.						
13.						
14.						
15.						
16.						
17.						
18.						
19.						
20.						
21.						
22.						
23.						
24.						
25.						
TOTAL						

Children's Questionnaire

THE GIFT OF COMPASSION

1. My greatest joy is showing love to those who are hurting.
2. I want to make sure everyone feels good.
3. I'm so idealistic that I'm sometimes unrealistic.
4. I don't always feel good about myself.
5. I am shy and quiet.
6. I am very softspoken.
7. It's hard for me to stand up for my own rights.
8. I am a daydreamer.
9. I try to be a friend to those who have no friends.
10. I am eager to please everyone.
11. I would rather be a follower than a leader.
12. I am an average student.
13. I love to read romance, fantasy, or mystery stories.
14. I am very loving.
15. I prefer noncompetitive sports or none at all.
16. I enjoy quiet imaginative play and games.
17. I realize that I am easily hurt.
18. I am eager to help people who are hurting on the inside.
19. I always look for the good in people and ignore the bad.
20. I want everyone to get along with everyone else.
21. It's easy for me to tell when someone is insincere.
22. I am very trusting of others.
23. I feel happy when others are happy and sad when others are sad.
24. I often pray for those who have needs or who hurt.
25. I don't like to be rushed in what I do.

Youth Questionnaire

YOUTH MOTIVATIONAL GIFT PROFILE SHEET

Gift	0	10	20	30	40	50	60	70	80	90	100
Perceiver											
Server											
Teacher											
Exhorter											
Giver											
Administrator											
Compassion											

NAME _____

AGE _____ GRADE _____ DATE _____

CLASS/GROUP _____

#1 GIFT _____

#2 GIFT _____

#3 GIFT _____

© *Copyright 1987, Don & Katie Fortune.*

260

Youth Questionnaire

THE GIFT OF PERCEPTION

	Never	Seldom	Sometimes	Usually	Mostly	Always	POINTS
	0	1	2	3	4	5	
1.							
2.							
3.							
4.							
5.							
6.							
7.							
8.							
9.							
10.							
11.							
12.							
13.							
14.							
15.							
16.							
17.							
18.							
19.							
20.							
						TOTAL	

Characteristics:

1. Quickly sees what is good or evil and hates evil.
2. Sees everything as either right or wrong.
3. Can easily tell the character of others.
4. Encourages others to be sorry for doing wrong.
5. Believes problems and difficulties can produce spiritual growth.
6. Has only a few or no close friendships.
7. Views the Bible as the basis for truth, belief, and action.
8. Boldly lives by spiritual principles.
9. Is frank, outspoken, and doesn't have much tact.
10. Is very convincing with words.
11. Feels bad when others sin.
12. Is eager to see his own blind spots and help others see theirs, too.
13. Desires above all else to see God's will done in everything.
14. Loves to encourage the spiritual growth of others.
15. Prays a lot for others and for God's will to be done.
16. Likes to dramatize what he "sees."
17. Looks inside self a lot.
18. Has strong opinions and beliefs.
19. Has strict personal standards.
20. Feels strong desire to be obedient to God.

Typical problem areas:

						TOTAL
1.						
2.						
3.						
4.						
5.						

1. Tends to be judgmental and blunt.
2. Forgets to praise others for accomplishments.
3. Pushy in trying to get others to grow spiritually.
4. Doesn't like opinions and views that differ from his own.
5. Struggles with self-image problems.

Youth Questionnaire

THE GIFT OF SERVING

Characteristics:

1. Is quick to meet the needs of others.
2. Especially enjoys working with hands.
3. Keeps everything neat and in order.
4. Remembers details easily.
5. Enjoys having people at his house.
6. Wants to complete what is started.
7. Has a hard time saying no to requests for help.
8. Is more interested in meeting the needs of others than own needs.
9. Enjoys working on projects that can be finished in a short time.
10. Shows love for others in deeds and actions more than words.
11. Needs to feel appreciated.
12. Tends to do more than asked to do.
13. Finds highest joy in doing something that is helpful to someone.
14. Does not want to lead others.
15. Has a high energy level.
16. Cannot stand to be around clutter.
17. Wants everything to be perfect.
18. Thinks serving is the most important thing in life.
19. Would rather do a job than ask someone else to do it.
20. Likes to help others who are in leadership get the job done.

	Never	Seldom	Sometimes	Usually	Mostly	Always	POINTS
	0	1	2	3	4	5	
1.							
2.							
3.							
4.							
5.							
6.							
7.							
8.							
9.							
10.							
11.							
12.							
13.							
14.							
15.							
16.							
17.							
18.							
19.							
20.							

TOTAL

Typical problem areas:

1. Upset with others who do not offer to help out with needs.
2. May forget to help family by being too busy helping others.
3. May become pushy in eagerness to help.
4. Hard to accept being served by others.
5. Easily hurt when not appreciated.

1.	
2.	
3.	
4.	
5.	

TOTAL

© Copyright 1987, Don & Katie Fortune,

	Never	Seldom	Sometimes	Usually	Mostly	Always	POINTS
	0	1	2	3	4	5	
1.							
2.							
3.							
4.							
5.							
6.							
7.							
8.							
9.							
10.							
11.							
12.							
13.							
14.							
15.							
16.							
17.							
18.							
19.							
20.							

TOTAL

1.	
2.	
3.	
4.	
5.	

TOTAL

Youth Questionnaire

THE GIFT OF TEACHING

Characteristics:

1. Likes to present truth in a logical way.
2. Always likes to check out the facts.
3. Enjoys studying.
4. Enjoys learning the meaning of words.
5. Likes to use biblical illustrations to make a point.
6. Does not like Scripture to be used out-of-context.
7. Wants truth to be established in every situation.
8. Able to analyze without personal feelings getting in the way.
9. Easily develops and uses a large vocabulary.
10. Believes facts are more important than feelings.
11. Always wants to be sure that what is learned is true.
12. Prefers helping believers grow as opposed to witnessing.
13. Feels this gift is the best one for a strong Christian life.
14. Solves problems by using principles found in the Bible.
15. An excellent student.
16. Self-disciplined.
17. Emotionally self-controlled.
18. Has only a few close friends.
19. Has strong beliefs and opinions.
20. Believes truth has the power to produce change in people.

Typical problem areas:

1. Tends to forget to apply truth in practical ways.
2. Slow to accept viewpoints of others.
3. Tends to feel smarter than most others the same age.
4. Tends to be a "know-it-all."
5. Easily sidetracked by new interests.

	Never	Seldom	Sometimes	Usually	Mostly	Always	POINTS
	0	1	2	3	4	5	
1.							
2.							
3.							
4.							
5.							
6.							
7.							
8.							
9.							
10.							
11.							
12.							
13.							
14.							
15.							
16.							
17.							
18.							
19.							
20.							

TOTAL

1.	
2.	
3.	
4.	
5.	

TOTAL

Youth Questionnaire

THE GIFT OF EXHORTATION

Characteristics:

1. Loves to encourage others to live fully and happily.
2. Watches for the response of others when speaking.
3. Would rather apply truth than research it.
4. Prefers learning things that can be used in practical ways.
5. Loves to tell others what to do in order to grow.
6. Loves to work with people.
7. Encourages others to develop in their ability to help others.
8. Finds truth most often in experience.
9. Loves to help others with their problems.
10. Will stop helping others with their problems if they don't change.
11. Prefers teaching that can be applied to life.
12. Believes trials and problems can help people grow.
13. Accepts people as they are.
14. Is positive about everything.
15. Prefers to witness through the way he lives his life rather than talking about it.
16. Makes decisions easily.
17. Completes what is started.
18. Wants to clear up problems with others quickly.
19. Expects a lot of self and others.
20. Needs a close friend to share ideas and thoughts with.

Typical problem areas:

1. Tends to interrupt others in eagerness to give opinions.
2. Will use Scriptures out-of-context in order to make a point.
3. May tend to give the same advice again and again.
4. Speaks out boldly on opinions and ideas.
5. Can be too self-confident.

264

	Never	Seldom	Sometimes	Usually	Mostly	Always	POINTS
	0	1	2	3	4	5	
1.							
2.							
3.							
4.							
5.							
6.							
7.							
8.							
9.							
10.							
11.							
12.							
13.							
14.							
15.							
16.							
17.							
18.							
19.							
20.							
							TOTAL

1.				
2.				
3.				
4.				
5.				
				TOTAL

THE GIFT OF GIVING

Characteristics:

1. Gives freely of money, things, time, and love.
2. Loves to give quietly, without others knowing about it.
3. Wants to feel a part of the ministry he gives to.
4. Prays a lot for the salvation of others.
5. Delighted when his gift is an answer to someone's prayer.
6. Wants gifts to be the best he can give.
7. Gives only by the leading of the Holy Spirit.
8. Gives to support and bless others or to help a ministry.
9. Sees having people in his home as an opportunity to give.
10. Has ability to handle money wisely and well.
11. Quick to help where a need is seen.
12. Prays about the amount to give.
13. Believes in tithing and in giving more besides.
14. Loves to share the Gospel more than anything else.
15. Believes God will take care of all his needs.
16. Works hard to earn money so more can be given away.
17. Good at making money.
18. Careful not to waste money on self.
19. Not easily fooled.
20. Has both natural and God-given wisdom.

Typical problem areas:

1. May try to control how money given is used.
2. Pushy in trying to get others to give.
3. May upset others who do not understand how and why he gives.
4. May spoil someone by giving too much.
5. May become stingy.

	Never	Seldom	Sometimes	Usually	Mostly	Always	POINTS
	0	1	2	3	4	5	
1.							
2.							
3.							
4.							
5.							
6.							
7.							
8.							
9.							
10.							
11.							
12.							
13.							
14.							
15.							
16.							
17.							
18.							
19.							
20.							

TOTAL

1.	
2.	
3.	
4.	
5.	

TOTAL

Youth Questionnaire

THE GIFT OF ADMINISTRATION

Characteristics:

1. Loves to organize anything.
2. Can explain ideas and organization to others clearly.
3. Is glad to be under authority in order to have authority.
4. Will not try to take leadership unless given by those in authority.
5. Will take leadership when needed if there is no leadership.
6. Enjoys working on long-range goals and projects.
7. Can easily see the broad picture of what needs to be done.
8. Knows how to pick the right people to get a job done.
9. Enjoys getting others to do things and to grow in responsibility.
10. Doesn't mind criticism as long as things get done.
11. Has great interest and enthusiasm for whatever he does.
12. Finds greatest fulfillment and joy in working toward a goal.
13. Is willing to let others get the credit in order to get a job done.
14. Prefers to move on to something new once a goal is completed.
15. Constantly writes notes to self.
16. Is a natural and good leader.
17. Knows when to change ways of doing things and when not to.
18. Enjoys working with and being around people.
19. Wants to see things completed as quickly as possible.
20. Does not enjoy doing the same things over and over again.

Typical problem areas:

1. Becomes upset when others do not work together well toward a goal.
2. Can hold in hurts due to being a target for criticism.
3. Can sometimes "use" people to accomplish own goals.
4. Can tend to drive self and neglect personal needs.
5. Can neglect home chores due to intense interest in activities.

	Never	Seldom	Sometimes	Usually	Mostly	Always	POINTS
	0	1	2	3	4	5	
1.							
2.							
3.							
4.							
5.							
6.							
7.							
8.							
9.							
10.							
11.							
12.							
13.							
14.							
15.							
16.							
17.							
18.							
19.							
20.							
						TOTAL	

1.		
2.		
3.		
4.		
5.		
TOTAL		

Youth Questionnaire

THE GIFT OF COMPASSION

Characteristics:

1. Great ability to show love.
2. Always looks for the good in people.
3. Senses the spiritual and emotional condition of others.
4. Attracted to people who are hurting or in distress.
5. Takes action to remove hurts and relieve distress in others.
6. More concerned for mental and emotional hurts than physical hurts.
7. Helps others have right relationships.
8. Loves to give others the better place or opportunity.
9. Careful with words and actions to avoid hurting others.
10. Can easily tell when others are insincere or have wrong motives.
11. Drawn to others with the gift of compassion.
12. Loves to do thoughtful things for others.
13. Trusting and trustworthy.
14. Avoids conflicts with others.
15. Doesn't like to be rushed in a job or activity.
16. Usually cheerful and joyful.
17. Ruled by heart rather than head.
18. Rejoices to see others blessed and grieves to see others hurt.
19. A crusader for good causes.
20. Prays a lot for the hurts and problems of others.

Typical problem areas:

1. Has a hard time making decisions.
2. Can easily take up another person's offense.
3. Feelings are easily hurt.
4. Concern for the suffering of others can produce depression.
5. Can be taken advantage of by others.

© *Copyright 1987, Don & Katie Fortune*

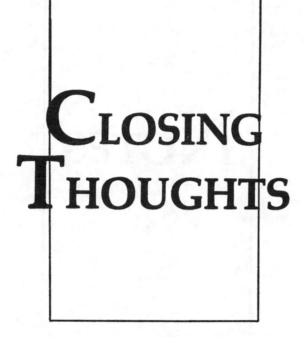

CLOSING THOUGHTS

You have learned about the motivational gifts, discovered your own, and seen how they can function in the Body of Christ. Now the application is up to *you*!

We can honestly say that what we have learned about the motivational gifts has been and continues to be extremely useful in every aspect of our lives. It has enriched our relationships, increased our understanding and acceptance of others, equipped us to minister more effectively, enabled us to cooperate with God's plan for our lives, and allowed us the freedom to be ourselves.

We trust this book has enriched your life, drawn you closer to Jesus, and truly enabled you to be free to be *you*, and to carry out the biblical command, "Each one should use whatever gift he has received to serve others, faithfully administering God's grace in its various forms . . . so that in all things God may be praised through Jesus Christ . . ." (1 Peter 4:10–11, NIV).

NOTES

1   Edward Ziegler, "The Mysterious Bonds of Twins," *The Reader's Digest* (January 1980): p. 78.

2   George Ricker Berry, *The Interlinear Literal Translation of the Greek New Testament* (Grand Rapids, Mich.: Zondervan Publishing House, 1973).

3   James Strong, *Strong's Exhaustive Concordance of the Bible* (New York: Abingdon Press, 1970).

4   Kenneth Wuest, *Word Studies in the Greek New Testament*, Chapter 12: Romans in the New Testament (Grand Rapids, Mich.: William B. Eerdmans Pub. Co., 1955).

5   Emily Binning, *Gordon Takes a Wife* (Lynnwood, Wash.: Women's Aglow Fellowship, 1977), pp. 136–137.

6   Steve Lightle, *Exodus II* (Kingwood, Tex.: Hunter Books, 1983), pp. 60–61.

7   Howard Pitman, *Placebo* (Bassfield, Miss.: Mississippi Christian Broadcasting, Inc., 1980), p. 33.

8   Used with permission.

9   Albert W. Lorimer, *God Runs My Business* (Old Tappan, N.J.: Fleming H. Revell, 1941), pp. 131–132.

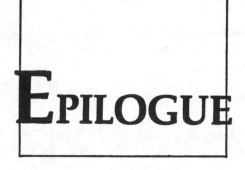

EPILOGUE

Here is a study plan designed to help teach the material in this book. While it is designed as a 13-week study, it may be lengthened or shortened to fit any time frame. Assign the chapters and the questions in advance of the discussion time.

1. First week: Read chapters 1–2

Chapter 1: *Three Categories of Gifts:*

a. What nine gifts are mentioned in 1 Corinthians 12:7–10? Define each one.

b. What are the functions of the five gifts that are listed in Ephesians 4:11–13? How do these gifts differ from the ones in 1 Corinthians 12?

c. How do the seven gifts found in Romans 12:6–8 shape our personalities?

d. How does Romans 12:1–5 provide a good basis for operating our motivational gifts.

e. How does 1 Corinthians 12:28–31 relate to the lists of gifts? Is love essential?

Chapter 2: *Everyone Has a Gift:*

f. In what ways should others benefit from your motivational gift?

g. When do we receive our motivational gifts? What is the evidence?

h. How does a motivational gift affect a person's viewpoint?

i. In what ways are different basic needs met by the seven motivational gifts?

2. Second week: Read chapters 3–5

Chapter 3: *Placed in His Body*

a. How do the seven gifts relate to different parts of the body?

b. Describe someone you know and the way his gift reflects his position in the body.

c. What is the difference between the "speaking gifts" and the "serving gifts?"

Chapter 4: *We Minister in All Areas*

d. In what sense can we all function in all seven areas of the motivational gifts?

e. Why can some people minister better and more naturally in some areas?

Chapter 5: *If I Have a Gift, Why Haven't I Known It?*

f. Why might a person not know about his/her motivational gifts?

g. What are some of the hindrances to the flow of a person's motivational gift?

h. How is a motivational gift empowered so that it is used for God's purposes?

3. Third week: Read chapters 7–9

Chapter 7: *Characteristics of the Perceiver*

a. What are the differences between a perceiver, a prophet, and the gift of prophecy?

b. Why do perceivers hate evil but welcome brokenness?

c. Why do perceivers put so much emphasis on what the Bible teaches?

d. What are blind spots? Do you have any? How can you get rid of them?

e. Why is intercession the most important ministry of the perceiver?

f. Why are perceivers so introspective? How does it help them? Hurt them?

Chapter 8: *Problems of the Perceiver*

g. Why isn't it okay to be open and blunt if it is based on truth?

h. Why would perceivers tend to have self-image problems?

Chapter 9: *Biblical Perceivers*

i. Who are the Old Testament people that might have been perceivers? Why?

j. Why is John the Baptist a good New Testament example of a perceiver?

4. Fourth week: Read chapters 10–12

Chapter 10: *Characteristics of the Server*

a. What types of things do servers do that may not be recognized as ministry?

b. What should a server do if he/she gets over-extended?

c. How can others adjust to the perfectionism of a server?

d. How can a server parent rob his/her children of learning to be responsible?

e. Why was Moses' gift of serving an asset to God's plan for the Israelites?

Chapter 11: *Problems of the Server*

g. How can we help servers feel more loved and appreciated?

h. How can you gracefully tell a server you don't want his help with something?

Chapter 12: *Biblical Servers*

i. What do you think Jesus appreciated about Martha's serving gift?

j. Why did Mary's and Martha's gifts clash?

5. Fifth week: Read chapters 13–15

Chapter 13: *Characteristics of the Teacher:*

a. Why do teachers insist on such extensive researching of everything?

b. How can a teacher's objectivity fit him for jobs that others could not do well?

c. Is it possible to change a teacher's opinions? How?

d. Why would a teacher have difficulty participating in assertive evangelism?

Chapter 14: *Problems of the Teacher:*

e. In what ways might a teacher be less effective at teaching than an exhorter?

f. How can others cope effectively with a legalistic or dogmatic teacher gift?

Chapter 15: *Biblical Teachers:*

g. What traits in Apollos indicate that he was a teacher?

h. What do you know about Luke that reveals his gift of teaching?

6. Sixth week: Read Chapters 16–18

Chapter 16: *Characteristics of the Exhorter:*

a. Why do people usually like to be around exhorters?

b. Why do you think exhorters feel life-experience is as valid as Scripture?

c. What qualities make the exhorter an exceptional counselor?

d. Is the exhorter's tendency to accept everyone an excuse for compromising?

Chapter 17: *Problems of the Exhorter:*

e. What justification is there for using Scripture out of context?

f. How can others cope with the overtalkativeness of an exhorter?

Chapter 18: *Biblical Exhorters:*

g. Why would Barnabas stand by John Mark, who had deserted them once before?

h. In what ways did Peter demonstrate the characteristics of an exhorter?

7. **Seventh session: Read Chapters 19–21**

Chapter 19: *Characteristics of the Giver:*

a. How many ways can a giver give?

b. Why is a giver most suited to be involved in evangelism?

c. Why should God enable givers to be so gifted and successful in business?

d. Is wisdom exclusively the possession of the giver? Why?

Chapter 20: *Problems of the Giver:*

e. How can a giver be helped to "cut the strings" after he has given financially?

f. In what ways can a giver's generosity have a negative effect on his family?

Chapter 21: *Biblical Givers:*

g. What clues do we have to Abraham's motivational gift of giving?

h. Since apostles often have more than one strong gift, what were Paul's?

8. **Eighth session: Read chapters 22–24**

Chapter 22: *Characteristics of the Administrator:*

a. How do you think administrators relate to authority?

b. Why is a visionary capacity vital to the gift of administration?

c. Why do administrators continually keep lists of things to do?

d. How can we know if a person who desires leadership is really qualified?

Chapter 23: *Problems of the Administrator:*

e. How should an administrator deal with criticism?

f. Why do administrators sometimes get their priorities out of order?

Chapter 24: *Biblical Administrators:*

g. How did Joseph's sharing of his dream both get him into trouble and into God's plan?

h. Why would David and Nehemiah be considered administrators?

9. **Ninth session: Read chapters 25–27**

Chapter 25: *Characteristics of the Compassion Person:*

a. In what ways is the compassion gift both a blessing and a problem to have?

b. What draws compassion people to those who are hurting or in distress?

c. Why do compassion people trust even those who have proven untrustworthy?

d. What conflicts could develop in a relationship between a compassion person and someone with one of the more analytical gifts?

e. Which gifts include intercession; how can people with these gifts work together?

Chapter 26: *Problems of the Compassion Person:*

f. Why are compassion people the most easily hurt?

g. Why is it difficult for a compassion person to be firm or to plan ahead?

Chapter 27: *Biblical Compassion People:*

h. To what extent did the Good Samaritan show compassion?

i. Although Jeremiah was a prophet by call, how do we know he also had the gift of compassion?

10. **Tenth session: Read chapter 29**

Chapter 29: *Jesus' Characteristics*

a. Was Jesus' perception greater than ours or does the Holy Spirit enable us to have similar perception today?

b. Why do you think Jesus put such emphasis on servanthood?

c. Why did Jesus base so much of His teaching on the Old Testament?

d. How did Jesus determine who to encourage and who to condemn?

e. In what ways was Jesus' teaching on the good news of the Kingdom of God central?

f. Did Jesus just "let things happen" or did He have a plan for His ministry?

g. Discuss a variety of ways in which Jesus showed compassion. Which was best?

11. **Eleventh session: Read chapters 30–31**

Chapter 30: *Living Your Gift*

a. How might each gift cause a person to respond if a child brought home a notice that his schoolwork was poor?

b. What are some marriage conflicts that may result when people with two opposite gifts marry?

c. What other interpersonal relationships might involve conflict? What can you do?

d. How can knowledge of the motivational gifts be useful in counseling?

e. Do all of the motivational gifts approach witnessing the same way? Why or why not?

Chapter 31: *Every Christian a "Minister"*:

f. In what way is every Christian a "minister"?

g. Should people with every gift teach? How will their approaches differ?

h. What are some possible areas of ministry for those with each gift? What have you done?

i. How do talents relate to the motivational gifts?

12. **Twelfth session: Read chapter 32**

Chapter 32: *Careers and Jobs:*

a. How do your built-in traits reflect your motivational gifts?

b. What did you do in childhood that was a result of your built-in traits?

c. What should you do if you find your traits are not fulfilled in your job?

d. What are the jobs or careers that your testing showed you'd be successful in? Are you doing anything along those lines right now? Have you in the past? What does this indicate to you about your future?

13. **Thirteenth session: Read chapter 33 & Closing Thoughts**

Chapter 33: *Your Children's Gifts:*

a. Why would server, giver, and compassion children learn better when separated from the more outgoing perceiver, teacher, exhorter, and administrator children?

b. How would the parenting styles of perceivers differ from styles of compassion people?

c. What special challenges would teacher parents have with a server child?

d. Have you discovered your children's gifts or the gifts of children you know? How has this helped you understand them better? Work with them better?

e. Have you discovered the gifts of any teenagers? Does it help to explain any of their actions or attitudes? What can you do to improve those relationships?

Closing Thoughts:

a. What insights have you gained from this study of motivational gifts?

b. How do you view the Body of Christ now?

ADDITIONAL MATERIAL AVAILABLE

To assist you in testing yourself, your children or others, or in presenting the material in this or other books by Don and Katie Fortune in a teaching or sharing situation, the authors make the following items available:

1. *Adult Questionnaire Scoring Set* (16 pp.). This includes the seven adult testing sheets from *Discover Your God-Given Gifts*, along with a profile sheet for final scoring. Tie-breakers (enabling a person to determine which gift is stronger when scores are close or the same) are also included.

2. *Youth Questionnaire Scoring Set* (16 pp.). Designed for teenagers (grades 7–12) and college-age young adults, this set is based on the material in chapter 6 of *Discover Your Children's Gifts*. It includes the seven scoring sheets for teens, a profile sheet and tie-breakers.

3. *Junior Children's Questionnaire Scoring Set* (16 pp.). Designed for grade-schoolers (grades 4–6), this test should be adminis-

tered by a parent, teacher or other adult. It is based on the material in chapter 5 of *Discover Your Children's Gifts*. Tie-breakers included.

4. *Primary Children's Questionnaire Scoring Set* (16 pp.). Designed to be completed by parents of primaries (grades 1–3), this testing set is based on material in chapter 4 of *Discover Your Children's Gifts*. Tie-breakers included.

5. *Children's Survey Testing Sheets: Preschool* (16 pp.). This packet includes three sets of scoring sheets from the material in chapter 3 of *Discover Your Children's Gifts*. Use these to help determine the gifts of children from toddler through kindergarten age. The tests can also help determine the gifts of older children and help adults clarify their own scores by comparing the survey characteristics with those from their own childhood.

6. *Objective Questionnaire Testing Set* (16 pp.). Designed to be used for objective (not

teaching) testing situations. The adult questionnaire is arranged randomly so a person taking the test cannot tell how the gifts relate to each characteristic. Tie-breakers, scoring key and decoder sheet included.

7. *Ministry Discovery Set* (16 pp.). This set contains expanded material from chapter 31 of *Discover Your God-Given Gifts* and a listing of ministries most fulfilling for persons with each gift. Selected material from chapter 30, "Living Your Gift," helps the user put gifts into practical action.

8. *Occupational Success Testing Set* (16 pp.). This set contains information from chapter 32, "Careers and Jobs," of *Discover Your God-Given Gifts*, along with a detailed analysis of the 180 most common careers and jobs, showing the degree to which each gift is likely to be successful. Also included is an evaluation of built-in traits that bring joy and satisfaction to persons with each gift.

9. *Secular Objective Questionnaire Testing Set* (16 pp.). This test is arranged randomly and designed to be used in situations where secular adult objective testing is desired. Christian terms and interests have been replaced by generic ones. Tie-breakers, scoring key and decoder sheet included.

10. *Children's Gifts Teaching Tape Set* (6 cassettes). Nine hours of seminar teaching on the book *Discover Your Children's Gifts*, recorded on six 90-minute cassette tapes and packaged in an attractive case. By following the teaching outline in the back of the book, the tapes can be used for teaching others. The following syllabus is recommended for use with the tapes.

11. *Children's Gifts Seminar Syllabus* (48 pp.). This workbook is designed for use in seminars or with the seminar teaching tapes, and covers the subjects discussed in *Discover Your Children's Gifts*. Many charts and practical application ideas included.

12. *Forms & Charts Packet* (32 pp.). This includes enough forms and charts from Part III, "Practical Insights," in *Discover Your Children's Gifts* to keep records for a family of four or five children. In 8 1/2" x 11" size it constitutes a permanent family record, but individual forms or charts can be removed. (It does *not* contain the motivational gifts testing sets.)

13. *The ABCs of Christian Parenting* (parchment). This inspirational reminder, taken from *Discover Your Children's Gifts*, makes a thoughtful gift for new parents or anyone with children. It is available on 9" x 12" parchment-type paper suitable for framing.

14. *Variety Packet, Children* (13 items). This packet contains one each of the above items: all testing and discovery sets, syllabus, tapes, a parchment and the Forms & Charts Packet—everything needed to teach the material from *Discover Your Children's Gifts*.

15. *Motivational Gifts Seminar Tape Set* (6 tapes). This set includes nine hours of seminar teaching on motivational gifts based on the book *Discover Your God-Given Gifts*, recorded on six 90-minute cassette tapes and packaged in an attractive case. The following syllabus is recommended for use with the tapes.

16. *Motivational Gifts Seminar Syllabus* (48 pp.). This attractive workbook is designed for use in motivational gifts seminars or with the seminar teaching tapes above, and covers the material and subjects in *Discover Your God-Given Gifts*. Testing sheets and tie-breakers for adults included, as well as biblical examples and practical application material.

17. *Video Teaching Tape Sets* (two tapes per set). Each of these two sets contains material from the nationally broadcast Canadian TV program *It's a New Day*, featuring Don and Katie Fortune. Each of the seg-

ments, in an interview format, is about 45 minutes long but can be shown in shorter units. Each is informal and lively, including introductory and life-related material, and can be used in teaching a smaller group.

The first set contains five segments on the motivational gifts, covering the adult testing material for all seven gifts from *Discover Your God-Given Gifts*. The second set contains four segments on the book *Discover Your Children's Gifts,* covering the characteristics for all seven types of gifted children. To order specify *Adult Gifts* or *Children's Gifts* teaching videos.

18. *Foreign Language Adult Questionnaire Scoring Sets* (8 pp. each). The adult testing sets have been translated so far into Danish, Finnish, French, German, Indonesian, Japanese, Korean, Polish, Portuguese, Norwegian, Russian, Spanish and Swedish. More translations are in process. Inquire about special permissions for missionaries and those teaching in foreign countries. To order specify the language needed.

19. *Free Information Packet #1.* Information about the procedure for having the authors present a motivational gifts seminar (or other subject) for a group, church, retreat or conference.

20. *Free Information Packet #2.* Information about the authors' books, tapes and materials on various subjects.

21. *Variety Packet, Adult* (11 items). This packet contains one each of the above items 1–9 and 16–17: testing material, syllabus, tapes and everything needed to teach the material from the book *Discover Your God-Given Gifts.*

22. *Discover Your Children's Gifts* (book, 296 pp.). Here is how to discover the gifts God has built into every child according to Romans 12:6–8. This book, a comprehensive study complete with study guide, is enlightening and practical. It is a valuable tool for parents, grandparents, youth workers, teachers, daycare providers, Sunday school teachers, Christian education leaders and anyone involved with children or youth of any age. The book is being used by parents, pastors and educators around the world.

23. *Discover Your Spouse's Gifts* (book, 352 pp.). Here is how the discovery of the motivational gifts of Romans 12:6–8 can enhance a marriage relationship. Based on an extensive marital survey conducted by the Fortunes, the book gives valuable information on how the gifts affect marriage, how to identify problems that stem from not knowing about the motivational gifts and how to overcome those problems and release a couple into the freedom and joy of a God-given, God-gifted marriage.

24. *Survey Your Marriage* (16 pp.). Based on an extensive marriage survey conducted by the Fortunes, this personal copy of the survey will enable you and your spouse to pinpoint the differences you have and the problem areas in your marriage. It will give you insight and understanding that will greatly enhance your marital relationship. It is also an excellent tool for couples' groups or classes and in premarital or marital counseling. The survey is based on the twenty most common categories of problems in marriage.

25. *Marriage Seminar Tape Set* (6 tapes). Nine hours of seminar teaching on the book *Discover Your Spouse's Gifts*, recorded on six 90-minute cassette tapes and packaged in an attractive case. By following the teaching outline in the back of the book, the tapes can be used for teaching others. The following syllabus is recommended for use with the tapes.

26. *Marriage Seminar Syllabus* (48 pp.). This attractive workbook is designed for

use in marriage seminars or with the seminar teaching tapes above, and covers the material and subjects of the book *Discover Your Spouse's Gifts*. Dual motivational gift testing sheets for couples are included, as well as a personal copy of the marriage survey and practical application material. Ideal for teaching couples who want to make their marriages better.

27. *The ABCs of Christian Marriage* (parchment). This inspirational reminder, taken from *Discover Your Spouse's Gifts*, makes a thoughtful gift for engaged couples, newlyweds or any Christian couple. It is available on 9" x 12" parchment-type paper suitable for framing.

28. *Dealing with Anger* (tape and book). Katie Fortune shares a life-changing teaching based on Matthew 5:21–26 on how to get free from the negative effects of anger in the heart. Couples and individuals will discover the scriptural key to dealing with anger. Christian counselors will have a tool for helping people with the number-one problem: buried anger.

For orders or a free price list write:

Don and Katie Fortune
Heart to Heart International Ministries
P.O. Box 101
Kingston, WA 98346
For phone inquiries or orders call
(360) 297-8878
web site: heart2heart.org
e-mail: fortune@heart2heart.org